MORMONIS

MORMONISM

The Story of
A New Religious Tradition

JAN SHIPPS

University of Illinois Press
Urbana and Chicago

© 1985 by the Board of Trustees of the University of Illinois
Manufactured in the United States of America

C 5 4 3 2

This book is printed on acid-free paper.

Library of Congress Cataloging in Publication Data

Shipps, Jan, 1929–
Mormonism: the story of a new religious tradition.

Bibliography: p.
Includes index.
1. Mormon Church—History—Addresses, essays,
lectures. 2. Church of Jesus Christ of Latter-day Saints—
History—Addresses, essays, lectures. I. Title.
BX8611.S49   1985 289.3   84–2672
ISBN 0–252–01159–7 (alk. paper)

For

A. W. S.

Contents

Temple Square in Salt Lake City, showing the Bowery as well as the
recently completed tabernacle, c. 1865

Preface

EARLY CHRISTIANS THOUGHT of themselves in Hebraic terms. As the saints—for that is what the Bible calls them—of Solomon's day rejoiced when fire came down from heaven and the glory of the Lord filled the house during the consecration of the temple, so at Pentecost the "latter-day" saints of early Christianity rejoiced in God's goodness when a rushing mighty wind filled all the house and cloven tongues like as of fire sat on each of them. But as Christianity developed, as Jews and Greeks were together "in Christ" brought beneath the covenant that God had made with Abraham, it gradually became clear that the way espoused by the apostles included important elements that were not a part of Israel's tradition. Without fully and consciously realizing that they were doing so, the followers of Jesus established a new religious tradition.

This book tells the story of yet another assembly of saints whose history, I believe, is in many respects analogous to the history of those early Christians who thought at first that they had found the only proper way to be Jews. Despite the surprising similarity between some of the modern cultural manifestations of Mormonism and American evangelical Protestantism, Mormonism started to grow away from traditional Christianity almost immediately upon coming into existence. It began as a movement that understood itself as Christian, but as "the new dispensation

of the fulness of times" commenced with the publication of the
Book of Mormon, the "restoration" of the Aaronic priesthood, and
the recognition of Joseph Smith as prophet, these nineteenth-
century Latter-day Saints (as they came to be called) embarked on
a path that led to developments that now distinguish their tradition from the Christian tradition as surely as early Christianity
was distinguished from its Hebraic context.

By no means is this the first time a sustained argument has
been advanced to make the case that Mormonism ought not to be
classified as a part of *traditional* Christianity.[1] Indeed, since the
1830s opponents of Mormonism have been trying to prove that
Mormonism is not Christian in any sense. Some of its adversaries
have used theological reasoning to define Mormonism as heresy,
thereby mounting a challenge to the Mormon claim that the only
legitimate means of becoming a member of a Christian church is
through baptism by the authority of the LDS (Latter-day Saint)
priesthood. Others have gone further. Basing their conclusions
on a grand array of historical data, much of it drawn from LDS
sources, they have argued that Mormonism could not possibly be
Christian because the movement rests on a foundation of subterfuge, chicanery, deception, and trickery, and therefore must be defined as fraud. Furthering modern arguments along these lines is
neither the tenor nor the burden of the present work. As opposed
to addressing issues of heresy or fraud, what follows here is an argument that Mormonism is a separate religious tradition and that
it must be understood and respected on its own terms.[2]

Although I was trained to write history, this book reflects the
fact that I have been teaching religious studies as well as history
for the past decade. It is filled with historical data, but because
Mormon history itself is treated as text and subjected to inter-
pretive analysis, it is as hermeneutical as it is historical. While
the presentation is roughly chronological, its objective is not simply narration of the Mormon story with emphasis on religious experience, but explication of how this movement developed into a
new religious tradition. As is the case with any work of interpretation, readers will more easily follow the lines of the argument when they are familiar with the "text." For that reason, "A
Chronology of Nineteenth-Century Mormonism" has been prepared to serve as an appendix to this book. Readers who are un-

familiar with the general sweep of Mormon history will, in addition, wish to consult one of the best of the recent histories of the LDS movement: *The Story of the Latter-day Saints* by James B. Allen and Glen M. Leonard or *The Mormon Experience: A History of the Latter-day Saints* by Leonard J. Arrington and Davis Bitton.[3]

The theoretical works of Thomas Kuhn, Mircea Eliade, and Peter Berger, the literary criticism of Frank Kermode and Northrop Frye, and the analytic example provided by John Gager's study of the social world of early Christianity are all important to the argument advanced in the chapters of this book.[4] Yet the work of none of these scholars provided an exact model to be tested or a set of principles by which interpretation should proceed. My approach issued, instead, from a consideration of LDS historical materials within the broad comparative framework provided by religious studies as that discipline is currently pursued in public universities in the United States.[5]

Calling first for a reexamination of the data for the purpose of teasing from it the Saints' perceptions of what had happened, what was happening, and what could be expected to happen in the future, this approach also called for an examination of the impact of these perceptions on individual and corporate behavior. In addition, it required careful scrutiny of these perception-consequent action combinations with an eye to identifying patterns that would facilitate in-depth comparison of the Mormon experience with the experience of peoples in other times and places who were likewise caught up in the religious movements whose motive forces drew power from the gospel of the God of Abraham. Finally, the approach used in this study called for the development of a framework of interpretation which would permit an assessment that would bear directly on the troublesome question of whether Mormonism has become just another religion of the American mainstream, an idiosyncratic subdivision of Christianity, or whether it is a separate and distinct religious tradition in its own right.

While the resulting argument is fundamentally analytical, I decided early on that it ought not to be set forth in technical language, but in a style that itself would carry the argument forward. As often as seemed necessary to separate the "text" from my act of interpreting it, I inserted phrases such as "so the words said," "the general perception was," "for all practical purposes, they," and "it seemed to them." But I made an earnest effort to avoid distancing my interpretation from LDS historical data: I searched out direct quotations that expressed ubiquitous ideas and used them in the presentation; I paraphrased perceptions in words that might have been used by nineteenth-century Mormons themselves; and, as far as possible, I tried to establish contexts that would have been recognizable to the Latter-day Saints who lived in the times and places in question. Moreover, because parallels among Hebraic, Christian, and Mormon history are significant to my analysis, I described comparisons of the experiences of these various peoples with language as often drawn from the Judeo-Christian scriptures as from anthropology, sociology, or everyday life.

A disadvantage of this manner of proceeding is its tendency to make my argument appear somewhat apologetic at times—an irony since I am not a Mormon—but that disadvantage is far outweighed by the effective means this stylistic strategy provided for reconstructing the picture of early Mormonism *as perceived from the inside*, a reconstruction that is crucial to the illumination of parallel patterns of development in early Christianity and Mormonism.

The overarching plan of the work is as follows. A narrative prologue supplies an introduction, bringing the story of the Mormon prophet, his family, and his little flock—the metaphor was Joseph Smith's—up to the publication of the Book of Mormon and the formal organization of the church. Unlike subsequent chapters, this one uses a strict chronological approach because that is the best way to place Mormonism's foundational claims in context, and it is the only way to consider the integral relationship between magic and religious seership in Smith's early life. Of more significance to the argument of this book, close attention to chronology discloses the presence in Smith's life of trance as a response to divine calling, and it isolates a period of private spiritual preparation that preceded the active initiation of his prophetic ministry, thereby pointing to elements in the Mormon prophet's career that parallel elements of the career patterns of persons who spoke for God in biblical times.

The second chapter initially diverts attention away from the Mormon prophet to the Book of Mormon and the *historical* beginnings of the LDS movement. Describing the state of religion and culture wherein the Book of Mormon had to make its way, this chapter considers the various responses that were generated by the claims made in the book. It demonstrates that a belief that the book is a true record implied much more than acceptance of the historicity of the document by showing how such belief led directly to an acceptance of Joseph Smith's prophetic role, membership in the Church of Jesus Christ whose organization was foretold in the Book of Mormon, and union with like believers in the community of Latter-day Saints.

A comparative perspective is adopted in the third chapter. Before dealing with early Mormonism in comparative context, however, the character of cultural situations in which new religious movements flourish is delineated and definitions are established for the descriptive terms religion, church, denomination, sect, and cult. Then, taking the experience of the followers of the early Christian apostles as guide and recognizing that, even as they continued to expect the arrival of the *eschaton*, their acceptance of the reality of the resurrection of Jesus ushered early Christians into a new world, this comparative analysis places the first Latter-day Saints on the threshold of a new age. Examining subsequent Mormon history from that point of departure makes it clear that it is an open canon, represented by the Book of Mormon and a prophet in their midst, *plus* the historical experience of the early Latter-day Saints that distinguishes Mormonism from all other existing religious traditions.

Taken together these first three chapters describe what may be thought of as Mormonism's foundational tripod, a metaphorical support unit composed of prophetic figure, scripture, and experience—Joseph Smith, the Book of Mormon, and the corporate life of the early Saints. Just as a real tripod only supports weight when all three legs are in place, so the growth and development of this religious and cultural movement rested on all three of these elements. Accounts that focus attention more or less exclusively on Joseph Smith or one of the other "legs" of the tripod fail to provide an adequate explanation for the survival and endurance of this important religious and cultural movement.

The question of whether Mormonism was a renewed version of apostolic Christianity or whether it was a more radical movement that accepted the "restoration of all things" created tension within Mormonism from the very first. Chapter Four deals with this issue, showing that Mormonism started to move away from primitive Christianity very early in its history. A type of Mormonism that is primarily a movement of reformation rather than radical restoration survives as the "Reorganization," whose institutional form is the Reorganized Church of Jesus Christ of Latter Day Saints with headquarters in Independence, Missouri. Yet, as is demonstrated with comparison and contrast between Mormonism and the Christian (Disciples of Christ) movement, this LDS form also differs from traditional Christianity, although not as thoroughly as does the form of Mormonism institutionalized as the Church of Jesus Christ of Latter-day Saints with headquarters in Salt Lake City, Utah.

Implied throughout this work is the notion that what happened to Mormonism as it came into existence is typical of the process through which new religious traditions pass as they are established as something other than transient religious movements. Nowhere in this work is this notion more precisely worked out than in Chapter Five, which contains an account of the canonization of the Mormon story. Although a clear distinction is drawn between the long and agonizing process by which the Christian scriptures were canonized and the settling of the Mormon canon of scripture during Joseph Smith's lifetime, a close look at the fate of Lucy Mack Smith's history of Joseph Smith and his family reveals that an informal canonization process continued long past the prophet's death and, indeed, continues still.

Chapters Six and Seven concentrate on Mormonism around the turn of the century. Looking backward to the period when plural marriage (and geographical distance) established such a firm boundary between the Saints and the non-Mormon world that the Saints in Utah were able to live outside the ordinary American political process, and looking forward to the twentieth century, when Mormonism would enter the mainstream of American life, these chapters deal with the transition from one of these states of affairs to the other. When it occurred, this transition was extremely difficult for the Saints, and determining exactly how it happened has also proved to be extremely difficult for scholars. Using History of Religions theory to illuminate this transition period, these chapters suggest that when the Saints lived in the Great Salt Lake Basin in the nineteenth century, they lived "in the kingdom," outside the constraints of ordinary time. In order to survive and grow into an important religious tradition, however, the practice of plural marriage had to be relinquished and the political kingdom given up. Chapter Six deals with the trauma of surrender and the movement out of sacred into ordinary time, while the final chapter suggests, through a detailed analysis of an LDS sermon, set in the context of General Conference, how Mormonism was able to move out of its own "apostolic era," to transform itself and gear up for the long run.

I knew practically nothing about the Latter-day Saints and absolutely nothing about Mormonism when I moved to Logan, Utah, in 1960. In the years since my accidental entrance into the Mormon world, I have carried out a wide variety of research and writing projects in Mormon history. At the same time, I have been befriended by large numbers of Latter-day Saints (persons from all across the activity spectrum of the LDS Church) and Latter Day Saints (persons connected in one way or another with the Reorganization). This book reflects both my own research into specific aspects of the Mormon past and countless extended conversations with Mormons about Mormonism that have taken place across the last two decades.

Parts of any book a long time in the making—as this one has been—are likely to have been presented to the public in some form. This is true of this work. Chapter Two is a radically revised version of the presidential address that I delivered in Canadaigua, New York, to the annual meeting of the Mormon History Association in April 1980. Chapter Four is based on papers that were presented to the American Society of Church History in March 1980, and at the Sunstone Theological Symposium in August of that year. Chapter Five is a revision and expansion of a paper entitled "Mother Smith's History" presented to the annual meeting of the Mormon History Association in 1979. Most of Chapter Six was presented as "In the Presence of the Past," a Charles Redd Lecture delivered at Brigham Young University in 1979 and subsequently published; it appears here with the permission of the Charles Redd Center for Western Studies.[6] In addition, Chapters Two, Four, and Seven were presented more or less in their present form in April 1982 in Boise, Idaho, at a Circuit Rider Seminar sponsored by the Eastern District of the Idaho-Washington Conference of the United Methodist Church.

Since this work is more the result of my thinking about Mormonism than the outcome of a particular research project, its preparation did not lead to my incurring the usual debts for assistance with resources and research problems that are ordinarily acknowledged in prefaces to historical studies. I am, however, indebted to a far greater number of scholars who opened their hearts and minds as well as the results of their research to me than I can even begin to recognize by listing their names here. Nevertheless, for good or ill, I would claim more credit for this book than I should if I did not acknowledge the importance of searching discussions with Douglas D. Alder and Paul M. Edwards; Alfred L. Bush and Klaus J. Hansen; Thomas G. Alexander, James B. Allen, Leonard J. Arrington, Maureen Ursenbach Beecher, Davis Bitton, Alma Blair, Everett L. Cooley, Robert B. Flanders, Lawrence Foster, Marvin S. Hill, Dean Jessee, Robert Paul, Marvin B. Rytting, and D. Michael Quinn, many of whom also criticized early drafts of one or more of the papers that became chapters for this work. In addition, Hollis R. Johnson, Uwe Hansen, and Ned C. Hill (the presidency of the Bloomington Stake of the LDS Church during the years in which this book came into being) saw to it that my theorizing, as they called it, was constantly corrected with knowledge about the reality of Mormon life.

Richard L. Bushman and Martin E. Marty read an early version of the entire manuscript. Their valuable suggestions for its improvement, for which I am very grateful, were important factors in the process of revision. Martha Taysom, who teaches church history courses at the LDS Institute of Religion in Bloomington, Indiana, also read the manuscript in its entirety. Her willingness to assist in this way is much appreciated.

The illustrations were selected with the assistance of William

W. Slaughter, Donald Schmidt, Madelon Brunson, and Alfred
Bush, all of whom have a wide acquaintance with and knowledge
of the visual record of Mormonism. The jacket illustration is the
work of the outstanding woodcut artist Dorothy Mandel.

A fortunate joint appointment in history and religious studies
in the Indiana University School of Liberal Arts at Indiana University–Purdue University at Indianapolis led me to extend my consideration of the LDS past beyond the parameters of the social, intellectual, and religious history of the United States to the much
larger religious studies sphere. This appointment was made possible with funds provided for the purpose of adding religious studies to the School of Liberal Arts curriculum by Lilly Endowment,
Incorporated. It is not at all too much to say that ultimately this
book is one of the fruits of that bequest. Other more direct assistance included a sabbatical leave granted by the university in
1978–79 that gave me time to shift my research from straight history to history and religious studies, and research grants from the
LDS Church History Division and the IUPUI Center for American Studies that allowed me extremely important stints of research in the archives of the Mormon Church in Salt Lake City.

In countless ways across the past decade, James F. Smurl, Row-
land A. Sherrill, and E. Theodore Mullen, Jr., the other three
members of our religious studies faculty, have all served as teachers, as well as friends and colleagues. Responding to casual rumina-
tions and written drafts with useful observations, asking hard
questions, and in departmental colloquia subjecting early versions of four of the chapters to rigorous analysis and criticism,
they made an enormous difference in the shape of my argument
and the style of this work. Of particular importance was Professor
Mullen's warning that I was making a distinction that was too
rigid between the Judaic character of Utah Mormonism and the
New Testament character of the Reorganization, a warning that
echoed reservations first voiced by my friend and colleague
Stephen J. Stein, who teaches religious studies at Indiana University, Bloomington. While this difference is surely important, continuing to place great emphasis on it could have prevented me
from asking more fundamental questions about Mormonism.

Although its grounding in religious studies moves this work

away from history to some extent, I wish also to acknowledge the help and encouragement of my history department colleagues, most especially Donald L. Kinzer and Ralph D. Gray.

Ross Marrs and George Davis, reverend scholars as well as ministers in the United Methodist Church, were both willing to make the effort to understand enough about Mormonism to help me conceptualize and explore the comparisons between the nineteenth-century Mormon world and the worlds inhabited by the Israelites, the Jews, and the Christians in biblical times. I am grateful to them for this assistance, and for putting up with a parishioner with such a deep and abiding interest in Mormonism.

Elaine Childs and Marilyn Gunnion typed early drafts of these chapters. Katherine Amy Phillips assisted with the preparation of the bibliography and index, and Anne Fraker, who works with me in the Center for American Studies, helped with proofreading the index and assisted in many other ways. Mary Kuonen and Patty Ebbing prepared the much-revised manuscript for the press. All were extremely helpful, working more cheerfully and expeditiously than I had any right to expect. I appreciate them as persons and I appreciate their work.

Finally three women, all close friends and valued colleagues, were instrumental in helping me to get this work out of my files and into final form. Peggy Fletcher, editor of *Sunstone* magazine and *The Sunstone Review*, pushed; Elizabeth Dulany, assistant director of the University of Illinois Press, pulled; and Gretchen Wolfram, newswoman extraordinaire, warned me when what I was writing seemed about to turn into dense academic prose. I thank them all.

JAN SHIPPS

Bloomington, Indiana
Spring, 1984

MORMONISM

A nineteenth-century portrait of Joseph Smith

Chapter One

Prologue

Historical chronologies of Mormonism ordinarily open by identifying Joseph Smith as the Mormon prophet and describing the three foundational events that get the LDS story under way. Such accounts first cite Smith's reports of visions of heavenly beings manifested to him in the 1820s when he still lived with his parents on a farm in Palmyra, New York. Then they go on to tell about the coming forth of the Book of Mormon, a document said to have been miraculously translated from hieroglyphics engraved on golden plates whose location had been revealed to Smith by an angel.[1] And they describe the formation, in 1830, of the religious institution that was the forerunner of both the Church of Jesus Christ of Latter-day Saints and the Reorganized Church of Jesus Christ of Latter Day Saints, plus a variety of sectarian forms of Mormonism. That this is no ordinary story is made clear, however, by the extraordinary (supernatural) character of two of these three occurrences that are said to have set it in motion.

That Mormon history is not ordinary history either is demonstrated in the multitude of historical accounts of the LDS movement that have been written across the last 150 years, accounts in which these foundational phenomena take on meanings that differ dramatically according to the context into which they are introduced. When the narrative backdrop describes a world wherein apostasy has reigned supreme for nearly 2,000 years, for example, Smith's visions, the appearance of the Book of Mormon, and the organization of the church present themselves as light breaking into darkness, light "poured upon the earth in a stream of effulgent glory."[2] Yet these reported visions, the prophet's explanation of the origin of the Book of Mormon, and even the organization of the church appear as agents of darkness if they are placed in a post-Enlightenment setting in which humanity had been ushered into a new age, one that had renounced "superstition" and started to glorify self-evident "truth" based on observation and logic.

To be more precise, in the LDS histories adopted as authoritative by the Church of Jesus Christ of Latter-day Saints, the ancient Judeo-Christian past is set forth as the background of Mormonism. Brigham H. Roberts and Joseph Fielding Smith, who wrote the most important official accounts of the Mormon past, both begin the LDS story with the foundation of the world. Their timelines move forward through a series of "dispensations" from Adam to Noah, Noah to Abraham, Abraham to Moses, and Moses to John the Baptist. Then they describe a "dispensation of the meridian of time" marked by the ministry of Jesus of Nazareth. According to the writers of these priestly narratives—Roberts and Smith were both General Authorities of the LDS Church—this "meridian of time" dispensation turned the world into a new path, only to have that path blocked by a "Great Apostasy" which caused the removal of the ancient priesthoods and the true Church of Jesus Christ from the earth. They picture the world being plunged into darkness as a result, a darkness lasting for roughly 1,500 years. In their histories of the Latter-day Saints, this darkness sets the stage for the appearance of Mormonism. A new "dispensation of the fulness of times" opened with the coming forth of the Book of Mormon (which meant the reopening of the Judeo-Christian canon), the reintroduction of prophetic leadership for the people of God, the re-formation of the Church of Jesus Christ, the restoration of the priesthoods of Aaron and Melchizedek, and the gathering of the Saints.[3]

This "light breaking into darkness" motif appears, in addition, in LDS histories, official and unofficial, that open with Joseph Smith's 1838 account of his early visions. In his report of the first of these—the one canonized as the First Vision—Smith said that

while he was praying in a wood near his home on a spring morning in 1820, he felt himself surrounded with darkness so thick
that "sudden destruction" seemed imminent. As the powers of
darkness intensified, however, he "saw a pillar of light . . . above
the brightness of the sun" which, when it rested on the fourteen-
year-old lad, allowed him to see two "personages" who revealed
themselves as "the Father and the Son." In this vision, Smith was
told not to join any of the existing "sects, for they were all wrong."
Consequently, said Smith, he refused to become a church member, explaining that in a vision he had been so commanded. This
caused the future prophet to be enmeshed in enmity (darkness),
"suffering severe persecution at the hands of all classes of men."
Smith's report (as published in the Pearl of Great Price, a work the
Saints regard as scripture) continues with the description of a
light illuminating his darkened bedroom on the night of 21/22
September 1823. Into this light, said Smith, came a personage
whose name was Moroni and who, in three sequential visits, revealed that God had a work for the young man, now aged seven-
teen, to do. This work was the translation of the Book of Mormon,
which, the LDS histories say, brought light to those who had been
sitting in darkness for a very long time.

Early histories of Mormonism written by non-Mormons often
worked out the opposing motif. Placing this same extraordinary
story in the context of a world enlightened by science, the Protestant Reformation, and America's "lively experiment" with religion, the authors of such works described Smith's visions and his
explanation of the Book of Mormon's source as the products of a
diseased imagination, if not the elements of a gigantic fraud. Consequently Mormonism was pictured in such accounts as a mix-
ture of superstition and subterfuge that conceals the light of
truth. As such works of this sort said, it pandered to the super-
stitious, the gullible, and the fearful, at least in the beginning.
The development of the Mormon movement was therefore described as a menace that would, if unopposed, reverse humanity's
forward progress, turning the world backward to the "dark ages."[4]

Books and articles about the Saints that were written in the
nineteenth century by antagonistic Gentiles (i.e., persons who
were not part of the Mormon community) rarely failed, at some
point, to accuse Mormonism of "blinding" its adherents so effec-

tively that when they heard Smith's report of his visions and his explanation of the origins of the Book of Mormon, they could not distinguish truth from falsehood. Furthermore, such works nearly always placed the organization of the church against a backdrop picturing the accelerating development of democracy in Jacksonian America. This setting makes the rigid ecclesiastical rankings that came to be a part of Mormonism appear to be the basis of a hierarchical social system, a system typically interpreted as a dark cloud threatening to put out the splendid light illuminating the American scene during the early republic's halcyon days.

This demonstration of what happens when identical accounts of the foundational events of Mormonism are set down within different contexts is presented here at the outset because the fact of the matter is that the "facts" of LDS history do not necessarily speak for themselves. It is as important to remember that the very same descriptions of the very same events can take on radically different meanings when they are placed in different settings as it is to keep in mind that "inside" and "outside" perceptions of what was happening differed at practically every point in LDS history.

While the occurrences here identified as foundational events were indeed the effective beginning of Mormonism, a proper prologue to a study of Mormonism does not open with the visions of the Mormon prophet, the coming forth of the Book of Mormon, and the organization of the church, but with the story of the life and hard times of Joseph Smith's family. Although he was the third son, rather than the eldest, the prophet was the namesake of Joseph Smith of Topsfield, who was born in 1771 in Essex County, Massachusetts. A New England farmer and sometime entrepreneur, Joseph Smith, Sr., came from a family whose members had resided in Essex County for four generations. In 1796 he married nineteen-year-old Lucy Mack, the daughter of Lydia and Solomon Mack of Cheshire County, New Hampshire, a family whose members had likewise resided in New England for several generations.

If this marriage did not unite two leading New England households, it nevertheless brought together two venerable families of the region. The groom's grandfather, Samuel Smith, had held responsible positions in Topsfield, serving multiple terms in the state legislature and as selectman and town clerk, in addition to serving as a militia captain in the American Revolution. His son Asael, Joseph's father, moved from Topsfield to Derryfield, New Hampshire, where he served several terms as town clerk. He, too, fought in the Revolution, settling afterward in Tunbridge, Vermont, where, at the time of his son's nuptial, he was a substantial landowner and respected community leader. The bride's paternal grandfather, Ebenezer Mack, had held "a large property and lived in good style" in Lyme, Connecticut, until he met financial problems severe enough to force him to apprentice his son Solomon to a neighboring farmer.[5] This meant that Lucy's father had little or no schooling. Yet at one time or another in his adulthood Solomon held significant properties also, including farms in Lyme and Marlow, New Hampshire, and a schooner large enough to accommodate thirty passengers. While these were all lost by her father through accident or ill fortune, Lucy's brother Stephen succeeded at both farming and business, and at the time of his sister's wedding was a prominent citizen of Tunbridge.

During the first two decades of their marriage, nine children were born to the parents of the lad who would become the Mormon prophet.[6] They were fortunate that only one of the nine, a son named Ephraim, failed to survive infancy. But they were not so fortunate in other ways. In those same twenty years the life of the family was so marked with wretched luck, bad health, and economic disaster that the Smiths were forced to move from place to place in Vermont and New Hampshire at least eight different times. Finally, in 1816, when Joseph Smith, Jr., was ten years old, the family joined the grand out-migration from New England across the Adirondacks to western New York that had started at the close of the American Revolution and continued as the construction of the Erie Canal acted as a magnet for settlement in that area.

Seeking a better means than they had yet found to secure a livelihood, Joseph Smith, Sr., his wife, Lucy, and their children stopped about twenty miles east of Rochester and rented a house in the village of Palmyra. They lived two years in town, working at whatever came to hand in order to survive and get together enough cash to make a down payment on a farm. Then, when they had accumulated enough capital, they arranged to buy a farm in nearby Manchester. As had happened to the family several times before, however, once again the members of the family made a valiant effort to move back into the ranks of property holders, only to be deceived by their creditors. They were never dispossessed from the holding which they had improved and on which they built a comfortable home, but neither were they ever able to obtain a title to the farm in Manchester that they believed was rightfully theirs.

Thus it was that the Mormon prophet grew up in a family that had lost status, one that, as the saying goes, had seen better days. His parents apparently worked very hard and they were persons of considerable learning (as is revealed by surviving holograph letters written by his mother and by the fact that his father knew enough to have been hired to teach school in Sharon, Vermont). But Joseph and Lucy were unable to prevent the drift that carried the Smith family away from the solid center of respectability toward the fringes of polite society. This was particularly the case after they left New England, since the family connections that had helped to preserve the respectability of their branch of the family were effectively abandoned when the prophet's parents decided to emigrate to western New York. There, as landless settlers, they were easily relegated to marginal status.

Although a different approach to religion might have helped the Smith family maintain its status in New England, the family was never a part of respectable, mainline Protestantism of the Presbyterian, Congregational, Baptist, or Methodist variety. Instead, the Smiths were a part of a heterogeneous assemblage of Christian "seekers" who were believers of a very special kind. Often intensely religious, in the sense of being pious and devout, the persons who fit securely in this category seem either to have had a history of having moved into and then back out of various evangelical denominations and groups organized on the basis of "no creed but the Bible," or else to have gone to the other extreme, refusing to affiliate with ecclesiastical organizations of either type. Although Christianity's apostolic period was the main source of their inspiration, many of these people were heirs to the early American religious heritage of magical noninstitutionalized religious practices, practices that were described by Jon Butler in 1979 in an article in the *American Historical Review* and to which Marvin Hill referred in asserting that necromancy and religious faith were not incompatible in nineteenth-century America.[7] As did the religious lives of many of their forebears, the religious lives of people like the Smith family held in suspension both a reliance on magic and the occult arts and a thoroughgoing acceptance of the truth of the claims set out in the Judeo-Christian scriptures. This made them receptive to ideas that existing churches would have defined as unorthodox; it made them seekers after truth wherever it might be found.

By crossing the Adirondacks, the Smith family entered into what, in the early nineteenth century, was an unrestricted arena as far as religion was concerned. In western New York the various Christian denominations contended openly for members. Revivals swept across the land with such regularity that it became known as the "burnt" district because the fires of religion had burned over it so many different times. The resulting emphasis on religion encouraged the development of a pattern of Bible study that made Christian primitivism flourish; it favored the creation of new religious movements that did not fit into the denominational framework; and it allowed Masonry (complete with mytho-logical, doctrinal, ritual, and social dimensions that made it a proto-religious movement) to grow and prosper to such an extent that it generated an important anti-Masonry movement. Furthermore, conditions in this region produced an atmosphere of experimentation that made it likely that novel religious ideas—which would have been dismissed out of hand in more settled situations—would here receive serious consideration.

For many years now, serious students of Mormonism have recognized the importance to the story of Mormon beginnings of the situation in western New York during the future prophet's childhood and adolescence. In recounting what happened, however, scholars typically describe the Burned-over District primarily in terms of its impact on Joseph Smith, Jr.[8] In so doing, they fail to represent fully the religious and psychic as well as social and economic impact that living in the district had on the Smith family, and how living in a family that was searching for truth wherever it might be found intensified the impact that the region's religious environment had on the future prophet.

During much of the decade of the 1820s, the Smith family was virtually a microcosm of the religious macrocosm in which it was immersed. The senior Joseph was a curious combination of deist and seeker. His father had given him a copy of Thomas Paine's *Age of Reason* that he seems to have read with great interest. Yet he was also influenced by dreams which—according to his wife's history of the family—were filled with transparent symbols of an impending restoration of truth to the earth and which started him on a search for true religion outside the pathways of orthodoxy. Smith *père* held himself aloof from organized religion, as did his eldest son, Alvin, but Lucy Mack Smith and three of her children (the family's second and fourth sons, Hyrum and Samuel, and eldest daughter, Sophronia) joined the Presbyterian Church in Palmyra. This brought an intense biblicism directly into the family circle, and it made the family members aware of the various theological arguments concerning the degree of congenital depravity human beings are heir to, as well as introducing them to the struggle between enthusiasm and conservatism that marked the early nineteenth-century experience of this denomination. Hyrum joined the Masons, too, adding that element to the multiplicity of religious ideas presenting themselves for discussion within the Smith ménage. Moreover, magic and the occult were so fascinating to the prophet's father—and perhaps also to Alvin and other members of the family—that the more esoteric components of the western New York religio-cultural situation were additional ingredients in the immediate familial milieu in which Joseph Smith, Jr., grew to manhood.

If chronological accounts of Mormonism proceed directly from descriptions of the family's move from New England and characterizations of the region in which the Smiths settled to the young prophet's story, focus is not kept on the family unit long enough to describe young Joseph's experiences in the context of the religious ambience within the Smith family circle. Although the world, as represented in Joseph Smith's own history by a clergyman of a popular Christian denomination, scoffed, Joseph's family thought that unbelief closes the way to knowledge, and the teenager's accounts of his visions were, for that reason, apparently accepted without question. The Smiths welcomed Joseph's announcement that he had obtained a treasure trove that "contained the fulness of the everlasting Gospel"; they believed in him when he said that "a great and marvelous work [was] about to come forth unto the children of men"; and they strongly supported his efforts to make this work available to humanity in the latter days. Their immediately positive reactions to the surprising information imparted to them by one of their own number makes the Smith family's response to the prophet so critical to the LDS story that accounts of Mormon beginnings are incomplete when so much emphasis is placed on Joseph Smith, Jr., that his family recedes into the background.

Although he remembered having reported it at the time it occurred only to members of his own family and to one member of the clergy in Palmyra, fourteen-year-old Joseph Smith's "First Vision" is now widely regarded as the initial episode in Mormon history.[9] Fixed in time and place in Smith's canonized account as having been manifested in a grove of trees on the family farm on the morning of a beautiful clear day in the spring of 1820, this theophany answered the lad's question about which of the "sects" were right and which were wrong. When the two personages appeared to him in that "pillar of light," they told him that he must not join any of the existing denominations for they were all wrong, an injunction that kept him from becoming a Presbyterian and, as it turned out, moved him closer to the position on religion taken by his father.

When he wrote his history for posterity the Mormon prophet summarized the events of his life during the decade of the 1820s. He pursued his "common vocations in life," he said, even though he was "persecuted" because he insisted that a vision had been manifested to him in what is now called the "sacred grove." Yet Smith said he beheld a second vision during the night of 21/22 September 1823. This time it was a vision of an angel who identified himself as Moroni, "a messenger sent from the presence of God" to tell of records written on gold plates which, along with two special stones called the Urim and Thummim, were buried in a hill not far from the Smith family farm. From Moroni the young man learned that "the possession and use of these stones were what constituted 'seers' in ancient or former times, and that God had prepared them for the purpose of translating the book" that was engraved in "Reformed Egyptian" characters on the gold plates.

As often as the stories of Joseph Smith's visions are repeated, it
is surprising that very little emphasis is placed on Smith's description of how he was affected by these two experiences in
which he received his divine calling. At the conclusion of his description of the 1820 experience, Joseph said, "When I came to
myself again, I found myself lying on my back looking up to
heaven . . . I had no strength." Then, recalling the aftermath of
the night of 21/22 September 1823 in which his interviews with
the angel Moroni "must have occupied the whole of that night,"
Joseph said his strength was so exhausted that when he tried to
work alongside his father as usual he found he could not. Leaving
his father's side, he started back to the house, only to fall "help-
less to the ground, and for a time [to be] quite unconscious of anything." It stands to reason that it was the phenomenon of visionary trance to which Smith referred, and if this is, in fact, correct,
then these trances, coming in response to divine calling, parallel a
similar trance in which Saul became Paul on the road to Damas-
cus. Possibly they also parallel instances of "possession trance"
that legitimated prophetic figures in pre-exilic Israel.[10]

When he was told of the existence of the gold plates and the
Urim and Thummim in the 1823 vision, Joseph Smith was also
told by the angel Moroni that he had been called to the task of
translating the engravings on the plates with the aid of the "ancient seers." This was an unusual assignment, but it does not
appear quite so strange when it is placed in historical context.
Smith's "First Vision" caused him to stay away from the orthodox
Christianity of his day. As he worked alongside his elder brothers
and his father—who was particularly predisposed toward the miraculous and willing to search for truth in unorthodox places—
the lad came into contact with the folk magic that was very much
present in his region of the country. Prior to his having reported
the vision in which he learned about the existence of a record
graven on plates of gold, Joseph had found a "seerstone," a smooth
stone "the size but not the shape of a hen's egg," whose magical
properties reputedly made possible the location of lost objects and
metals hidden beneath the surface of the earth.[11] His possession of
this occult article, which he found while helping his brother
Alvin dig a well for one Willard Chase, allowed the Smith family
to take up what was known in those days as "money-digging."

Because Smith's efforts to find ordinary buried treasure were gradually transformed into a search for treasure of infinitely greater value, he later dismissed his youthful treasure-hunting activities as trivial and unimportant, but they were recalled in later years by neighbors of the Smith family, who connected them to Joseph's claim of having found plates of gold. In one of the many affidavits about the Smith family during the 1820s that Philastus Hurlbut collected in 1833 for publication in *Mormonism Unvailed* [*sic*], Willard Chase claimed that the prophet told him "that if it had not been for that [seer]stone . . . he would not have found the book." Lucy Harris, the daughter of one of the prophet's very first followers, suggested that Martin Harris also believed that Smith's gold treasure had been located with the stone, in which Joseph could see "anything he wished." This same belief was later held by some of Smith's followers, for Hosea Stout wrote in his diary in 1856 that Brigham Young "exhibited the Seer's stone with which The Prophet Joseph discovered the plates of the Book of Mormon."[12]

If such evidence does not establish a *direct* connection between the prophet's having possessed a seerstone and his having gained possession of a treasure whose secret had to be unlocked with "stones [that] were what constituted 'seers' in ancient or former times," chronology establishes an *implicit* connection. Joseph's 1820 vision was followed in 1822 by his finding a seerstone. In 1823, he reported to his mother and father that he had learned of the existence of a cache of gold plates, but he said he was unable to gain possession of them until 1827. He was, nevertheless, permitted (or required) to make annual visits in September 1824, 1825, and 1826 to see the plates in the place where they were buried and to talk with the angel Moroni. During those same four years, the Joseph Smiths, father and son, were very much engaged in the hunting of treasure, and in one instance in 1826, their failure to find any led to a trial in Bainbridge, New York, in which the younger of the two was charged with being a disorderly person, a "glass looker," and/or an impostor.[13] Then, in September 1827, Joseph Smith, Jr., said that he had gained possession of the gold plates and the Urim and Thummim, an instrument that apparently functioned in the manner of a seerstone, revealing a long-lost story to the young prophet.

According to his mother's reminiscences, Joseph had told his family about the plates and described the importance of their contents to them long before he actually obtained the treasure. Joseph's story may have amazed his parents and siblings, yet any questions they had were obviously answered within the family circle, for the response of the family to the announcement that one of their own had been selected to translate a mysterious record that would be their means of salvation shows a family united in the belief that "a marvelous work and a wonder" was about to come forth. Members of the family who had joined the Palmyra Presbyterians stopped attending the services of that church as their expectations about the impending restoration of the apostolic form of Christianity took hold in their religious imaginations. And all the family members extended such assistance as they could manage to further the work of the one of their number through whom they believed God had started to speak anew to their generation.

In January 1827, some eight months before he reported that the plates were in his possession, Joseph married Emma Hale of Harmony, Pennsylvania, and brought her back to live with him on the Smith family farm in Manchester. Emma was the daughter of Isaac Hale, a man who had formed his opinion of Joseph when the Smiths were engaged in the search for treasure that had led to the Bainbridge court trial. He very much disapproved of Joseph's money-digging activities and he very much disapproved of the match. Yet his daughter seems also to have accepted her new husband's calling without question, and, as did his family of lineage, she seems to have supported him in his efforts to accomplish what he told her he had been called to do. As the story goes, Emma went along when Joseph took a horse and wagon borrowed without permission from Joseph Knight, Sr., to fetch the Urim and Thummim and the gold plates. Moreover, when the news that he possessed the plates had stimulated so many attempts to get them away from Joseph that he decided he would have to leave Manchester and go elsewhere to prepare the translation of the record, Emma braved her father's disapproval by traveling with her husband back to Harmony, Pennsylvania, where his work of translation might proceed without impediment.

The members of Joseph's own family and his wife were not the only persons who were involved with him in preparing the Book of Mormon for presentation to the world. Other active participants in the work that went forward between fall 1827, when Joseph said the plates and the ancient seers were entrusted to him, and spring 1830, when the Book of Mormon was published, were Martin Harris, a prosperous farmer from the Palmyra region; Joseph Knight, Sr., a friend of the Smith family whose home was in Colesville, New York; Oliver Cowdery, a young schoolteacher who came to board with the Smiths in Manchester after Emma and Joseph left for Pennsylvania; and various members of the family of Peter and Mary Whitmer, who lived in Fayette, in Seneca County, New York. These were all persons who not only came to believe that Joseph had gold plates, but also to accept his claim that the plates were actually a book whose text contained the fulness of the gospel that would lead to salvation. For that reason, it is not surprising that they brought provisions or money, or provided free room and board, so that Joseph could work at translating, rather than at plowing fields and harvesting crops, nor that they were willing to do much more.

Despite extant reminiscences of several of the persons involved, an air of mystery surrounds what went on as the Book of Mormon and Mormonism itself came into being.[14] It is clear, however, that Harmony, in the Susquehanna country in northern Pennsylvania, was the central locale of action between December 1827 and June 1829. In the latter summer, Joseph and Emma moved north to Fayette, New York, where they boarded with the Whitmer family until the translation of the book was completed at some point early in 1830. Oliver Cowdery, who served as Smith's chief scribe from 7 April 1829 forward, boarded there as well. Other persons who had started to follow Joseph also made their way to Fayette. In addition, the parents of Joseph Smith and one or another of his siblings occasionally visited from Manchester, keeping the family in close touch with the progress of the translation of the record.

A number of references to the gold plates are found in the historical record—Joseph said that they were carried south hidden in a forty-gallon barrel of beans, for example, and Lucy Smith remembered later that they were sometimes kept in a red morocco trunk on Emma's bureau—but, despite a great deal of somewhat naive speculation, the importance of the plates to the process of translation has never been established. The ancient seers and/or Joseph's seerstone seem, rather, to have been the key to the procedure by which the Book of Mormon came into existence. "Through the medium of the Urim and Thummim, I translated the record by the gift and power of God," said Joseph Smith in an 1842 statement that is consistent with descriptions of his having dictated the text of the Book of Mormon to various scribes as he sat with his face buried in his hat, wherein he had placed a seerstone. Emma Smith and Oliver Cowdery both recalled that this was the way Joseph worked, adding that he could work that way for hours on end. Joseph never indicated when, or if, he had to consult the "Reformed Egyptian" hieroglyphics that were said to have been engraved on the gold plates that he said he had, but invaluable evidence survives to explain exactly how the gift of translation worked.

The exhilaration that Oliver Cowdery felt in the spring of 1829 as he recorded the words that were spoken by Joseph led him to petition for a similar gift of translation. God responded, said Joseph Smith, with a revelation to Cowdery promising that he would "receive a knowledge concerning the engravings of old records" through a manifestation of the Holy Ghost "which shall come upon you and which shall dwell in your heart." Although this revelation made it clear that this manifestation of knowledge "in your mind and in your heart" was to be his gift, Cowdery apparently tried his hand at translating in the manner of Joseph Smith. His lack of success led to a second revelation, also given through Joseph Smith, in which God clarified the translation process:

> Behold you have not understood, you have supposed that I would give it [the gift of translation] unto you when you took no thought, save it was to ask me; but behold I say unto you that you must study it out in your mind; then you must ask me if it be right, and if it is right, I will cause that your bosom shall burn within you: therefore, you shall feel that it is right; but if it be not right, you shall have no such feelings, but you shall have a stupor of thought that shall cause you to forget the thing which is wrong: therefore, you cannot write that which is sacred, save it be given you from me.[15]

Although the hieroglyphics may not have been necessary to the translation procedure, they were very important in an episode involving Martin Harris and two eminent scholars in which the divine origin of the gold plates and the ancient record was verified for Joseph. Harris was the prosperous yet credulous Palmyra farmer who extended the financial support that allowed Joseph and Emma to leave Manchester in 1827, and he soon followed them to Harmony, where he became Joseph's scribe. In 1828, in response to a vision that he had had, in which he was commanded to show a document containing "characters which [Joseph] had drawn off the plates" to knowledgeable scholars, Harris traveled to the East to show such a document to Professor Samuel L. Mitchill of Rutgers and Professor Charles Anthon of Columbia College. Because the report Harris brought back focused attention on the scholars and not on what they had said, the significance of this episode was overlooked for many years. Mitchill said that he could not read the document, while Anthon—having asked to see the plates themselves rather than the incomplete copy, and having learned that this would be impossible—told Harris that he could not read a "sealed book."[16]

These results no doubt disappointed Harris, but the scholars' inability to read what he said he had copied from the plates did not disappoint Joseph Smith. Quite the reverse. In his thinking, as revealed in a note in his own hand written on the back of the sheet containing the characters, the statements of Mitchill and Anthon were convincing evidence that the record engraved on the plates was, in fact, the sealed book that the learned could not read, the book "delivered to him that is not learned," which preceded "a marvelous work and a wonder" that God would inaugurate, according to prophecy recorded in Isaiah 29, on the day when the book comes forth. Then, the Old Testament prophet had said, the deaf shall "hear the words of the book, and the eyes of the blind shall see out of obscurity, and out of darkness, the meek also shall increase their joy in the Lord, and the poor among men shall rejoice in the Holy One of Israel."

Martin Harris somewhat inadvertently played an even more crucial role in bringing Mormonism into being when he persuaded Joseph to let him take the first 116 pages of the text of the Book of Mormon from Pennsylvania back to Palmyra to show his wife and family. Harris had been investing his time and his substance in support of Joseph Smith's work. His motivation in asking for this privilege was probably his desire to prove to his family that the work was "of God." This Joseph Smith no doubt realized. Possibly he even anticipated needing to call on Harris's financial resources so that the Book of Mormon could be published. Yet Joseph was exceedingly reluctant to disregard the charge he had received to be personally responsible for the plates (and, by extension, the text of the record) until they should be returned to the heavenly messenger from whom they had been given into his hand. If he let the plates (or the text) go carelessly or through any neglect of his own, Joseph feared being "cut off"; the Urim and Thummim and the plates might be taken from him, and he would be powerless to fulfill his calling.

When Harris continued to importune for permission to show the foolscap pages to his wife, who was suspicious of the Smith family and unsympathetic to the work at hand, Joseph decided, however, that it would be best to "inquire of the Lord through the Urim and Thummim if he might not do so." Joseph first received a negative answer, but Harris was so adamant about needing to convince his wife that the work in which he was engaged was divinely mandated that Joseph kept reiterating his inquiry through the Urim and Thummim until he became convinced that he had permission to let Harris take the writing home. He required the scribe to promise to show the text to members of his immediate family and to no one else, however. This Harris did, solemnly covenanting with Joseph to abide by these conditions, and in early June 1828, he left for Palmyra carrying with him the only existing copy of the first 116 pages of the text of the Book of Mormon.

A tragic conclusion to Emma's first pregnancy (in which she had a long and very hard labor, only to give birth to a baby that lived less than a day) initially kept Joseph's mind off the fact that he had allowed the Book of Mormon text to leave his hands. For two weeks he thought of little else than the death of the child and the dreadful illness of his wife. But as Emma regained her health, Joseph started to worry about what he had agreed to and the fact that he had not heard from Martin Harris in nearly a month.

Therefore, as soon as he felt it safe to leave Emma in her mother's care, he started for the Palmyra area to retrieve the manuscript. But soon after he reached the Smith farm in Manchester, Joseph learned, to his great dismay, that the 116 pages had disappeared and that Harris, who had broken his covenant, showing the pages to many persons, had absolutely no idea what had happened to them. This knowledge almost drove Joseph to despair, for he believed that all was lost. "He wept and groaned and walked the floor continually," his mother said, and "all the family [was] in the same situation of mind . . . for sobs and groans and the most bitter lamentations filled the house." The expectations of Joseph and his family that had been "so fondly anticipated . . . the source of so much secret gratification had in a moment fled."

A close reading of Joseph Smith's own history, the revelations dated 1828 and early 1829, especially as printed in the Book of Commandments, and Lucy Mack Smith's history of her son reveal how vitally important to the development of Joseph Smith's religious career was the loss of the forepart of the Book of Mormon manuscript and Smith's reaction to the loss. Worried beyond all consolation, the future prophet immediately returned to Pennsylvania. The trip gave him plenty of time for reflection. He must have thought about how he had ignored the negative answers he received when he initially inquired through the Urim and Thummim whether he should let Martin Harris take the manuscript home to show his wife and family, for as soon as he reached home, "he commenced humbling [himself] before the Lord," pouring out his soul in supplication that he might "be forgiven of all that [he] had done contrary to [the Lord's] will." [17]

Joseph later told his mother how contrite he had been, adding that an angel came as he was praying and took both the plates and the Urim and Thummim from him. The angel had informed him, however, that if he would be "humble and penitent" it was possible that these things could be returned to him. "Repent of that which thou has done which is contrary to the commandment which I [the Lord] gave you," Joseph said he was told, for "thou art still chosen and art again called to the work."

The authors of most historical accounts move from a description of the loss of the 116 pages of manuscript directly to what many call the "convenient" revelation, in which Joseph was told not to retranslate the story from the same plates he had used before, but to translate the story as it was recorded on "the plates of Nephi." Then authors go on to describe the subsequent completion of the text of the Book of Mormon. In so doing, they fail to recognize the significance of the period between late summer

1828 and early spring 1829 as a time when Joseph Smith seems to have come to terms with his calling.

The connection (or lack thereof) between ordinary magic and the working of the divine hand was not clarified in the earliest days of Mormonism. The Book of Mormon and Smith's religious claims were rejected by many of the persons who had known him in the 1820s because they remembered him as a practitioner of the magic arts. Yet if Martin Harris, Oliver Cowdery, and Smith's own father may be taken as typical, some of Joseph's earliest followers accepted his book and his claims for precisely the same reason. The retrospective account of his life that Smith wrote in 1838, from the standpoint of having successfully established himself as a prophet, fails to mention any questions Joseph entertained regarding this issue. Yet it stands to reason that Smith, too, might sometimes have wondered about the nature of the connection between magical practice and manifestations of divinity despite his convictions about the reality of his visions and the assurances his father gave him that they were "of God."

If the episode in the early spring of 1828, when Harris carried the document on which the characters had been copied to show them to the scholars, helped Joseph to see what he was doing in the context of Isaiah 29, as the notation on the back of the document indicates that it did, the loss of the manuscript pages that summer and the period of deep reflection that followed allowed Joseph to resolve any remaining doubts as he came to a full comprehension of the nature of his gift. While he said that the plates and the ancient seers were returned to him on 22 September 1828 (exactly one year from the day on which he had first reported that they were in his possession), Joseph did not immediately begin translating, even though he had received the revelation in July that had solved the worrisome problem that might have arisen if a second translation had been compared with the one that had been lost. He could have set to work immediately with his wife serving as scribe, but he went, rather, "to laboring with his hands upon a small farm" that summer, an occupation that encouraged contemplative thought and led him to a clearer understanding of what lay ahead.

From the standpoint of theology, comparison of this period of bucolic introspection in Joseph Smith's life and the forty days that

Jesus spent in the wilderness would be improper. From a structural perspective, however, when the goal is determining developmental patterns in religious leadership, these two periods of retrospection are reasonably parallel. Forward progress on the translation stopped to allow Smith this period of spiritual preparation. As did the wilderness period in the life of Jesus, this period immediately preceded the inauguration of Smith's public ministry.

By February 1829, when Joseph Smith, Sr., and Lucy arrived to visit Joseph and Emma and, incidentally, to learn what was going on, Joseph had become fully aware of what he had to do. This is clear because he started translating again, and because a revelation to his father, probably given through the Urim and Thummim, announced triumphantly that "a marvelous work [was] about to come forth among the children of men." This revelation called the senior Joseph into the service of God. "For behold the field is white already to harvest: and lo, he that thrusteth in his sickle with his might, the same layeth up in store that he perisheth not, but bringeth salvation to the soul."[18]

While the time for the work to begin had clearly come, the plan of procedure was not spelled out until a revelation a month later directed Joseph to finish translating the record before taking on other tasks. ("For I [God] will grant unto you no other gift until my purpose is fulfilled in this, for I will grant unto you no other gift until it is finished.") Thereafter, the revelation said, Joseph would be ordained and would go forth to deliver God's words "unto the children of men," for "this generation shall have [God's] word through you." That is, upon completion of the record, Joseph would be called upon to carry out the prophet's task, meaning that he would—as prophets have done down through the ages— speak for God. In addition, three witnesses would be called and ordained, unto whom God would "show these things and they shall go forth" with God's word as given through Joseph Smith. "And behold, whosoever believeth in [God's] word will [he] visit with the manifestations of [his] spirit, and they shall be born of [God] and their testimony shall go forth. And thus if the people . . . harden not their hearts," God promised to work a reformation among them and establish his church among them, "like unto the church which was taught by [his] disciples in the days of old." But if hearts were hardened against the word, as spoken by Joseph and the witnesses, if people failed to repent and believe, "they would be delivered up unto satan," or, as a later edition of the revelation stated, "consumed away and utterly destroyed by the brightness" of the Lord's return to the earth.

Interspersed among the various parts of the programme in this extraordinarily important revelation (section 5 in the Doctrine and Covenants of both the LDS and RLDS churches) are warnings to Joseph "to repent and walk more uprightly before [the Lord] and to yield to the persuasions of men no more." Perhaps of greater moment, the revelation included warnings about what Joseph must say to Martin Harris. This man had been impressed by Joseph's supernatural abilities as early as 1824 and, for all practical purposes, had been Joseph's patron even before he gained possession of the plates. Yet he had to be told, the revelation said, that Joseph had entered into a covenant with God not to show the things he had been given to any person save those to whom God commanded that they be shown. Harris, who wished to be one of the witnesses, would not be allowed to view the plates unless he humbled himself and agreed that he would say, "Behold I have seen the things and I know of a surety that they are true, for I have seen them, and they have been shown unto me by the power of God and not of man." The revelation continued, "And I [the Lord] command him that he shall say no more unto [people] concerning these things, except he shall say, I have seen them and they have been shown unto me by the power of God. And these are the words which he shall say. But if he deny this . . . behold he is condemned."

Coming as it did, at the end of his period of reflection, this revelation cleared away what might be described as the debris from the Mormon prophet's early career. It dealt with a problem (i.e., Martin Harris) that, in the words of the revelation, was "lying in wait to destroy [Joseph]" even as it reminded him of the significance to his generation of the contents of the record he was translating. This revelation also allowed Joseph to look forward to fulfilling a calling as a prophet who would speak for God, to anticipate the church being established as in apostolic days, and to expect, in the end, "the brightness of the Lord."

During the eighteen months between the end of September 1827 and the end of March 1829, the nature of his calling was

clarified and the character of the record that he said he had found
was verified for Joseph Smith. Yet other than the section that was
lost, not much appears to have actually been done on the translation of the Book of Mormon. After 7 April 1829, however, the
work progressed with amazing rapidity. The change in the pace of
activity was not entirely due to the fact that Smith's time of se-
clusion and reflection were at an end, for Oliver Cowdery's assumption of the scribal task seems to have been the catalyst that
inaugurated such an astonishing acceleration in the work that the
entire book, which would run to nearly 600 pages, was ready to go
to the printer early in 1830.

Cowdery, who may have been a distant relative of Joseph Smith
through Joseph's grandfather, Solomon Mack, had heard about the
plates and the ancient seers from Joseph, Sr., and Lucy Mack
Smith. He found the story fascinating enough to go to Pennsylvania to investigate, possibly because he had had some success
using a divining rod and was, thus, interested in the folk magic
that was so popular in that time and place.[19] Since he arrived on
5 April and started to act as Smith's scribe two days later, it is obvious that he was quickly convinced of the worth of what Joseph
was doing and, incidentally, that 6 April was an important day for
the LDS movement in 1829, as well as in 1830.

As their dating gives only the month (April 1829) in which
three revelations were manifested to Cowdery through Joseph
Smith, no determination can be made of the relative importance
in Cowdery's decision to join in the work of translation, on the
one hand, and Smith's own account of the significance of the project, on the other. Perhaps it was somewhat difficult for Cowdery
to distinguish between Joseph as revelator and Joseph as persuasive rhetorician. Yet the revelations surely carry great weight
in explaining the intensity of Cowdery's labors across the twelve
months between 7 April 1829 and 6 April 1830, the period between the beginning of his assumption of the scribal task and the
formal organization of the Church of Jesus Christ. Although one
of these communications from the divine was disappointing in its
directions to Cowdery to simply serve as Smith's amanuensis
rather than translate from the record himself, the others assured
Cowdery that he was called to assist in bringing forth a great and
marvelous work; that the words he was writing were true; that he
and Joseph Smith together held the keys to the ancient scriptures

that had been hidden away for nearly 2,000 years; and, in the earliest printings, the revelations also told Cowdery that his work with the divining rod was "of God," a gift that was not unrelated to the work he was currently carrying out.

But while these revelations set what Cowdery and Smith were doing apart from the ordinary business of life, revelation was not required to alert the two men to the momentous nature of their activity. The excitement of discovering a "new witness for Christ" in the words of the story that fell from Smith's lips made the two willing to work at a feverish pace for long hours every day. In addition, as the translation proceeded, exhilarating vistas were opened to them: the announcement of the coming forth of a prophet, whose name, like that of his father, would be Joseph, may have been more or less routine, given the role of Joseph Smith, Jr., in the translation process, but the prospect of the restoration of the priesthoods of Aaron and Melchizedek and the forming again of the church of the lamb of God, as it had existed in apostolic times, raised the expectations of Smith and Cowdery to dizzying heights. In the long run, it is significant that a revelation came to Smith and Cowdery to settle the issue of whether John, the beloved disciple, had "tarried in the flesh or had died," for it foreshadowed revelation's future function in articulating doctrine and settling doctrinal issues. Yet such revelation was not needed in the spring of 1829 to signify to Smith and Cowdery the impending opening of a new dispensation of the fulness of times.

As often happens when the spirit makes itself known to one portion of humanity, the excitement that infected the lives of Joseph and Oliver Cowdery soon became epidemic, and in the remainder of Smith's "little flock" revelation was very much a part of the story. Expectations mounted as revelation was manifested, either through the Urim and Thummim or simply through Joseph Smith himself, informing the various members of the Smith and Whitmer families that a marvelous work and a wonder was about to come forth, that the field was white to the harvest, and that humanity was called to repentance as a necessary prelude to accepting the religious and secular implications of the story contained in Smith's "golden bible."

Several persons, including Joseph Smith's brother Hyrum, were called to preach repentance to their generation. But for the nonce that was all that could be preached, since the church was not yet organized and doctrinal questions were not settled. Before that would happen, the text of the Book of Mormon had to be completed; its legitimacy as a translation of the engravings on golden plates had to be established through the testimony of witnesses; and the theological ground had to be prepared for the organization of the church.

All three requirements were fulfilled virtually simultaneously. During the summer of 1829, as Emma and Joseph Smith and Oliver Cowdery boarded at the home of Peter and Mary Whitmer, Smith and Cowdery worked tirelessly at the translation. That summer, also, two sets of witnesses were called to see the plates. A trio composed of Cowdery, Martin Harris, and David Whitmer testified in the words of a formula specified in a revelation to Joseph Smith that they had been shown the plates by the power of God and not of man. And a second set of witnesses—eight in number, including five members of the Whitmer family plus Joseph Smith's father and his brothers Hyrum and Samuel—declared in a more prosaic, but no less sincere, fashion that they had "seen and hefted" the plates.

On 15 May 1829 a revelation was manifested to Smith and Cowdery in which the priesthood of Aaron (the Levitical priesthood) was restored to the earth, making baptism under a new and everlasting covenant possible. That was the same month in which Hyrum Smith was called to preach. And soon thereafter Oliver Cowdery and David Whitmer were called into the ministry and assigned to search out and identify potential apostles.

All this made possible the organization of the church. But that formal action did not take place until the publication of the book containing "all those parts of [God's] gospel which [his] disciples desired in their prayers should come forth" had been announced.[20] Then, as is shown in Chapter Two, the Mormon movement could begin.

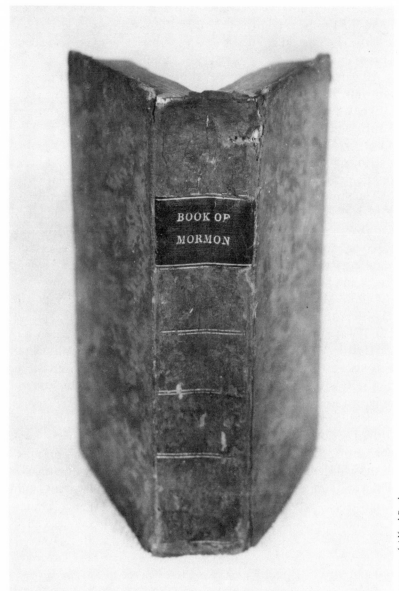

A first edition of the Book of Mormon

Chapter Two

In the Beginning . . .

In THE BEGINNING there were words filling page after page after page with unpunctuated prose. About Near Eastern peoples who came to America in Old Testament times, the words told of the Jaredites, who came to the western hemisphere at the time of the destruction of the "great tower," when "the Lord confounded the language of the people and swore in his wrath that they should be scattered upon all the face of the earth." They told, too, of the descendants of Mulek, the "son of Zedekiah," who settled in the north. But most especially, the words on the foolscap paper told the strange sad tale of the family of Lehi, a Hebraic patriarch who escaped being carried into bondage by leaving Jerusalem before the Babylonian desolation in 587 B.C.E.

Bringing the Torah with them, plus prophecies of the "holy prophets" and genealogical records engraved on brass which established Lehi's Abrahamic lineage through Joseph, the son of Jacob, this family traveled across the great waters only to break into warring factions upon their arrival in the land that is "choice above all other lands." For nearly six centuries two peoples, called after the names of two of Lehi's sons, struggled with each other for supremacy, the Nephites generally being on the side of righteousness and the Lamanites being the wicked ones. The appearance of the resurrected Christ and his ministry (which included delivering the Sermon on the Mount) to these peoples in America initiated more than 200 years of harmony, keeping the story from being one of unrelieved hostility. But as in Jerusalem and Antioch, Rome and Constantinople on the other side of the globe, the memory of the ministry of Christ and possession of his gospel did not cause enmity among peoples to disappear entirely. So it came to pass that in the third century after the departure of Jesus from the earth, the words describe brother turning, as it were, once more against brother. An extended and dreadful battle ensued wherein the city of Desolation repeatedly changed hands. For a time it looked as if the Nephites would triumph, but in the story's tragic climax, the Lamanites destroyed the Nephites, root and branch. All except Moroni, who alone survived, to add "the sad tale of the destruction of [his] people" to the records somehow preserved by his father, Mormon, and, upon completion of that melancholy task, to "hide up the records in the earth." The victors likewise suffered, losing everything of value in the terrible battle and its aftermath. With access neither to history nor genealogy, in time the Lamanites—from whom, say the words, American Indians are descended—would forget their heritage as children of the wandering Aramean who went down to Egypt long ago.

Set in type in E. B. Grandin's Palmyra, New York, print shop, paged, put through the press, and printed in biblical fashion as a collection of books (here divided into chapters, but not further subdivided into verses), the words were published in 1830 as *The Book of Mormon: An Account Written by the Hand of Mormon upon Plates Taken from the Plates of Nephi.* Notwithstanding the title-page designation of Joseph Smith, Jr., as the author, the body of the work was bracketed with a preface and concluding testimonies which, by bearing witness to the existence of plates covered with engravings from whence the words had come, corroborated the assertion of the work's subtitle that the Book of Mormon was a translation.[1]

Carried about the countryside and sold or given away by the members of the Smith family and a few of Smith's friends, this curious book seemed to some of its readers to be a harmless romance, as historical novels were then quaintly called. Upon reading it (or even just hearing about it), others also concluded that it was fiction, but a monstrous fiction filled to overflowing with heresy.[2] The book convinced a select number of readers, however, that it was not ordinary—or even extraordinary—fiction. To them the Book of Mormon was precisely what it said it was: a translation of ancient records that had been written, sealed up, and hidden in the earth for more than fourteen centuries.[3]

These responses reflected a great deal more than conflicting opinion about literary merit and disagreement about narrative *vraisemblance*. In the last chapter of the final book of the work, words of Moroni exhort readers to "ask God, the Eternal Father, in the name of Christ, if these things are not true," adding assurance immediately thereafter that if one asks "with a sincere heart, with real intent, having faith in Christ," the truth of the contents of the Book of Mormon will be made manifest "by the power of the Holy Ghost."[4] Appended as they are to a book that represents itself as a record of God's dealings with his people in the western hemisphere, the sheep not of the fold described in the Old and New Testaments, the words of this exhortation made authenticity the critical query about which readers of the volume had to make up their minds. Making judgments about whether the book was interesting, informative, or worthwhile was not enough. The issue was much more fundamental: was this a Hebraic record once "hid up," but now brought forth to show the Indians that they were the "remnant of the House of Israel"; and brought forth, too, in order to demonstrate to "Jew and Gentile that JESUS is the CHRIST, the ETERNAL GOD manifesting Himself to all nations"? In other words, was this a "second witness"; was it "another testament of Jesus Christ"?[5]

All truth claims are potentially divisive. The truth claims at the very heart of the Book of Mormon guaranteed that this potential would be realized as soon as this "very strange book," as Parley P. Pratt called it, thrust itself into culture. Humanity ever since has been divided up, so to speak, into opposing camps, one peopled by individuals who treat the book as just a book and nothing more. Set over and against this population is a camp in which the network of truth claims in the work is treated as a valid description of what once was and what will be. Whatever their location on the continuum stretching between thinking that the book is "a 'silly mess of stuff' not worth the perusal" and thinking it "the most ingenious literary work ever put together," people in the first camp have regarded the book from the first as a nineteenth-

century document composed by a nineteenth-century man completely concerned with such nineteenth-century matters as anti-
Masonry and the ethnic origin of the American Indians.[6] The
other camp, however, has always been filled with people for whom
the Book of Mormon was and is, at one and the same time, a
nineteenth-century document and an ancient record, a book and
more than a book.

For such persons, the book has ever been "something of a wholly
different order, a reality which does not belong to [this] world,"
but something that is, nevertheless, a part of this world.[7] It is
manifested in the form of historical accounts of past events, a
form integral to everyday experience. Yet it has never lent itself to
the same process of verification that historians use to verify ordinary accounts of what happened in the past. The historicity of the
Book of Mormon has been *asserted* through demonstrations that
ancient concepts, practices, doctrines, and rituals are present in
the work; that the nineteenth century's overwhelming concern
with liberty and the working of the political process is absent
from it; that from the standpoint of archaeology, its account of
settlement and peoples "makes sense" and could have happened;
that the pre-Columbian compilers of the various books within the
work had distinct literary styles, and so on.[8] But such demonstrations point, finally, only to plausibility. Proof is a different matter.

From the first, individuals came to believe that the Book of
Mormon is an ancient document as they read it. "With a prayerful
desire to know the truth" Brigham Young read the work, and his
investigation resulted in a firm conviction "that the Book of Mormon is 'a divine record.'" Sidney Rigdon was convinced of its
truth after a fortnight's careful perusal of the volume and "much
prayer and meditation." After reading the work through twice,
George Q. Cannon remarked that "no wicked man could write
such a book as this; and no good man could write it unless it were
true and he were commanded by God to do so." A copy fell "acci-
dentally or providentially" into the hands of Willard Richards,
who also, in about ten days, read it twice through, concluding
that it was true. And many people still gain a testimony about the
truth of the Book of Mormon when they follow the injunctions of
the missionaries to ask prayerfully, as directed in Moroni 10:4, "if
these things are not true."[9]

Because the Book of Mormon's claim to historicity has been fully authenticated only in a fashion that does not lend itself to intellectual verification, it becomes a paradox whenever it is unquestionably accepted as a nineteenth-century translation of documents that had been buried for 1,400 years. Paraphrasing Mircea Eliade, to the people who accept its historicity, the Book of Mormon remains a book, yet by manifesting the sacred, it becomes something other than a book. While nothing distinguishes it from all other books except its claim to be a record of God's dealing with His people in the western hemisphere, "for those to whom [it] reveals itself as sacred, its immediate reality is transmuted into a supernatural reality." Its claims become something more than mere propositions; they become true.[10] But how? In what manner was this book, whose origin was explained in supernatural terms, transmuted into a record of actual events involving real people?

If it had been totally abstracted from everyday experience, this transmutation would have been too esoteric to analyze. But there was more than spiritual validation to the transaction in which Mormons became convinced of the historicity of the Book of Mormon. The work that Smith said he translated from records engraved on gold plates presented itself as the fulfillment of biblical prophecy to a world wherein the Bible was still culturally defined as an undoubtedly authentic record of actual events involving real people, a record whose prophetic predictions would be literally fulfilled. Skepticism's inroads made some people doubters, but Americans in the 1830s generally regarded the Bible as the actual "stick of Judah" to which, so Ezekiel had said, the "stick of Joseph" would someday be joined. Hence, when persons credited the Mormon claim that the Book of Mormon was the "stick of Joseph in the hand of Ephraim," the work took on a biblical character for them. They saw the events that it described as actual events involving real people, and they confidently expected that its prophetic pronouncements would literally come to pass.[11]

The assertion that the work was the "stick of Joseph in the hand of Ephraim" was not the only thing that tied the Book of Mormon to the Bible. Persons who accepted the volume's contents as reliable descriptions of past events also accepted at face value Joseph Smith's acount of how it came into being. Referring to the gold plates on which ancient records were engraved that had long been buried not far from his home, Smith had said that "Moroni, who deposited the plates in a hill in Manchester, Ontario county, New York, being dead and raised again therefrom, appeared unto me and told me where they were and gave me directions how to obtain them." He "obtained them and the Urim and Thummim with them," by means of which he translated the plates; "and thus came the Book of Mormon." Recognizing that this "resurrected angel," Moroni, can be regarded as the angel from the "midst of heaven" who is credited with "having the everlasting gospel to preach unto them that dwell on the earth, and to every nation, and kindred, and tongue, and people" further illuminates the situation. In the biblical culture that nourished early Mormonism, the story of how it came forth served to authenticate the Book of Mormon, while acceptance of the historicity of the work reciprocated by confirming Moroni's identification as the angel in Revelation 14:6.

Hearing testimony about the truth of the Book of Mormon having been revealed to individuals by "promptings of the spirit," by "a wonderful Heavenly Presence in the room," by the Holy Ghost, and so on, is not at all unusual in the world of modern Mormonism. In the twentieth century, however, accounts of spiritual verification of appearances of the angel Moroni to Joseph Smith have increasingly been overshadowed by testimony about experiential encounters that validate Smith's account of an 1820 vision in which he was visited not by an angel, but by the Father and the Son themselves. This is not to say that believers are starting to doubt the reality of Moroni's appearances; if they are certain that the record is both ancient and true, they do not doubt the explanation of how it came forth. But as far as Smith's so-called First Vision is concerned, more and more Mormons do not *believe* it happened: they *know*.

This development reflects the emphasis that has been placed on the 1820 vision across the last century.[12] Practically unknown until an account of it was published as a part of Joseph Smith's *History* in 1838—at least if earlier written accounts are used as a measure of how familiar the story of this vision was to early Mormons—this First Vision has assumed so much theological significance in Mormonism that it is now almost as important as any of the other elements—the Book of Mormon, Smith's revelations, the Books of Moses and Abraham—that set Mormonism apart as a unique faith.

Whether the Mormon story is related in a manner intended to establish its veracity or its fraudulent character—and as it always has been, the story continues to be told both ways—the narrative almost never begins nowadays with the coming forth of the Book of Mormon and the founding in 1830 of the organization from which the various Mormon churches have descended. Instead, a setting is generally established with an evocation of rampant revivalism as the source of a "war of words and tumult of [religious] opinions" that prevailed during the teen-age years of a young western New York farmer whose name, although he was not the eldest son, was like that of his father, Joseph. Then the story opens with accounts of Smith's First Vision that bestow substance on this theophany by locating it firmly in time, "on the morning of a beautiful, clear day, early in the spring of eighteen hundred and twenty," and space, a specific grove of hardwood trees near the place where the Smith family dwelt, outside the village of Manchester in Ontario County, New York, North America. Further granting essence to the vision, such accounts identify its genesis as a prayer for guidance about "which of all the sects was right," and the visionary experience itself as the source of Smith's subsequent contention that all the sects, by which was meant all the forms of Christianity then organized, were wrong.[13]

Since Smith's report of this divine response clears the way for the introduction of a new form of Christianity, it might appear that the 1820 vision has become central to the story of Mormonism's coming into being because it so effectively dispenses with other Christian claimants to legitimacy. But as the same message that existing creeds would all be abominations in God's sight when the record came forth out of the ground is also stressed in the Book of Mormon, it is obvious that overwhelming concern with Smith's 1820 vision cannot be explained simply as an effort to start the Mormon story with an impressive rationale for a new "sect to end all sects" or a new Christian church called into being in response to a new set of exclusive claims.

Close reading of many modern accounts reveals less emphasis on the sects all being wrong than on the implications of Joseph

Smith's having realized that the Father and the Son are two distinct personages with "bodies and parts." The vision's message that divinity still communicates with humanity is given great prominence. Smith's sincerity and piety are depicted. And, in one way or another, mainly through reminders that Mormonism started with the First Vision, all these accounts automatically place God in the position of inaugurating the Mormon saga.

That this way of relating Mormon beginnings did not make its appearance until the 1880s is established in the work of James B. Allen. Although he does not state it exactly in this fashion, Allen sees this development as a part of the process by which the Mormon story was canonized, a process well under way before Mormonism reached its first year of Jubilee. When the first generation of leadership died off, leaving the community to be guided mainly by men who had not known Joseph, the First Vision emerged as a symbol that could keep the slain Mormon leader at center stage. In time, the vision proved to be a symbol that was sufficiently multivalent to serve, on the one hand, as a "shared community experience . . . that every Mormon must respond to personally," and, on the other, as a disseminator of agreement about things historical and a preserver of unity about matters doctrinal.[14]

Across the last century the First Vision story has come to pervade not only Mormon history but Mormon culture. Dramatic renderings of the theophany are popular; artistic depictions are legion; children's books simplifying it have been written, as have scholarly books exploring its complicated theological implications. It has been celebrated in song, in poetry, and in prose. Yet because it is an extremely efficient vehicle for transporting the essence of Mormonism across generations and cultures, institutional considerations are as significant as sentimental and spiritual ones in explaining the ever-more-intense weight the First Vision is being made to bear.

Despite its effectiveness as the opening episode in telling the Mormon story, however, it is important to recognize that beginning an account of Mormon *history* with restatement and elaboration of Joseph Smith's 1838 account of the First Vision can be exceedingly problematic. Doing so almost always leads to an oversimplification of the cultural situation into which Mormonism irrupted.[15] It also suggests that a more or less complete theological system was revealed to Joseph Smith in embryo, hiding the dynamism of the developmental process by which Mormonism's present theological system evolved.[16] It obscures the centrality of the story of the appearances of Moroni and the coming forth of the Book of Mormon and, as a result, also obscures the extent to which Mormonism, through its demonstration that divinity had not ceased direct intercourse with humanity at the end of the apostolic age, responded to the concerns of the inhabitants of the biblical culture out of which it emerged.[17] Most important, telling the story the modern way tends to take the Book of Mormon away from the limelight, making Joseph Smith the focal point of the Mormon story. Whether intended or not, this has the effect of making Smith's spiritual experience serve to legitimate the Book of Mormon.[18]

In sum, when Mormon history begins with the First Vision, the result tends to be an account of a religious movement which, even as it differs dramatically on basic theological and doctrinal issues from other sects and churches, is analytically yet one more subdivision of Christianity inaugurated through the efforts of a charismatic leader. Surely the story of the vision is important, but too much emphasis on it takes the Book of Mormon away from the limelight, obscuring the fact that it was this "gold bible" that first attracted adherents to the movement. As crucial to the success of the whole Latter-day Saint enterprise as is Joseph Smith, it must never be forgotten that in the early years it was not the First Vision but the Book of Mormon that provided the credentials that made the prophet's leadership so effective. In order, therefore, to begin to comprehend early Mormonism, it is necessary to examine the cultural context that made this curious work so appealing to so many persons.

As indicated, much has been made of the situation in western New York in the first half of the nineteenth century as scholars have sought to explain the proliferation of new forms of religions that made appearances there.[19] But looking too closely at the "burnt" district can be misleading if we are to understand the wide appeal of the Book of Mormon. The situation throughout the union was unsettled and things were extremely fluid in this period when all America seemed to be streaming westward after

the Revolution. A new physical universe was there to contend
with. A new and somewhat uncertain political system existed
and Americans had to operate within it. The bases of social order
were in a state of disarray, and as a result of the nation's having
cut its ties with England and her history, a clear lack of grounding
in the past was evident. Quite clearly as important in the break-
down of a once reasonably stable cognitive and normative edifice
of knowledge and understanding of the way things are was the uncertainty that was the outgrowth of the development of skepticism, on the one hand, and direct contention among systems of
theology and doctrine, on the other. That uncertainty placed in
jeopardy the religious dynamic that for centuries—through formal or informal catechizing—had passed from one generation to
the next a body of unquestioned information about divinity, humanity, the system of right relationships that created the social
order, and the nature of experience after death.[20]

Certainly there was, as Martin Marty maintains, an informal
doctrinal consensus in the United States that mitigated the religious contention accompanying the development of voluntaryism
in the nation in the wake of disestablishment.[21] But the development not only of new religious movements in the first half of the
nineteenth century but of changes in traditional ones demonstrated conclusively that disagreement about fundamental matters
was in the air.

Very different reactions, but all fundamentally and profoundly
based in religion, developed in the culture to allow Americans to
deal with this disturbed situation. One of these reactions was essentially a revitalization of traditional Christianity, but, significantly, not revitalization through revivalism alone.[22] A dual form
of revitalization developed in traditional Christianity, an anti-
creedal *sola scriptura* movement that assumed the form of Christian primitivism, leading many Americans into the Christian
movement of Elias Smith, James O'Kelly, Barton Stone, and Alexander Campbell, and the great evangelical revival which, so Paul
Johnson argues in *A Shopkeeper's Millennium*, operated as an en-
gine to restructure the world as traditional paternalism gave way
before modern industrial society.[23] Both of these Christian revitalization thrusts were, at base, conservative and reintegrating.
Whether they were rooted in deeply intuitive, nonrational reli-

gious experiences, as in the evangelical world, or on more rational cogitation, as in the primitivist one, what one might call the content or the message or the imperative that issued from religious experience had the confirming effect in this context of reintegrating people into one or another form of changed, but nevertheless traditional, Christianity continuous with the post-Reformation Christianity brought from Europe to America during the colonial period.

Mormonism represented a very different reaction to the confused and disorienting situation in which Americans found themselves in the first half of the 1800s. It put itself forward in the familiar guise of primitive Christianity and initially appeared to appeal to the same constituency as the Campbellites. It drew, however, on so many elements other than the Judeo-Christian tradition that its adherents were not reintegrated into traditional Christianity but quite the reverse.

The work of Thomas Kuhn alerted historians as well as scientists to the "paradigm shift" phenomenon, where fundamentals and not just the details of understandings of reality are changed.[24] Not often has it been pointed out, however, that there is a difference between the chaos existing in the intellectual world, where observant students of the universe, scientists and philosophers, are in the habit of dealing regularly with abstractions, and the chaos existing in the less articulate world of everyday experience. In the former, theory is recognized as theory; in the latter, no clearly defined difference exists between the theoretical and the real. A paradigm shift that proposes a new theoretical understanding of the universe may occur in intellectual communities. But in the United States in the 1830s, among the readers who concluded that the Book of Mormon was exactly what it claimed to be, it was not an intellectual paradigm shift that altered existing understandings of the nature of the world and the construction of the cosmos. The Mormonites, as their contemporaries called them, moved out of the chaos of the early national period in America into a new dispensation of the fulness of times.

This they did by accepting a complex set of religious claims that brought speculation about the origin of the American Indian and America's place in the grand scheme of things into synthesis with the story of the Hebrews, generally as redacted by New Tes-

tament writers but with some Masonic lore worked in. Set out in
a book whose origins rested, in turn, on a synthesis of folk magic
and visions and revelations that were religious to the core, these
claims formed the basis of a new mythos in which the coming
forth of the book served as the agent that opened what had been
closed and ushered in the new dispensation. In the fullness of
time this mythos (the mythological dimension of Mormonism)
gave rise to other dimensions—social/institutional, ritual/liturgi-
cal, and doctrinal—of what would become a new religious
tradition.

In *Time and Myth*, John S. Dunne wrote that "there is some
profound link, it seems, between the story of a man's life and the
story of his world. The story of his world is his myth, the story in
which he lives."[25] In other words, there is a direct connection between the story of the world—that is, its creation and its past history—and everyday existence. People live inside stories, as it
were. Consequently, when the reliability of the story of the world
is questioned, the result is confusion in individual lives. In post-
Constantinian Europe, humanity lived inside a story of a world
firmly rooted in a particular Roman Catholic understanding of
the Christian gospel, an understanding that prevailed for more
than a millennium. But the Protestant Reformation called the reliability of that version of the story into question, while the Enlightenment raised doubts about the reliability of the story itself.
Although it took a very long time for the fundamental questions
that were introduced during the Reformation and Enlightenment
to trickle down to the popular level, as Gordon Wood has shown,
they had started to penetrate every aspect of American popular
culture in Joseph Smith's generation.[26] The evangelical thrust that
radically altered American Christianity during the period of the
Second Great Awakening made religious authority subject to the
democratic process, while skepticism questioned the basis of religious authority altogether.[27] A dramatic weakening of the link between the story of the world told in Christian terms and the story
of individual American lives was the outcome.

Given this cultural situation, it is easy enough to explain the
initial appeal of the Book of Mormon. As a "second witness to
Christ" it was a reassuring document. But the new scripture was
even more vulnerable to hard questions about its history and its

historicity than the Old and New Testaments, whose authority was under attack from skeptics and deists. For that reason if for no other, it is obvious that it was not the Book of Mormon alone which acted to alleviate the fears of potential Saints that the heavens had "turned into brass" and, therefore, that the voice of God would no longer be heard in the land.[28] Its assertion that, as the "stick of Joseph in the hand of Ephraim," it fulfilled Hebrew prophecy was extremely important, but perhaps even more important to its early readers was the fact that in the third chapter of Second Nephi the book set forth Joseph Smith's prophetic call. The coming forth of a "choice seer" who "shall be great like unto Moses" was predicted. Like that of his father, the seer's name would be Joseph; he would "write the writing of the fruit of [Lehi's] loins"; and he would act as God's agent to restore the house of Israel. As prophet, Smith turned these predictions into actualities. They validated the book and *vice versa*. It stands to reason, then, that the Book of Mormon *and* the subsequent events of Smith's extraordinary career *functioned together* to establish the authenticity of the book and to cement the link between a Hebrew-Christian understanding of the story of the world and the personal lives of the prophet and the people who became his followers.

A revelation dictated by Smith a dozen years after he dictated the contents of the Book of Mormon reminded the Saints that the Lord had given them "his servant Joseph to be a presiding elder over [the] church," that is, to be both high priest and president. He had, likewise, been given to them "to be a translator, a revelator, a seer, and a prophet,"[29] a surfeit of titles that might seem to suggest that, as far as titles were concerned, the divine economy was plagued with oversupply. (Or that an insecure prophet was seeking to buttress his power by adding to the number and variety of his positions.) But Smith's place at the center of nineteenth-century Mormon history suggests otherwise. With the abilities and powers inhering in the various positions whose titles he assumed, Smith filled the Old Testament roles of deliverer (Moses), military commander (Joshua), prophet (Isaiah), high priest (Eli), king (Solomon), and the New Testament positions of church founder (Peter) and apostle to the Gentiles (Paul). The correspondences are not so direct as they could have been had Smith con-

sciously attempted to model his leadership on a single biblical figure. Yet the pattern is clear enough to make it obvious that during
Smith's lifetime, leader as well as led—prophet as well as people
—were engaged in a process of renewal through replication that
gave the Saints a particular perspective on the biblical past and a
literal understanding of what happened in ancient times.

Whether Joseph Smith was prophet or fraud has been debated
ever since news of his "gold bible" spread across the New York
countryside in the late 1820s.[30] This interpretation of the nature
of the creative process that brought Mormonism into being will
not ultimately—or even intermediately—settle that disputed issue. But in proposing that Smith's story is best understood in the
context of his sequential assumption of positions/roles that allowed the Saints to recover a usable past, it suggests a way of
shifting the focus. By ordering the data so that it takes into account the intensity of the Mormon leader's study of biblical materials and the complex interactions between the stories of Israel
and early Christianity, on the one hand, and Mormon experience,
on the other, Smith is revealed in the context of what might be
described as an LDS *Gestalt*. The result is a picture of a seer who,
in becoming a "translator" (not only of a "new testament of Jesus
Christ" but of the Old and New Testaments as well), made the
biblical story meaningful and accessible to a doubting generation;
a prophet who spoke for God, comforting his people and gathering
them into a community so that the Lord could protect them as a
hen protects her chickens under her wing; a revelator who called
both church and temple into being; a presiding elder who was instrumental in bringing his people into institutional relationship
with each other; a high priest whose words and actions harnessed
spiritual energies to produce a physical temple where the "ordinances of the Lord" could be performed; and a king whose leadership made possible the organization of the political kingdom
of God.

Working out a program of matching the events of Joseph Smith's
life to biblical roles does not make all the problems that confront
the prophet's biographers disappear. But it does clarify the story of
early Mormonism because it reveals the movement as one in
which leader and followers were together living through—re-
capitulating—the stories of Israel and early Christianity. This ex-

periential process legitimated the prophet's centrality to the enterprise, which means that, *as far as history is concerned*, the question of whether Smith was prophet or fraud is not particularly important. Of far more significance for the purposes of this study is the fact that when Mormon history is examined within a framework that recognizes a process of replication of the biblical story, it becomes clear that the Book of Mormon, Joseph Smith's prophetic leadership, and the experience of the Saints were all crucial components in the creation of Mormonism. In the world into which this religious movement first thrust itself, divinity was a distant—perhaps even fictitious—presence. Operating together, these components brought this new religious tradition into being, reopening the canon and bringing God back into the history of the Saints in such a substantial way that within Mormonism, divinity is still as real as all the other realities of everyday existence.

A detail from a C. C. A. Christensen panorama showing the
"Miracle of the Quail"

Chapter Three

History as Text

W HEN GOD'S IN HIS HEAVEN and all's right with the world, the nature of divinity is not debatable. The nature of humanity is also settled and the proper divine-human connection is firmly established. An ordered and harmonious universe rests on a complex body of right relationships between humankind and the natural world, on the one hand, and among all manner of persons, on the other. While the pattern of these relationships is rarely articulated, it is universally understood because it follows naturally from cultural conceptions of reality that—in circular fashion—depend on a culture's particular conceptions of divinity, humanity, and the natural world. If things are at sixes and sevens, however, as they are during periods of crisis, dislocation, and change, the equilibrium of assumed agreement that created and supported culture is disturbed. Disordered status relationships develop as novel ways evolve to organize and conduct the business of society under stress. Order and harmony dissipate; tradition disintegrates; only confusion remains.

When answers to questions arising out of concern about property and place are worked out so that the rights and responsibilities of persons in society are clearly specified, order reestablishes itself, harmonizing old and new to make everything right with the world again, although in a far different, much more legalistic atmosphere. But describing the precise character of the network

of right relationships on which a culture depends and spelling out
the rights and responsibilities attending those relationships is extremely difficult. For that reason, attempts at such articulation
often founder on the variability of human beings and the complexity of the changed state of affairs. If that happens, if the rights
and responsibilities attending proper relationships cannot be
effectively clarified, then confusion veers over toward chaos, a
cultural situation that is not so much to be defined as a time in
which fundamental questions have no answers as one in which
every sort of question—important and unimportant—has too
many answers, all of them tentative and subject to modification.

Enough is known about the origins of most of the world's religions to make it clear that this kind of cultural chaos was a pre-
condition for the coming forth of the prophets and enlightened
ones whose words and deeds became the focus of the movements
that developed into major religious traditions. Yet similarity in
the contexts in which these religions came into being is not
always noted in general historical and theological surveys of the
religion of Israel, Hinduism, Buddhism, Confucianism, Christianity, and Islam. In fact, so much attention is normally concentrated
on the leaders and early followers that it is often hard to discern
the corresponding cultural patterns that nourished the different
movements. Consequently, the voices of Moses, Gotama, Jesus,
Muhammad, and the others may appear to have been heard at ran-
dom, in circumstances having nothing in common. Actually,
however, these voices were all first heard in troubled times and
places in which new peoples, new ideas, or new methods of
organizing political and economic life had so severely disturbed
the traditional network of right relationships that chaotic situations obviously existed.

Moreover, in addition to originating in cultural conditions that
had much in common, all these religions accomplished essentially the same thing as they developed. They transformed cultures that were dangerously close to being without form and void
into ordered universes. In a manner never easy to determine precisely, the inhabitants of the several cultures under stress came
to accept the messages spoken or written by the prophets or
enlightened ones as absolutely reliable information that, by extension, could answer all imaginable questions and provide solu-

tions to problems that had appeared insoluble. When the voice of a new religious leader became authoritative for a community, the darkness that had been on the face of the deep gradually disappeared. Chaos was banished; order and harmony were restored.

The perspective provided by the thousands of years since the occurrence of the founding events of the world's major religions makes it easy to identify this characteristic movement from chaos to order. But since the mystery of antiquity shrouds their times of beginnings and since most extant accounts of their histories bear heavy theological burdens, not much is known about what really happened as these religions were established. Details are lacking even about the development of Christianity and Islam, the two youngest world religions. Through close study of artifacts and careful consideration of surviving written documents from the standpoint of both linguistics and literary form, scholars are trying to extend existing knowledge about the process by which cultures were restructured and regained equilibrium as new religions acquired followers and started to be regarded by whole populations as sources of ultimate authority. But the serious problem of missing information presents an immense challenge to students of the history of pre-exilic Israel, for example, or early Hinduism, Buddhism, Christianity, and so on.

Students of Mormonism are not similarly confronted by the challenge of missing information. Because this movement started in the United States in the late 1820s and early 1830s, it is not difficult to establish the extent of cultural confusion, occasioned by dislocation and change that infected the milieu into which it came. In addition, there is evidence aplenty about the Mormons themselves since, as religious duty requires, they have been prodigious record-keepers from the very beginning, preserving for their posterity full accounts of what happened to them personally and what happened to the movement corporately. But if it seems, at first blush, that all this firsthand evidence would make describing the beginnings of Mormonism so simple that its story could readily serve as a modern analogue that could shed light on how the older religions started and became established, this is not exactly the case.

While neither temporal distance nor lack of evidence hamper the recovery of the Mormon story, conflicting data are a serious

problem. In addition to primary and secondary accounts written
by Latter-day Saints who were there when things occurred and by
Saints who became a part of the movement somewhat later, but
who heard the principals tell the story of what happened, the
genesis of Mormonism is described in a large number of contemporary accounts written by persons who had moved into and then
back out of close association with the Saints and by persons who
merely observed the movement from the outside. As a result,
rather than one story, there are several stories of Mormon beginnings from which to choose.

As has been indicated, alternative narratives about Joseph Smith
and the coming forth of the Book of Mormon evolved from these
conflicting sources. One of them is about ancient records engraved on metal plates translated by a young man chosen by God
for the task, and the other describes a work of nineteenth-century
fiction somehow produced by a ne'er-do-well member of a dis-
reputable farm family living on the fringes of society in western
New York. The impact of these opposing narratives has already
been explored and does not need to be reviewed here. Yet this is
the place to consider the amazing persistence across time of both
this elemental component of the Mormon faith-story and its an-
tithesis. Since the days of its first telling, intense efforts have been
made to explain the Mormon story away by citing contemporary
reports of the unsavory character of Joseph Smith and his entire
family, and by compiling a wealth of commonsense information
about obvious Book of Mormon parallels to other nineteenth-
century accounts tying the American Indian to Israel's lost tribes;
also by pointing out the book's descriptions of situations, incidents, characters, and theology suspiciously like those within its
so-called translator's ken, and its echoes of Masonic lore, its Isaiah
passages, and its bountiful anachronism supply. But while new accounts ringing the changes on the anti-Mormon version of Smith's
story have continued to appear, at what sometimes seem regular
intervals since Alexander Campbell first analyzed the Book of
Mormon in the *Millennial Harbinger* in 1831, and Eber D. Howe
published *Mormonism Unvailed* in 1834, the prophet's testimony
endures, unchanged in any particular, a stumbling block to scientific history and foolishness to many.

Thus, the story of Mormon beginnings appears to be an exception to the normal modern expectation that natural explanation based on objective evidence will be more persuasive than supernatural explanation growing from subjective accounts. Like the gospels that include the story of the resurrection of Jesus without supporting it with objective evidence obtained from persons outside the incipient Christian community, the Mormon story includes an account of the translation of the Book of Mormon supported only by the testimony of members of the incipient LDS community. In both of these instances, the story of a tradition's beginnings rests on a paradoxical event that has proved anomalous enough to sustain the weight of supernatural explanation across a long period of time. Furthermore, in the Christian tradition, the story of the resurrection of Jesus in the flesh has not only been kept alive within the community of faith, but it has been brought to life again and again outside it. So, likewise, the LDS account of the translation of sacred records by one who became a prophet has been preserved within Mormonism and also has over and over again proved persuasive to individuals outside the community, notwithstanding the commonsense arguments that, in an open and public manner, have repeatedly called into question the supernatural explanation that undergirds the Mormon story.

Parallels between Christianity and Mormonism are not limited to their both having been introduced into contexts of cultural crisis and both having faith-stories that rest on paradoxical events. Before others can be pointed up, however, explicit distinctions need to be made among the several terms generally used to refer to communities of faith gathered under different circumstances for different reasons. *For the purposes of this discussion*, the most economical and unambiguous means of making such distinctions is developing definitions that all refer to the usual categories or dimensions—mythological, doctrinal, ritual/liturgical, ethical, social/institutional, and experiential—that scholars have developed over the years to facilitate discussion of religion.[1] Here, however, these dimensions need to be ranked so that the most significant is the mythological rather than the experiential (the classification very often receiving greatest emphasis in studies of specific religious traditions, because it is the one that includes the reports of direct encounters with the sacred that are turned into the founding stories of new religious movements), the doctrinal (the area so often stressed in apologetic works), or the social/institutional (the dimension that was the main focus of both the sociological and historical study of religion for many years and the one that remains the primary focus of much of the sociological study of the topic). Moreover, besides elevating the mythological dimension to primacy in this instance, it is extremely important to keep in mind that when it is used in religious studies, mythological does not refer to fairy tales, fables, and other forms of patent untruth. It refers to *story*, to accounts of beginnings (dramatizing how the world came to be) and endings (holding out possibilities both of devastation and renewal), of sin and redemption, of heroes, heroines, and life lived out in the larger-than-life "olden days" when divinity is said to have dealt with humanity face to face, providing a foundation for culture.

Because the word *religion* is so general that it is difficult to use in a definite or precise sense, *religious tradition* will here be used as the umbrella category that will cover (1) all the corporate bodies and (2) individuals unattached to corporate bodies in whose systems of belief a particular story is central. Because Abraham's story and Israel's history are central to the mythological dimension of more than one tradition in Western religion, a distinction will be made here between the Jews, whose belief system rests on this story essentially as it is recorded in the Old Testament, and other traditions whose belief systems center on the same story plus significant additions or alterations. By this means the elements in the so-called Judeo-Christian tradition will be precipitated out, since the account of the resurrection of Jesus and the report of his everlasting existence at the right hand of God make it impossible to fit the Christian Messiah into any of the categories by which Old Testament figures are classified. As the Christian story is neither simply a reinterpretation nor continuation of the Hebraic-Judaic story, so the Mormon story departs significantly from the story of Abraham and the histories of Israel and Christianity as those stories are understood by Christians and Jews.

This departure started with the Book of Mormon. But even as it reiterated the Judeo-Christian story in a different framework, that work served as a conduit to bring Christianity's mythological base into the New World more or less directly. Other LDS additions and modifications are much more consequential. Alterations to the story that came in Joseph Smith's revelations, especially the Book of Moses, and his translations of the Bible and the Book of Abraham—this last accomplished by means of inspiration using an Egyptian papyrus as text—are the truly important counters to charges that the Mormon story is merely an idiosyncratic interpretation of the Christian story.

Church, denomination, sect, and *cult* are the other widely used technical terms that refer to communities of faith. In a study in which establishing classifications for the various LDS communities is one of the principal goals, their use is indispensable. Yet these are vexing terms in which subjective rankings stubbornly inhere. For that reason, it must be understood at the outset that when they are used in this study no value load is attached. Descriptions of faith communities as churches or denominations are usually interpreted as expressions of respect, while descriptions of the same communities as sects or cults are generally thought to be expressions of disrespect, with *cult* being the more pejorative term, but that is not the case here.

A long tradition of the study of religion in society has produced a body of well-developed and fully articulated theory which makes useful distinctions among these four terms, with particular regard for the social and psychological makeup of the different communities and for the manner in which churches, denominations, sects, and cults are related to the sources of power in their cultures. Much use is made of these illuminating distinctions in the following chapters (where appropriate reference is made to the works of the sociologists and anthropologists who worked these distinctions out), but this particular study places more emphasis on the distinctions that grow out of considering religion's mythological dimension.

Therefore, the term *church* will be used to refer specifically to institutions that assume direct responsibility for the whole of a tradition's story: for proclaiming it, keeping it alive through liturgy and ritual, and transmitting it from one generation to another; for preserving the story's integrity through canonization and systematic doctrinal statement; and for drawing from it pat-

terns, examples, and principles that will insure the arrangement
of a network of right relationships within the community, will
prescribe the proper relationships to maintain with the world outside, and will serve as the basis for an ethical code. *Denomination* also refers to an institution, one that is by and large a subdivision of a church, the more inclusive term. Denominations
likewise bear responsibility for a tradition's story, but as a result
of their various histories, the different denominations within a
tradition preserve the story in distinctive ways, emphasizing some
things and neglecting others. *Sect* refers to a group that coalesces
around a leader or leaders who find themselves in disagreement
with ecclesiastical authorities over matters that manifest themselves as concern about ritual and liturgy, institutional structure,
the pattern of relationships within and without the community,
or the nature of authentic spiritual experience, but are matters ultimately rooted in disagreement over interpretation of a tradition's story and the implications following therefrom. *Cult,* by
contrast, refers to a group that coalesces around a leader who
mounts a challenge to the fundamental integrity of a tradition's
story by adding to it, subtracting from it, or by changing it in
some more radical way than merely setting out a new interpretation of the events and happenings in the existing story.

Churches and denominations resemble each other, especially
in that—more inclusive than exclusive—they serve as unifying
agents in culture. By telling and retelling their tradition's story,
they perpetuate a common symbolic universe that strengthens
the life of the community. But unlike churches and denominations that are more or less contiguous with culture, sects and
cults separate themselves from the community, create alternative
symbolic universes, and erect and maintain virtually impene-
trable boundaries between inside and outside. The two are socially similar in the makeup of their membership, in their appeal to
the disinherited (whether relatively or absolutely deprived), and
in their tendency to become millenarian/millennial movements.
Yet sects and cults stand in opposition to the world on different
grounds. However much they are alike in the way their activities
turn out to sanction simultaneously the social, political, and economic aspirations of those who join and question prevailing cul-

tural assumptions about power and prestige, it is important to remember that a sect grows out of disagreement over how a tradition's story ought to be understood, i.e. over interpretation, while a cult's antagonistic stance rests on acceptance of a story changed in essentials, not just by means of interpretation. Notwithstanding its quarrel with denomination or church over the correct understanding of a tradition's story, a sect remains under the same categorical umbrella as its adversaries. But the same cannot be said about a cult. If it survives and grows, the altered story eventually becomes central to a new system of belief that serves as the foundation of a new religious tradition.

As recently as the decades of the 1960s and 1970s, history again proved the truth of the maxim that when cultural confusion starts to tilt toward chaos, prophets and enlightened ones appear on every hand. Insufficient time has elapsed to allow knowledgeable assessment of the potential staying power of any of the new methods of reaching blissful states, new means of assuring redemption, or new candidates to messianic leadership that attracted such amazing numbers of followers ten or twenty years ago. But looking back to this recent period of frenetic religious novelty is instructive, because it provides a valuable comparative perspective from which to view the proliferation of unusual, different, and sometimes bizarre religious movements in the United States in the period of the early republic, from 1800 to 1860. For that matter, the comparison can likewise be extended backward in time to the volatile religious situation in Palestine at the turn of the ages. Just as Sun Myung Moon was not the first or even the twenty-first person to claim a divinely issued leadership mandate in the contemporary world, Joseph Smith was not the first or even the twenty-first American prophet of his day, any more than Jesus was the first or even the twenty-first Jewish prophet to claim a divine calling in inter-testamental times.

The babble of voices of potential prophets and the concatenation of religious claims during these three periods led to the development of more faith communities than it is now possible to count. Yet of that enormous number, a very select few developed into significant religious movements, and most of those were sectarian groups—Pharasaic Jews, for example, Seventh-day Adventists, Christian Scientists, or the so-called Jesus Freaks—who gradually found comfortable places for their interpretations of their traditions' stories within the religious traditions that spawned them. Of the cultic movements whose members accepted radically revised or fundamentally altered versions of the faith-stories regnant in their cultures, only Christianity and Mormonism are now full-scale religious traditions. How and why did these two movements take hold and develop into religious traditions while many other movements of essentially the same character lost followers and failed to last more than a decade or two?

When this question is posed to persons within a faith community, their response to the *why* part of the compound query often refers—directly or indirectly—to the will of the divine; their answers to the *how* part are then advanced in light of an ontological argument that uses the movement's survival and growth as evidence that it is "of God" and that, therefore, the ultimate explanation of its survival and growth is that it was God's will. As reassuring as such reasoning is within the community of faith and as useful as it is as a missionary tool, it finally convinces only those who are within (and those who are ready to move into) the faith circle. And yet, because this matter of why and how one religious movement flourishes while a virtually identical counterpart does not is so perplexing to persons interested in religion as phenomenon that there is no shortage of alternative explanations or bodies of theory to fit them in.

Still another theory that would make it possible to predict whether, out of the multiplicity of relgious movements on the contemporary scene, Scientology, say, or Transcendental Meditation will be around 500 years from now is not being proposed here. Instead, in an important sense, Mormonism is being used here as a case study that falls generally into the ongoing wide-ranging exploration of the important question of what it is that makes one movement thrive while others wither and die. More specifically, an examination of Mormonism from this perspective fits into efforts currently under way to investigate the *process* by which religious movements survive and grow. But unlike many social science analyses that focus on a triad composed of (1) the cultural situation, (2) potential converts, and (3) leaders and their

claims, this one concentrates on what went on within the movement itself as Mormonism moved along the rigorous and treach-
erous path from cult to religious tradition.

Religion in nineteenth-century America was like a collage made
up of a huge number of diverse materials put together in a pattern
that made sense to the artist but that still appeared to many ob-
servers to be a jumble and little more. The one common element
that pulled American religion together was the religious history
of Europe. Despite the Reformation and a good deal of less for-
midable sectarian splintering, the story of European Christianity
provided a thread that, while it did not bind American religion together internally, did connect all the separate parts to the Apostolic era. European religious history was even shared by the Jews,
who, as descendants of the people shamefully treated for something their ancestors had reputedly done to Jesus, were also bound,
unhappily, to New Testament times. Latter-day Saints, however,
were not tied to the ministry of Jesus and the world of the early
church through the history of Christianity in Europe. Theirs was
a different past.

Actually, the very first Mormons did not merely have a past
that differed from the past of other ninteenth-century Americans;
they had no recent past at all. Just as the outcome of the American Revolution had left the former English colonies without a
usable political history, by designating all existing churches—not
just the Roman Catholic variety—as corrupt abominations growing out of a "Great Apostasy" that began in the days of the ancient
apostles, the Book of Mormon left the Saints with an enormous
1,400- to 1,800-year lacuna in their religious history. This huge
hiatus meant that parallels between their experiences and experiences described in the Bible came so naturally to the Saints that,
as immensely egotistical as it now sounds, even Sidney Rigdon's
observation that his agonizing imprisonment in Liberty Jail was
comparable to the sufferings of Jesus is not terribly surprising,
since the LDS pantheon of saints and martyrs did not include Joan
of Arc, Savonarola, and the "inhabitants" of Foxe's *Acts and Monu-
ments*, from which a more appropriate comparative referent might
have been found. Yet the profound historylessness of early Mor-

monism cannot be satisfactorily explained entirely in terms of
the Saints' conscious rejection of the institutional history of
Christianity.

Something more fundamental had happened, and, although it
involves dealing in abstractions to some extent, comprehending
what it was is so critical to this study that it needs to be spelled
out one step at a time:

1. History, the story of the past, is linear. It moves from step A
   to step B, from promise to consummation, from prophecy to
   fulfillment.

2. Since it was at one and the same time prophecy (a book that
   said it was an ancient record prophesying that a book would
   come forth) and (as the book that had come forth) fulfillment
   of that prophecy, the coming forth of the Book of Mormon
   effected a break in the very fabric of history.

3. This interruption of history's presumably inexorably linear
   movement wiped clean the slate on which the story of the
   past had been written, making a place for the story of a past
   that led directly up to "the new dispensation of the fulness
   of times" whose events would be recorded there.

4. Standing on the threshold of a new age, the first Mormons
   were, then, suspended between an unusable past and an uncertain future, returned as it were to a primordial state.

5. But as their future unfolded, the activities the Saints engaged in—reestablishing the covenant, gathering the Lord's
   elect, separating Israel from the Gentiles, organizing the
   church, preaching the gospel, building up the kingdom—
   took on such a familiar cast that it is plain to see that they
   moved out of the primordial present into the future by replicating the past.

6. This replication was not conscious ritual re-creation of
   events, but rather experiential "living through" of sacred
   events in a new age.

7. Although it seemed strange and even dangerous in the modern world of nineteenth-century America, this activity allowed the Saints to recover their own past, their own salva-

tion history, which, despite its similarity to words and acts, places and events in the biblical stories of Israel's history and the history of Christianity, was the *heilsgeschichte* of neither Christian nor Jew.

Analyzed in this fashion, this process may sound more complicated than it really was. People who base their understanding of reality on a new set of religious claims often (perhaps always) come to the conclusion that the past is utterly irrelevant in view of an imminent *eschaton*. In truth, however, the past is a matter of fundamental importance to new religious movements. The assertions on which they rest inevitably alter the prevailing understanding of what has gone before, creating situations in which past and future must both be made new. Believing that Jesus fulfilled Mosaic law and Hebrew prophecy with his life and death, early Christians, for example, could no longer share a vision of the past with other Jews. They were as much constrained to create a usable past for themselves in the years between 50 and 150 C.E. as were the Mormons between 1830 and 1930.

Actually, Christianity and Mormonism both rest finally on claims that in them Hebrew prophecy has been fulfilled. Jesus was said to be Messiah, the king who would rule Zion in righteousness, whose coming Isaiah had foretold. The Book of Mormon was said to be the "stick of Joseph in the hand of Ephraim" of which Ezekiel spoke as he described the coming of the undivided Kingdom of God. By recognizing this structural parallel, and by paying close attention to what happened as the early Christian saints appropriated a vision of Israel's past that could be ritually re-created to serve as meaningful background to the Christian story, it is possible to discern the pattern of reappropriation that allowed the Latter-day Saints to take as their own a vision of the past of both Israel and Christianity that now serves both directly and through ritual re-creation as meaningful background to the Mormon story.

While the difficulty of reconstructing exactly how things happened nearly 2,000 years ago frustrates the development of an elaborate theoretical model that could be rigorously tested, it is clear that in early Christianity, the pattern of recovery included

four principal activities: *reiteration* of Israel's story, with heavy
emphasis on the means by which the life and death of Jesus fulfilled Hebrew law and prophecy; theological *reinterpretation*,
based on consideration of the meaning of the story in light of
what was seen as the eschatological event of the ages, the resurrection of Christ; actual *recapitulation* of key events of the story
in a new setting; and appropriate *ritual re-creation* of the story in
a Christian context. Furthermore, it is also clear that through
these acts of appropriation, Christianity transformed Israel's past
so that it seemed as alien to the Jews as did the developing Christian tradition whose belief system was supported not only by the
proclamation of a resurrected messiah, but also by a particular vision of Israel's history that gave meaning to the life and death of
Jesus. In the nineteenth century the Mormons were engaged in
similar activities, out of which emerged a similar result. This
time, however, reiteration, reinterpretation, recapitulation, and
ritual re-creation of the significant events in Israel's past *and* the
significant events in the story of early Christianity were both
required.

Just as the early Mormons tended to be persons who were well
versed in the Judeo-Christian scriptures, and hence sufficiently familiar with both the story and prophecy to be sensitive to the
claims that were set forth in the Book of Mormon, so it was that
the first Christians were persons who not only knew what had
happened to Israel before their time, but knew prophecy intimately enough to appreciate all the fine points of the declaration
that Jesus was the long-anticipated Messiah. For that reason, and
since the Hebrew Bible served as the basic Christian scripture, it
is very likely that the sort of reiteration of Israel's story preserved
in chapter 7 of the Book of Acts occurred repeatedly in the initial
stages of the formation of the Christian community.[2] The Book of
Hebrews is perhaps the most explicit example of theological reinterpretation of key portions of the Old Testament story in the
Christian canon. But the entire New Testament makes it obvious
that, in addition to repetition of the assertion that Hebrew prophecy had been fulfilled, reinterpretation of Israel's story was an integral part of what was going on.

The community's recapitulation of the salvation history of the
Hebrews must be recaptured mainly through its reflection in

the construction of the gospels, which means that it is hard to determine precisely whether this (perhaps necessary) phenomenon preceded, accompanied (as is probable), or followed theological reinterpretation. Also difficult to determine with any precision is where Christianity's ritual re-creation of Israel's story entered the developmental sequence. Notwithstanding when they started, however, Christianity's activities of recapitulation and ritual re-creation are evident in the way that, as retold, the life of Jesus played out Israel's story once again. John the Baptist was clothed in Elijah's raiment, for example, and the miraculous circumstances surrounding his conception and birth practically parallel the story of the conception and birth of Samuel; Mary and Joseph carried Jesus down into Egypt, where the children of Israel once sojourned; the crossing of the Red Sea was symbolically repeated in the baptism of Jesus; the days He spent in the wilderness numbered forty as did the years the Israelites spent in the wilderness; like the tribes of Israel, the disciples Jesus led numbered twelve; He went up into a mountain, from which He dispensed the law; and so on. More directly, Christianity's recapitulation of Israel's story is revealed in the account of what went on at Pentecost. And while its incorporation into the community's ritual and liturgical life leaves the impression that the Eucharist recalls only the Lord's Supper, it is possible that, even though the communal meals in early Christian times probably were not consciously conducted as Passover meals, they were nevertheless recapitulations of events connected with the Exodus, the Passover, and God's miraculous provision of manna to the Israelites in the wilderness.

So delineated, the activities by which the early Christians appropriated Israel's past, made it an integral part of their ritual and liturgical life, and used it as the foundation for the development of a new religious tradition appear more spontaneous than calculated, more open than esoteric, more transparent than opaque. Because the LDS reiteration of the Hebrew-Christian story was inaugurated with the Book of Mormon, because its theological reinterpretation came through Joseph Smith's revelations and translations as well as through the sermons of Joseph Smith and Brigham Young and the sermons and writings of such persons as Orson and Parley Pratt, because the Saints were obliged to recapitulate the significant events in the stories of Israel and Christianity virtually simultaneously, and because the ritual re-creations of such extremely critical parts of the story as creation and redemption were introduced in the LDS temple ordinances that are not in the public domain, the process by which Mormonism recovered its salvation history from the Hebrew-Christian story is not nearly so open and transparent. For those reasons, despite the availability of an enormous body of primary source material, early Mormonism has proved to be almost impervious to objective study.

The Christian structural parallel suggests, however, a means of ordering the data that clarifies the picture of the reiteration and reinterpretation of Christianity's mythological dimension that was at the heart of early Mormonism. More important, the Christian pattern illuminates Mormon history by suggesting that Mormonism's ritual re-creation of the stories of Israel and Christianity rests not only on theological reinterpretation, but on a recapitulation of biblical events much more complex than scholars have heretofore recognized. When Russell Mortensen and William Mulder pulled together their extremely useful collection of source documents, published under the title *Among the Mormons* in 1958, they designated the sections of the book "Genesis," "Exodus," "Lamentations and Judges," and "Psalms," for example.[3] But as they made no effort in the editorial matter to argue that the Mormons had actually replicated these scriptural accounts, it is clear that the titles were simply descriptive labels suggesting a connection between the nineteenth-century Mormon experience and the events described in the Bible. This connection has also been noted by virtually every person who has ever attempted a narrative reconstruction of the Mormon past. But the extent to which the Saints recapitulated the Hebrew-Christian story by living it through again does not really reveal itself in chronological accounts of LDS history.

Linear recounting divides the first sixty years of Mormon history into chronological units that reveal an almost unrelieved movement from east to west in the United States and a consistent pattern of growth despite unceasing opposition. It describes important LDS doctrinal and institutional developments and concentrates heavily on the conflict between Mormonism and the national government, as well as the governments of the several states in which the Saints settled for a time. Told in this fashion, the story begins with Joseph Smith's First Vision in 1820, proceeds to the publication of the Book of Mormon, the organization of the church, and its subsequent removal from western New York to Kirtland, Ohio. The construction of the Kirtland temple, economic and political troubles in the Old Northwest, and Mormon settlement in Independence, Missouri, make up the second chronological segment. The Missouri period, which concludes with a Mormon war in which the Saints are driven back across the Mississippi River, dramatizes Mormon-Gentile conflict and points up fundamental differences in the character of the sociopolitical organization of Mormon and non-Mormon society. Accounts of the Nauvoo years following the Missouri episode stress this *Gemeinschaft-Gesellschaft* distinction, the introduction of plural marriage into Mormonism, and the murders in 1844 of Joseph and Hyrum Smith that bring the first linear unit of Mormonism to an end. The struggle for possession of the "mantle of the prophet" which led to an atomization of the movement opens Mormonism's second chronological unit. From that point forward there are several Mormon histories, not just one. But all the others are ordinarily treated as footnotes to the more dramatic story of the Saints' journey to the intermountain region and their establishing the State of Deseret there.

Narratives of the pioneer period are dominated by the Mormon War of 1857, the continuing practice of polygamy, the struggle for political hegemony between the Latter-day Saints and the representatives of the federal government, the "Raid," in which polygamous Saints were driven into hiding in order to escape imprisonment, and the "Manifesto," in which the president of the LDS Church acknowledged Mormon acquiescence to the government's demand for a cessation of the practice of plural marriage. Emphasis is placed on Brigham Young and other Mormon leaders, on the Saints' achievements in making the desert "blossom as a rose," on the sophisticated political and economic organization of the community, the systematizing of LDS doctrine, the efficient bureaucratic structure of the church, and so on.

While it is all fascinating, it is by and large an exterior story rather than an interior one. Nevertheless, whether it has been set out as a mass of undigested information in need of analysis or analyzed with great skill by scholars trained to apply the canons of professional/scientific history to the records the Saints left behind, most Mormon history has been written in this mode. As a result, although many details need to be filled in, the main outlines of the institutional history of Mormonism are well known, and the story of the interrelationships between Mormonism and American culture is reasonably clear. But exoteric history does not always provide satisfactory answers to questions about the essential differences between the Mormonism of the early period and modern Mormonism, or to queries about how each of the several forms of Mormonism differs from all the others. The answers to these and many other questions about the LDS past are related to Mormonism's recapitulation of the biblical stories of God's chosen people.

This recapitulation process started with the discovery of a book whose contents told Saints in the nineteenth century what had happened to the people of God who came to America before them in much the same way that the priests' discovery in the recesses of the temple of a book said to have been written by Moses told the people in King Josiah's reign about those who came to Israel before them. Then the process moved forward through a series of "reprises" of events in the Hebrew-Christian story. But because the Saints had both to appropriate Israel's story and *re*appropriate Christianity's appropriation of the same story, the process did not involve linear movement through the story from beginning to end. Hence, the "restoration" of the Aaronic (Levitical) priesthood in 1829 was followed in less than a year by the organization of a "Church of Jesus Christ." A temple modeled on the pre-exilic temple of Solomon's day was constructed in Kirtland, but in the initial ceremonies conducted there, the Christian ordinance of washing of the feet was introduced. More directly integrating old and new was an 1836 vision in which Joseph Smith and Oliver Cowdery, who had separated themselves from the congregation in the temple by retiring behind the veils surrounding the pulpit, were visited by "the Lord." The eyes of their understanding were opened, and they saw this personage, who spoke with a voice that "was as the sound of the rushing of great waters, even the voice of Jehovah," and yet one who—in accepting the temple as a place in which he would manifest himself to his people—identified himself by saying, "I am the first and the last; I am he who liveth, I am he who was slain; I am your advocate with the Father." In that same visionary episode, recalling Matthew 17, the prophet and his Second Counselor were visited by Moses, Elijah, and Elias, who committed into LDS hands the keys to the gathering of Israel and the "new dispensation of the fulness of times."[4]

The Saints started to build a City of God that would be the jewel of a literal kingdom organized on the Hebrew model. But when the Mormon kingdom was buffeted with troubles as dreadful as any with which ancient Israel had to contend, opinion among the Saints divided, as in the olden days, about whether God would continue to act inside history or outside it. Apocalyptic expectation likewise integrated the experiences of the Israelites and early Christians with Mormon experience, since no matter whether they looked back to the Book of Daniel or to Revelation, Saints came to believe that they were living in the world's "winding-up scene."

For complex reasons related to the fact that the Nauvoo experience was a recapitulation of the so-called Patriarchal Age for only a part of the Mormon population, Joseph Smith's murder was not generally perceived as a reprise of the crucifixion. He sealed his testimony with his blood, as Brigham Young said, but the result did not unify Mormonism. Instead, the prophet's death ushered in divisions in Mormonism that are as dramatic and potentially as long-standing as the sundering of Israel's northern and southern tribes, because the murder brought the recapitulation process to an abrupt halt in the experience of one part of the community, while the same murder exponentially intensified it in the other part. For the former, Mormonism ever afterward took on the character of primitive Christianity that it had had in the very beginning. For the latter, the prophet's observation that he was "going as a lamb to slaughter" apparently suggested suffering servant more than crucified messiah, Israel more than early Christianity, since his death turned these Latter-day Saints away from New Testament stories to an even more elaborate and direct reprise of Old Testament times.

Historical accounts of the corporate movement of the Saints from Nauvoo to the Great Basin are rarely written without mentioning that the Saints who followed Brigham Young westward resolved themselves into a Camp of Israel organized into companies with captains of hundreds, fifties, and tens over them, as had the ancient Israelites during their journey from Egypt to the Promised Land in Palestine. But the real extent of the Exodus-like character of the Saints' journey from Illinois to the Great Salt Lake Valley is only fully disclosed when it is remembered that an ice bridge over the Mississippi River facilitated the Mormon departure from Nauvoo. It is neither so wide nor so deep as the Red Sea, but at Nauvoo the river is more than a mile broad, and "running ice" had made crossing difficult in the days before the main body of Mormons was ready to leave. The fact that many Saints walked across the river without getting their feet wet is enough to serve as a means of separating the Mormon trek from all the other pioneer companies who left for the west from St. Louis, Quincy, and the other cities and towns along the river's edge, especially as more than one group of starving and desperate Saints reported miracles in which quail and a manna-like substance called honeydew kept them from perishing. Moreover, even as it continued in some ways for virtually forty years, while Saints from across the world traveled through the wilderness to the valleys of the intermountain region, this LDS exodus led directly to the building up of a latter-day Zion in the tops of the mountains, a kingdom with a relegous leader at its political helm and a temple at its center.

Full and complete records of the Mormon pioneer period contain so many references to the extensive use of militant "kingdom language" in the sermons and public statements of Joseph Smith, Brigham Young, Heber C. Kimball, Jedediah Grant, and other LDS leaders that some scholars are convinced that nineteenth-century Saints were engaged in a quest for empire. Others disagree, interpreting the often-used "kingdom language" as a metaphor, mere repetitive allusion to passages of scripture that refer to the Kingdom of God. A wide-ranging and sometimes rancorous scholarly debate that turns on whether references to the kingdom should be understood metaphorically or taken literally has developed in recent years. Recognition of the Exodus-like character of the Mormon trek and the kingdom-like character of Utah Mormonism during the pioneer period (note this narrowing from Mormonism, in general, to Utah Mormonism) will not entirely settle this issue, but it will make it obvious that, as recapitulations of episodes in

Hebrew history, these events took on an experiential character appropriately described as metaphorical only if metaphor is understood as something more than literary device.

In *Metaphors We Live By*, linguists George Lakoff and Mark Johnson provide a persuasive demonstration of their thesis that "our ordinary conceptual system, in terms of which we both think and act, is fundamentally metaphorical in nature."[5] Their demonstration is helpful here, for the River Jordan flowed north from Utah Lake into the Great Salt Lake, rather than south through the Waters of Merom and the Sea of Galilee to the Dead Sea, but it still coursed through Zion. Brigham Young was not king—after 1858 he was not even governor—but he might as well have been, since Latter-day Saints actually, if not officially, lived in a literal LDS kingdom over which an ecclesiastical establishment presided for nearly fifty years. Thus this delineation of the Mormon replication of the Hebrew-Christian past tends to support the contention that scholars across the years have underestimated the importance of the political kingdom of God.

At the same time, this manner of interpreting the historical data calls into question the intimate connection that most scholars posit between the patriarchal order of marriage (polygamy) and the LDS political kindgom. As printed in section 132 of the Doctrine and Covenants of the Church of Jesus Christ of Latter-day Saints, the Mormon prophet's revelation about plural marriage is dated 12 July 1843. This date seems to place the inauguration of plural marriage in the same time period as Smith's organization of a Mormon political kingdom. But it is ever more obvious that the revelation is given an 1843 date because it was first written down at that time. In reality, along with the introduction of the temple ordinances and the ordination of Joseph Smith, Sr., as patriarch (which led directly to the custom of conferring patriarchal blessings), plural marriage entered Mormonism in Kirtland. All were part of a latter-day recapitulation of the ancient Patriarchal Age, which, in the Bible, is separated from the kingdom-building of David and Solomon by a great span of years and which, in Mormonism, is analytically distinct from the creation of the political kingdom of God. This means that a literal plurality of wives was one of the main elements figuring in the Saints' recapitulation of the stories of Abraham, Isaac, Jacob, and Joseph, while the LDS experience of living in a kingdom that the Saints themselves controlled politically recapitulated the stories of David and Solomon, kings of Israel during a much later era.

By indicating that the prophet made separate inquiries about the plural marriages of Abraham, Isaac, and Jacob, on the one hand, and those of Moses, David, and Solomon, on the other, the opening verse of the revelation about the plurality of wives suggests that Joseph Smith was aware of the differences that existed between these two periods in Hebrew history. But Smith's distinction was not communicated to his followers. It was even missed by the scribe to whom the revelation was dictated, William Clayton, whose diary account says that the revelation showed "the designs in Moses, Abraham, David, and Solomon having many wives and concubines & c."[6] And the distinction apparently was not later recognized, even after 1852, when the revelation was finally published. Although the Latter-day Saints did not fully realize at the time that they were living through reprises of the ages of the Hebrew patriarchs and kings simultaneously, the distinction is nevertheless significant in the context of this study because it highlights the non-linearity and complexity of the recapitulation process.

The subliminal, often involuntary nature of the process is revealed in the final Utah-Mormon reprise of Hebrew history: exile. Equally outraged by evidence that the patriarchal order of marriage was a reality and that an unofficial yet actual Kingdom of God was organized, non-Mormons mounted an all-out campaign in the late 1880s to stop the practice of polygamy and destroy the political kingdom. Seen from a Mormon perspective, the "Raid" was a Gentile threat to turn to ashes all the Saints' accomplishments in building cities for habitation and making the barren land fruitful. An army of "greedy politicians," intent on dismantling the political kingdom, and an army of federal marshals, intent on casting polygamists into prison, drove Mormons from their homes and made Zion desolate. Some of the patriarchs hid in the mountains, others sought asylum in Mexico or Canada, but when the Corporation of the Church of Jesus Christ of Latter-day Saints was dissolved and its property (including the nearly completed temple in Salt Lake City) confiscated, the Saints acceded to the superior strength of the Gentile government. Appropriately, as befits the end of exile, the Saints were allowed to return to their homes and everyday pursuits on the condition that they would give up marital plurality and that their kingdom would thereafter take on the political status of client state.

As was the death of Joseph Smith in 1844, the end of the practice of plural marriage was an event of overriding importance in Mormonism. Before LDS Church President Wilford Woodruff's Manifesto was issued and accepted as authoritative by the Saints, Mormonism was one thing; afterward, Mormonism was something else. Unlike Smith's martyrdom, however, the demise of plural marriage was not an inexplicable event that was sudden and unforeseen. The issuing of the Manifesto was preceded by years of struggle with the larger culture over what was permissible in the United States insofar as the organization of the Mormon kingdom and the behavior of the Saints was concerned. For that reason, chronological narrations of Mormon history must always explain this event in terms of cause and effect. In the context of this work, however, the matter of whether the Manifesto was the result of divine revelation or whether it was an extreme instance of religion accommodating itself to the world is far less important than the fact that the promulgation of this document and the informal political accords that accompanied its appearance brought the Mormon recapitulation of the Hebrew-Christian story to a close. With Zion and Babylon come to terms, the past was filled up. Complete.

Henceforth that past would be continually reiterated and sometimes reinterpreted. But its replication would come in the form of ritual re-creation, which differs fundamentally from recapitulation in that in ritual re-creation the Saints consciously and purposely played out the story of what had once happened to Israel in order to call up to modern memory the times when God tested, or tried, or was good to his chosen people. With temples and priesthood in place and sacred ordinances ever ready to signal renewal of divine-human covenants, the necessity of recapitulation, of living through the particular events of Hebrew-Christian history, disappeared. But the story of Mormonism's recapitulation of that past stayed very much alive as it moved out of experiential reality into Mormon history.

As temple ceremonies kept ancient times and the covenants of the new dispensation alive in Latter-day Saint minds, so festival, pilgrimage, and the recital of the stories of the nineteenth-century past preserved the vitality of the pioneer period. Moreover, because that history recapitulated more ancient pasts, it opened out to reveal Mormonism's reappropriation of Christianity's appropriation of Hebrew history and, especially in the case of the Saints who went to the Great Basin, its own direct appropriation of Israel's story. In "The Ritualization of Mormon History," an important article published in the *Utah Historical Quarterly* in 1975, Davis Bitton described the rapidity and "cumulative intensity" with which the Saints ritualized their past.[7] But there is still more to be said about this process, because it not only allowed the Saints to take hold of their own past, it also gave them a tenacious hold on the reality of the biblical story. For example, even as Mormonism continued the activity of recapitulation, an annual 24 July festival developed. Each year the Saints reenacted the fulfillment event of the LDS exodus, reentering the Salt Lake Valley with appropriate ceremony, thus symbolically reentering not only the Great Basin but also the Promised Land. Episodes in the Mormon past that reflected other sacred events, such as temple buildings or the journey through the wilderness, also called the Saints to pilgrimage, making eventual historical restoration inevitable at Kirtland, Nauvoo, Mt. Pisgah, and all the many other sites where LDS pioneer events took place. More important, because the nineteenth-century Saints had engaged in reestablishing the covenant, organizing the church, preaching the gospel, living the patriarchal order of marriage, and building up the kingdom—in short, in replicating sacred story—Mormon history itself took on a sacred character.

As a result, Mormonism's salvation history begins with the story of Abraham, the beginning point of the salvation histories of Judaism and Christianity, but it extends across the LDS experience in the pioneer period. It happened in the here and now, in the United States less than two centuries ago. And yet the story of the LDS past is in many ways as much a "historical product of a visionary tradition" as is the Bible, a work in which, according to literary critic Northrop Frye, religious and historical saga is continuously reshaped. Specifically, in *Fearful Symmetry* Frye writes that "the Gospels consolidate [the] vision of the [Old Testament]

Messiah into the vision of Jesus, who has the same name as Joshua, and the proof of the events in Jesus' life, as recorded in the Gospels, is referred not to contemporary evidence but to what the Old Testament prophets had said would be true of the Messiah."[8] The modern critical mind makes reference to the biblical accounts rather than contemporary evidence well-nigh impossible in the scholarly reconstruction of the Mormon past. Yet in its popular recital within Mormonism, the same pattern of referring to biblical prophecy operates in Mormon history.

The framework of interpretation in this work makes it possible to see, then, that accounts of Mormon history that reflect the experience of the Saints themselves consolidate and reshape the vision of Old and New Testaments in much the same way that accounts of the experience of the early Christian community consolidated and reshaped Israel's story. Moreover, it is equally true that as early Christianity's experience gave it a unique understanding of the gospel of the God of Abraham, so Mormonism's pioneer experience figures more prominently than has been recognized in the development of the Latter-day Saints' unique understanding of the "principles of the gospel." While Mormonism's transition from cultic movement to religious tradition follows the pattern by which other traditions made the transition, its unique understanding of "the gospel," which rests on its history as well as its theology, turns the story of Mormonism into a story that has meaning for all persons interested in religion as generic phenomenon.

The LDS temple, Logan, Utah, 1887

The RLDS auditorium, Independence, Mo.

Chapter Four

Reformation and Restoration

Aᴅᴅʀᴇssɪɴɢ ᴛʜᴇ sᴛᴜᴅᴇɴᴛs at Brigham Young University in 1979, W. Grant Bangerter declared, in a talk entitled "The Best of All Good News," that the Mormon restoration has to have been "the greatest news event since the resurrection of Jesus Christ."[1] The text of this talk was selected for publication in the sesquicentennial issue of the LDS Church's official magazine, the *Ensign*. It gives no indication that the observation about the restoration was made with careful consideration of the manner in which it might fit into LDS theology. But even though Bangerter's remark was not a statement of doctrine, it still has theological significance because it points up the truly radical character of the Mormon restoration. For that reason, Bangerter's declaration should not simply be dismissed as hyperbole inspired by the devotional context in which it was delivered.

If Elder Bangerter had been engaged in a scholarly exposition, his statement could be described as thoroughly revisionist since the usual pattern which scholars bring into play in treatments of LDS restorationism is the making of comparisons between Mormonism—especially Mormonism in its institutional forms—and other Christian restorationist groups—especially groups subscribing to "true church" doctrines.[2] Bangerter made, instead, an implicit comparison between the beginning of Christianity and the beginning of Mormonism, which, whether he intended the comparison or not, is, from the standpoint of theology and religious studies, a much more useful point of departure for examining Mormonism as a restoration movement.

While the fact is very often overlooked within certain forms of confessional Christianity, the study of its beginnings makes it abundantly evident that Christianity began as a restoration movement.[3] The Old Testament was its scripture, and its early claims were cast in an undeniably Judaic mode. But as indicated at the beginning of this work, the actual practical experience of early communities of believers shaped and transformed Christianity to such an extent that, even as it held fast to its reappropriation of the Hebraic past (to its reappropriation of Judaism's mythological dimension, to be more precise), Christianity and Judaism became separate religious traditions.[4] Mormonism also began as a restoration movement, and its reappropriation of the Judeo-Christian past has likewise endured. Yet unless the radical character of the Mormon restoration is taken into account, and unless careful attention is paid to the particular way in which Mormonism was shaped and transformed by the actual practical experience of the community of belief, Mormonism can all too readily be misunderstood as little more than an elaborate idiosyncratic strain of the nineteenth-century search for primitive Christianity. When a comparison between the beginnings of Christianity and Mormonism is used as a starting point for study of the Mormon restoration, it calls for an examination which begins with the hypothesis that as Christianity was *sui generis*, despite clear parallels to other movements which may accurately be categorized as forms of Jewish restorationism, so Mormonism, despite manifest parallels to other forms of Christian restorationism, is likewise *sui generis*.

An approach from this perspective means that it is not necessary to ignore the fact that Mormonism drew for inspiration not only on the Old Testament and the New, but also on the American experience in general, the experiences of the family of Joseph Smith in particular, and on Masonry and certain forms of magic and folk religion as well.[5] But it is necessary to recognize that Mormonism is derivative and synthetic only insofar and in the same fashion that other religious traditions are derivative and synthetic. Locating and identifying its components can facilitate understanding, but this approach demands acknowledgment that Mormonism cannot be reduced to the sum of its parts any more than Christianity can be reduced to the sum of its parts or Judaism to the sum of its parts. Moreover, while there can be no doubt about Mormonism's similarity to other restorationist forms of Christianity that came into being at about the same time and place, this approach likewise calls for an admission that trying to fit the Latter-day Saints into the standard categories (church/sect/denomination; Eastern Orthodox/Roman Catholic/Protestant; evangelical/liturgical; and so on) used in classifying these and other Christian groups requires so much qualification that it does not really illuminate the Mormon restoration. Finally, this approach holds that the Mormon restoration can best be comprehended if it is placed in the larger context of radical restoration movements, which, from time to time across the ages, have so reordered experience that humanity has been able to see anew the hand of God in history.

Restoration movements do not spring from the primordial past fully formed. The process is more natural than that, natural enough to be studied in a way that will make it possible to see (1) how a set of restoration claims is advanced to initiate the process, and (2) how response to those claims develops into a religious movement. But if the process is natural enough to be studied, it is nevertheless so very complex—aye, even mysterious—that unless its beginnings are examined within a clear theoretical framework, it can appear to be completely supernatural and thus amenable only to observation, not to analysis.

Developing such a theoretical framework must begin with a general consideration of restoration claims. What is their nature? In what context are they put forward? More important, what does the acceptance of a set of restoration claims mean in the lives of single individuals and in the history of communities of individuals united by that acceptance? And how, for these single individuals and communities, are these claims transformed into "objective facts" and operating principles?

By their very nature radical restoration claims are exclusive: they admit no alternative versions of truth. As discussed in the last chapter, they issue up in times of confusion when the worldview marketplace is crowded with contenders for primacy—in

genuinely pluralistic religious and cultural circumstances in
which multiple belief systems abound and in which cultural and
religious disorder is aggravated by the shifting of the social, political, and economic bases on which society has long rested—such
claims posit a return to an original situation wherein the proper
relationship between humanity and divinity was clearly and
firmly established. When they are accepted wholeheartedly, restoration claims banish confusion and make possible the passage
from chaos to cosmos, settling with unassailable authority the
tumultuous questions which at once generated and reflected the
chaos. They offer believers persuasive explanations allowing
them to determine which of several possible belief systems they
ought to adopt, which of several religious institutions is legitimate, which rituals and ordinances are necessary and proper, and
which human beings possess authority to speak and act for divinity. Yet because restoration claims are, finally, simply claims—
propositions—until a primal community of believers comes to
accept them as an accurate description of an original situation
wherein the terms of association between humanity and divinity
stood pure and undefiled, the study of restoration movements
calls for investigation of the process by which believers transform
restoration claims into objective facts and operating principles.

If the course of individual acceptance of a set of firmly established claims—personal conversion—is the object of study, the
image of rebirth is illuminating. Its utility is shown, for example,
not only by looking at ritual in primitive cultures, but by noting
that one way to understand Matthew's report of Jesus' words
"Truly I say unto you, unless you turn and become like children,
you will never enter the kingdom of heaven" is to note that in becoming "as a little child," a new believer reorders existence, growing into faith. The claims of restoration become so central to such
a person that the way they are comprehended both alters the person's behavior and, by providing a new perspective from which to
experience all of life, actually reconstructs reality. This suggests
that in individual lives, more or less canonized restoration claims
can become facts and principles when individuals act *as if* they
actually are facts and principles. But even cursory examination of
the experience of an initial community of believers in a new restoration movement reveals that when a new set of restoration

claims is transformed into a set of objective facts and operating principles around which a whole society may be organized, an infinitely more complicated process is set in motion.

Instead of starting over as little children, the pristine community of belief enters collectively into a new world. Because restoration claims postulate a return to an original situation, their immediate effect on the community that accepts them is, as will be shown in Chapter Six, the obliteration of history and the regeneration of time.[6] Standing, as it were, on the threshold of a new age, at the beginning of a new dispensation, this primal group receives the restoration as it is in the process of becoming, which means that the manner in which its members perceive the restoration and respond to its imperatives will operate both to shape and modify the restoration claims as the movement achieves stable form. Moreover, as they are the first to perceive and react, their perception of and response to the restoration sets this group, which is "once again at the beginning," apart from those who follow them in the faith.

The experience of the original group becomes profoundly important in that—whether or not they were persuaded to accept the restoration on the basis of rational argument or by some intuitive, nonrational means—their belief makes the beginning of the restoration possible. Consequently, their acceptance itself becomes, in time, a part of the original set of restoration claims. Their belief validates the claims and at the same time becomes, as the belief of the early Christian apostles demonstrates, an infinitely repeatable paradigmatic act wherein the claims of the restoration are continually transformed into facts and principles through an endless chain stretching across the stream of time. New believers banish cultural and religious confusion by coming to accept—either on the basis of rational argument or by some intuitive, nonrational means—the reality of the restoration.

Before moving from the general to the specific, from this theoretical framework to the Mormon restoration, it is important to note the difference between radical restoration movements, which make possible new beginnings in all the dimensions of religion—mythological, doctrinal, ritual, social, and experiential—and restoration movements, which, through processes of reformation, reinterpretation, and reintegration, revitalize religious traditions. In many of the world's religions differences would be so subtle that making distinctions between the two types of movements might be difficult. But in Christianity the difference is clearly discernible, because it is easy to comprehend the difference between a re-formation of the church and a restoration of the gospel, of which re-formation is only a part. Seeing that, it is possible to see also that while re-formation does make renewal possible, it is, finally, renewal that is continuous with history in that its purpose is to rectify the mistakes of the past on the basis of information already available within the tradition. Radical restoration involves a changing of the means of, or the reopening of, communication between divinity and humanity. In that sense and for that reason, it breaks through the ongoingness of experience, tearing across history's seamless web to provide humanity with a new world wherein God is actively involved.

While Mormon restorationism differs in fundamental ways from other nineteenth-century movements classified as restoration movements, enough similarity existed to make fairly common the conversion of members of other restorationist groups to Mormonism—Sidney Rigdon and his Mentor congregation spring immediately to mind—and, as records of Mormon apostasy suggest, the conversion of Mormons to other restorationist groups.[7] Most especially there was a similarity in appropriations of the Judeo-Christian scriptures and the history of the early Christian church. On the surface, the restoration claims advanced by Joseph Smith and the Latter-day Saints were not unlike those advanced, for example, by Alexander Campbell and the Disciples of Christ.[8] Both groups accepted the fathership of Abraham and both accepted the Sinaitic Covenant. The members of both groups believed that theirs was the true church, organized according to what they took to be the pattern laid down in the apostolic age; and both groups stood on the simple principles of faith, repentance, and baptism for the remission of sins.

Yet because the LDS restoration claims may not be fully comprehended apart from the manner of their presentation to the world, the similarity is more apparent than real. As opposed to the claims which Campbell deduced solely from the scriptures in completely "rational" fashion and which he presented in the form of logical arguments in the pages of the *Millennial Harbinger*,

Mormon restoration claims were embedded in the Book of Mormon. A curious combination of salvation history, doctrinal explication, and *ex eventu* prophecy, this book proposes not only to relate the story of the American experiences of an ancient Hebraic people who came in sailing ships to the western hemisphere from Israel's northern kingdom, but also to picture the sorry religiocultural state that would prevail in the days wherein the record should be found, translated, and published to the world. Because the opening of the record would—so both the text and the book's title page made clear—reveal to the Indians their true identity as a remnant of God's chosen people through Ephraim's rather than Judah's line, and because it would, at the same time, convince both Jew and Gentile of the truth of the Judeo-Christian scriptures, the coming forth of the Book of Mormon was presented therein as the preeminent event toward which all history had been tending, at least since the Resurrection, and perhaps since the division of Israel's monarchy nine centuries before that.

"Wherefore at that day when the book shall be delivered" unto a prophet whose name like that of his father shall be Joseph, then will God remember his covenants which he has made with the children of men that he may set his hand again the second time— the first was, of course, the ministry of Jesus—to recover his people. "And it shall come to pass that my people which are of the house of Israel shall be gathered home unto the lands of their possessions; and my word shall also be gathered in one."[9] As Ezekiel prophesied, the sticks of Joseph and Judah would grow together, and if "the Gentiles shall hearken unto the Lamb of God in that day . . . he shall manifest himself unto them in word and also in power." They, too, will be "grafted in" and "numbered among the seed [of Abraham] . . . and the house of Israel shall no more be confounded."[10] When the Book of Mormon "shall come forth from the Gentiles," two churches only will be there: one, "the church of the Lamb of God"; the other, "the church of the devil."[11] The contents of the record will show the power of the Eternal Father unto the Gentiles, "that they may repent and come unto him and be baptized in his name and know the true points of his doctrine [so] that they may be numbered among his people, Israel."[12] Then "the power of the Lamb of God [shall descend] upon the Saints of the church of the Lamb, and upon the covenant people of the Lord." And they shall be "armed with righteousness and with the power of God in great glory."[13]

Integrated into a complex narrative that can capture the imagination in much the same way the Old and New Testaments capture the imagination—an allegation to which evidence drawn from the lives of the community of the Mormon faithful bears eloquent testimony—these restoration claims had extraordinary power when the Book of Mormon first spoke "out of the ground" unto the children of men.[14] No matter whether believers accepted the Book of Mormon on rational grounds or whether its historicity was confirmed to them "by the ministering of angels" and they came to believe in some nonrational fashion, accepting the book at face value meant accepting its restoration claims. And as the number of believers multiplied, the organization of the church, which the Book of Mormon called the Church of the Lamb, followed naturally. Yet when prophecy was turned into reality, the church that would become the Church of Jesus Christ of Latter-day Saints did not come into existence in a form Saints would recognize today.

Although its legal organization did not take place until the spring of 1830, two 1829 events prepared the way for the institutionalization of Mormonism. In the middle of May of that year, Joseph Smith and Oliver Cowdery reported that the Aaronic priesthood had been conferred on them by an angelic visitor, and that this visitor foretold a subsequent restoration of the Melchizedek priesthood as well. Then, in June, a revelation came to Joseph Smith, Oliver Cowdery, and David Whitmer wherein they learned that twelve apostles would be called to go into all the world to preach the gospel to every creature, that in building up the church they should take upon them the name of Jesus Christ, and that as many as repent and are baptized in his name, and endure to the end, "the same shall be saved."[15] One component appropriating Old Testament institutions literally and another drawing on the New Testament directly together paved the way for the Latter-day Saint church, and, as events in the spring of 1830 illustrate, this contrapuntal pattern became a part of its very foundation. "The Articles and Covenants of the Church of Christ," obtained, Smith said, "by the spirit of prophecy and revelation," called for the formation of a church almost as closely modeled on the church de-

scribed in the Book of Acts as the one established by Alexander
Campbell and the Disciples of Christ. Yet on 6 April, the day of its
formal organization, the new church received a revelation—likewise given through First Elder Smith—that superimposed literal
prophetic leadership on this New Testament church.[16]

In an important *Dialogue* article, Melodie Moench investigated
the popular notion subscribed to by many modern Latter-day
Saints that the Mormon self-conception of Israel is drawn from
the Old Testament. She concluded that despite strong parallels
between modern Mormons and the Israelites, early Mormons
used scripture in much the same way that nineteenth-century
Protestants used scripture, seeing the Old Testament mainly
through the eyes of the Apostle Paul and the authors of the synoptic gospels. This suggests that early Mormon images of Israel were
refracted through perceptions of Israel recorded in New Testament writings.[17] However, again using the Disciples of Christ for
comparative purposes, a comparison of the Book of Mormon restoration promises/prophecies with the restoration claims set forth
in the *Millennial Harbinger* reveals that although it is true that
Mormon conceptions of Israel reflect New Testament understandings, there is a crucial difference in the Mormon and Disciples of
Christ restoration notions. The Disciples base the connection between Israel and the church on the principle that the division
among Abraham's progeny is a division between Israelite and
Gentile, with the latter coming beneath the covenant by virtue of
the New Testament promise that the salvation of God has been
extended to the Gentiles.[18] The connection established between
Israel and the church in the Book of Mormon does not, on the
other hand, depend so directly on the New Testament promises to
the Gentiles: in the Mormon restoration, membership in the
Church of Jesus Christ means that the Saints are literally adopted
into Israel and are thereupon brought into the covenant by virtue
of their membership in the tribes of Israel.[19] This means that,
while for the Disciples the organization of the church according
to the New Testament model was an end in itself, in Mormonism
the proper organization of the church of Jesus Christ was to be
but one of the opening events in the new dispensation of the fullness of times, the first step in a process that not only included the
restoration of the church, but the restoration of Israel thereafter.[20]

Because this unusual understanding of the relationship between the church and Israel had to be made to fit into an institutional framework patterned on the New Testament church,
wherein a very different conception—or at least a very different
popular perception of a different conception—of the church/Israel
relationship prevailed, a certain amount of what must be recognized as theological tension was embedded in the foundation of
Mormonism. Without a doubt, this tension was heightened by
the difficulty engendered by the need to mesh a belief in a *literal*
restoration of the Aaronic and Melchizedek priesthoods and, more
important, an open canon and the leadership of a living prophet
into an ecclesiastical organization whose blueprint was the one
set out in the Book of Acts. But the tension was not, finally, simply structural tension, as is indicated by the fact that, while the
tension was relieved somewhat, it did not disappear either in response to several early revelations—all, in essence, declaring that
"no one shall be appointed to receive commandments and revelations in this church excepting my servant, Joseph Smith, Jr."—
or as a result of an 1835 revelation on priesthood, which specified the rights and duties of the members of the Aaronic and
Melchizedek priesthoods and tied the various offices of the church
to priesthood place. Instead, the tension signaled the theological
stress arising from the effort made in early Mormonism to hold
within it two different understandings of the church.

On the one hand there was a conception that did not differ significantly from traditional understandings of the church as the
body of Christ, an organization in which, as a July 1830 revelation
specified, "all things shall be done by common consent, by much
prayer and faith, for all things you shall receive by faith." Entrance
into this body was made possible by repentance, baptism by immersion for the remission of sins, and receipt, as a revelation in
December of that same year stated, of "the Holy Ghost by the lay-
ing on of hands, even as the apostles of old." A contrasting conception made the church, on the other hand, a body—as yet another revelation given two years later made clear—"established in
the last days for the restoration of [God's] people." As the institution facilitating an actual and material as opposed to spiritual restoration of Israel (whose members could claim actual and material as opposed to spiritual inheritances in Zion), the church was

understood to be a "house of order." Entrance thereunto required repentance, baptism by immersion, and so on, but also the administration of ancient ordinances not described in the New Testament, but a part of those "plain and precious things" that the Mormons believed were left out when the New Testament scriptures were published to the world.

It would be very easy here to draw too hard and fast a distinction between these two conceptions, making one depend so much on the Old Testament that Mormonism's Christian connection is implied more by its institutional name than anything else, while making the other depend so much on the popular understanding of the primitive New Testament church that it implies nothing more than a figurative and mystical connection with Israel. Actually, much of the theological tension in early Mormonism resulted from the stress generated by literal as opposed to figurative interpretations of the church/Israel connection, both of which are potentially present in the Pauline corpus. Read afresh, in the light of Isaiah and Ezekiel (particularly chapters 11, 34, and 37 of the latter), rather than within a framework of post-Augustinian and, more important, post-Reformation hermeneutical assumptions, Paul's letters (most especially those to the Christians at Galatia and Rome) lend themselves to literal as well as figurative understanding.[21] When Galatians 3: 7 is used alone as a proof text, for example, its "know ye therefore that they which are of faith, the same are the children of Abraham" can suggest a spiritual—i.e. figurative—ingathering in the last days. But placed alongside Paul's elaborate discussion of "Abraham our father as pertaining to the flesh" in Romans 4 and his use of the image of the olive tree in Romans 11, the gathering of "the children of Abraham" may be taken as pointing to an actual—i.e. literal—restoration of Israel's bloodline. Although the complex LDS recapitulation of the stories of Israel and early Christianity during the nineteenth century left behind records of an experience that does not admit of easy analysis, recognition of a fundamental theological tension within Mormonism allows a clearer picture to emerge of the way in which the response of the first generation of Latter-day Saints to Mormon restoration claims transformed those claims into facts and principles.

Mormonism actually came into being in 1828 and 1829 be-

fore the Book of Mormon was published. News of the work spread
across the western New York countryside, and stories related by
close associates of Joseph Smith about the "great and marvelous
work" that was about to come forth filtered into the ranks of
the community of seekers, who either stood apart from existing churches or moved to and fro among them. The field, as a
whole series of very early (principally 1829) revelations stated,
was "white to the harvest," and those who believed the promises
of the new gospel were enjoined to thrust in a sickle and reap
while the day lasted.[22] As soon as the Book of Mormon came from
the press in Palmyra it was carried—by "godless vermin," a Protestant minister said—with surprising rapidity not only through
western New York, but also in northern, southern, and eastern directions.[23] In a very short time the first Mormon converts were
made and a Mormon community started to form.

The Mormon practice of keeping elaborate records started so
early that the recovery of the general nature of this early group has
been possible. The dissertations of Mario DePillis, Marvin Hill,
and Gordon Pollock together make it very clear that in the beginning, new Mormons were responding to signs of authenticity
similar to those which led converts into other less radical restoration movements.[24] Concentrating particularly on the response
to the restoration of the Aaronic and Melchizedek priesthoods,
DePillis found that early converts saw therein an institution that
answered their quest for authority, but since his writing reveals
that DePillis himself understood the priesthood as synonymous
with the church, as it is in Roman Catholicism, it is not surprising that he did not explore the manner in which early Mormons
thought that these Old Testament priesthoods ought, in practical
terms, to fit into the church. Other facets of the work of DePillis
speak more directly to the character of the early LDS community,
almost anticipating conclusions reached both by Hill and Pollock
that the earliest response to Mormonism was a response to its al-
lure as a form of primitive Christianity.

That the movement was seen in this way from the outside is
indicated by a letter written, just six weeks after the church was
formally organized, by a German Reformed minister from Fayette,
New York, the small town in which the organization took place.
He said that "already in this region more [copies of the Book of

Mormon] have been sold than one would have expected," and its effects "already extend upon members of various Christian persuasions. Some members of the Lutheran, Reformed, Presbyterian and Baptist congregations have given this book their approval, have been baptized by immersion, and formed their own sect. Because they baptize by immersion they are winning over many members of the Baptist Church (including General as well as Particular Baptists), first because of their teachings about the universal grace of God and lastly because of their agreement in attitude toward the proper subject of holy baptism."[25] That Mormonism was likewise seen from the inside as almost synonymous with apostolic Christianity is dramatically illustrated in letters written by Joseph Smith's mother in 1829 and, more important, in 1831. After describing the Book of Mormon and the means by which her son was called to translate the records, Mother Smith said that God has "now established His Church upon the earth as it was in the days of the Apostles. He has now made a new and everlasting covenant, and all that will hear His voice and enter . . . shall be gathered together in the land of promise. . . ." Intimating without actually saying so that those who were preaching the Mormon gospel were able to cast out devils, take up serpents, drink any deadly thing, and heal the sick, she outlined the story of Pentecost, noting that Peter told the multitude to "repent and be baptized, and the promise was that they should receive a remission of sins and the gift of the Holy Ghost." In the later letter, she continued, "this is the gospel of Christ, and His Church is established in this place and also in Ohio."[26]

Giving the title *Joseph Smith, the First Mormon* to her 1977 biography of the Mormon prophet, Donna Hill aptly and economically captured the model of the process by which the Mormon community responded to LDS restoration claims, a model provided by Smith himself. As the Book of Mormon came into being, he apparently accepted its message implicitly, becoming the first Book of Mormon convert. With no doubts whatsoever he seems to have awaited the unfolding of events predicted for the days in which the record should come forth. While it is not likely that anyone will ever know exactly how the prophet reacted to the revelations that started to transform Mormonism almost as soon as the church was organized, one lens through which to view

Smith's perception of the developments in 1830 and following is
his famed 1844 statement: "No man knows my history. I cannot
tell it; I shall never undertake it. I don't blame anyone for not believing my history; if I had not experienced what I have I could
not have believed it myself." This autobiographical summary of
his life can be taken to indicate that perhaps the prophet was as
astonished as many of his followers at the direction developments
took in Mormonism.[27] Rather than fulfilling the early expectations
of his followers, who were baptized by immersion and joined the
Saints believing that they were being admitted to the only true
primitive and apostolic New Testament church, he led them toward the creation and acceptance of a very different sort of Latter-
day Saint church.

That many very early LDS theological positions and worship
practices differ little, if at all, from those of the popular Protestantism and forms of primitive Christianity of Joseph Smith's day is
one of the most significant recent emphases in Mormon studies.
The work of Robert Matthews, Thomas Alexander, Mark Thomas,
Timothy L. Smith, and Melodie Moench underscores that of
Marvin Hill and Gordon Pollock as it directs attention to the parallels between the Church of Jesus Christ, which would afterward
add "of Latter-day Saints" to its name, and other churches of the
time who also regarded themselves as the New Testament Church
of Christ. But even as this work draws scholars toward readings of
the Mormon scriptures and the writings of early Saints with eyes
sensitive to trinitarian nuances and ears attuned to New Testament phrasing, the *experience* of the Mormon pristine community of belief must be kept constantly in mind. This is particularly
true with regard to the gathering concept. Less than six months
after the organization of the church, when people responded in
such numbers to the "repent and be baptized" part of the LDS
message, a revelation from God spoke to the Saints about the
"bring[ing] to pass the gathering of mine elect" as a prelude to an
ending, when "the heaven and earth shall be consumed and pass
away and there shall be a new heaven and a new earth." Stated in
New Testament terms, this message (now printed as section 29
in the Doctrine and Covenants of the LDS Church) can be read as
a prime example of the way in which the Saints and other Chris-

tians of that day—and across the ages—appropriated Old Testament concepts by way of the New Testament reappropriation of those concepts.

But another revelation concerning the gathering of the Saints was given three months later. While it likewise expressed conceptions found in the New Testament, it said that "the day would soon come when the veil would be rent" so that the Saints "should see the Lord's face." In the meantime, the Saints were enjoined to go into Ohio, where, said the Lord, "I will give you my law and there you shall be endowed with power from on high . . . for I have a great work laid up in store, for Israel shall be saved."[28] This the Saints did, drawing, to a surprising degree, even in this first corporate movement, on the Old Testament Exodus pattern. Essentially, therefore, they engaged in *action* appropriate to the literal Israel of the Old Testament rather than to the symbolic Israel that came into existence in the Graeco-Roman world of early Christendom.

It is difficult to determine exactly how long it took for the theological tensions buried in the Saints' conception of the restoration to surface. But it is fairly clear that a considerable proportion of early Mormon apostasy had its roots in the disappointment that awaited those persons who came into the church expecting to find it based as closely as possible on the apostolic model. After 1831, promised land notions and millennial expectations were fused in Mormonism. As Joseph Smith led the "Mormonites" westward to establish an incipient Ohio "Zion," he was also engaged in "translating" the Old Testament. As he did so, his concern was increasingly a concern about the relationship of the Mormon movement to ancient Israel, a concern that transferred itself to the Mormon primal community of faith, making the symbolic literal and the metaphorical real. Significantly, the greatest accomplishment of the Saints in Kirtland was not the building of a city of God, as would happen in about the same space of time in Nauvoo, Illinois, a decade hence, but the construction of a house of worship. Appearing for all the world to resemble from the outside the exterior of a New England meeting house, a church, this handsome building had internal arrangements indicating absolutely that it was not a church. It was a temple, which, by transforming into material reality that most tangible of all Old Testa-

ment symbols, came to symbolize the direction toward which the
Mormon restoration would tend in the future.

Scholars often refer to the dedication of the Kirtland temple as
the Mormon Pentecost. This designation is justified by considering the rituals accompanying the dedication, especially the ritual
of the washing of the feet, as well as in the way in which the
group mystical experience that lasted three days functioned in
the creation of Mormonism. Still, while there can be no question
of the importance of the dedication, it is plain to see that as the
fulfillment of the prophecy that the "veil would be rent" accompanying the revelation calling for the literal gathering of Israel, the
Kirtland temple dedication was not merely a powerful Pentecost-
like experience that legitimated the Mormon restoration simply
as a restoration of the true and apostolic church.

The transfiguration-like experience, in which the Lord appeared
to Joseph Smith and Oliver Cowdery to accept the temple as a
place where his name should be and where he would manifest
himself in mercy therein in precisely the same fashion that God
had manifested himself to his chosen people in Solomon's temple,
was the central feature of the dedication. Moses and Elias (or
Moses, Elijah, and Elias) appeared also and committed to the
Saints the keys to the new dispensation of the fulness of times as
well as the keys to the gathering of Israel and the dispensation of
the *"gospel* of Abraham," saying that in the Saints and their seed
all generations thereafter should be blessed.[29] In essence a fulfillment of the prophecy that had been set forth in an August/Sep-
tember 1830 revelation describing the priesthood of Aaron, this
transfiguration experience tied Mormonism to the Old Testament
traditions and Hebraic scriptures as much as the transfiguration
on the high mountain described in Matthew 17 tied Christianity
to the traditions of the Old Testament.[30] Whether or not this experience was mediated through the New Testament, it pointed to
the flourishing afterward of the conception of Mormonism as the
restoration of Israel that would become the ruling conception of
Mormon restorationism in the years to come.

The extraordinary development in the doctrinal and ritual dimensions of Mormonism that took place in Nauvoo in the last
two or three years of Joseph Smith's life has led to an interpretation of the Nauvoo period as the flowering of the "fulness of the

gospel" through which the Saints came to see themselves not as forming a New Israel but as establishing a very real connection with an ancient one. Although this interpretation is no doubt an accurate reading of what happened, it is nevertheless true that the patriarchal blessing became an integral part of Mormonism in Kirtland and that it is in this ritual that the Saints learn their Hebraic genealogical lineage by being informed, through the medium of inspiration available to the person occupying the patriarchal office, of the particular portion of Abraham's family, the particular tribe, to which they belong. Moreover, since plural marriage started in Kirtland and since, in embryo at least, the Mormon endowment ordinance was introduced there as well, literal connections with Israel were clearly a part of Mormonism before the prophet fled from Ohio to Missouri.[31]

As a footnote to this sketch of how the actual experience of the Latter-day Saints shaped the way in which Mormon restoration claims would be transformed into reality, one further thing needs to be pointed out. Many of the Saints who came into the church expecting it to be an apostolic church were never completely comfortable with the church conceived of as the literal restoration of Israel, which in time incorporated the patriarchal order of marriage and secret temple ordinances. Some of these New Testament–oriented Saints (as they might be described) drifted out of the church. Others were forced out. But large numbers remained in the church until a May 1844 revelation said "there is no such thing as immaterial matter, all spirit is matter" (making literalism as opposed to the symbolic supreme), and until the outcome of the struggle for succession to LDS leadership following the June 1844 death of the prophet Joseph Smith removed all possibility that the balance might shift backward toward the Mormonism of the New York period.

With regard to the latter, no clear and unambiguous set of directions existed to assist the Saints in identifying a new leader after Smith's death. On different occasions and under different circumstances, the prophet had ordained four different men to preside over the church. In addition to ordaining these four—Sidney Rigdon, David Whitmer, Oliver Cowdery, and Hyrum Smith—the prophet had given the Quorum of the Twelve administrative authority over the church equal to the authority of the First Presi-

dency. And, as the recent discovery of a long-lost document at-
tests, the Mormon leader also gave his eldest son, Joseph Smith
III, a blessing that invested him with the right to be the first Mormon prophet's "successor as President of the High Priesthood: a
Seer, and a Revelator, and a Prophet." Under these circumstances,
an intra-Mormon succession struggle was inevitable, and such a
struggle in fact occurred, stretching across many years. The conflict between the Saints and the outside world that erupted in the
wake of Smith's death obscured its extent and intensity, however.

While the Quorum of the Twelve assumed immediate responsibility for both church and community, with Quorum president
Brigham Young taking effective charge of the troubled situation,
significant divisions within the Mormon community have been
papered over by the popular, officially sanctioned story of how
"the mantle of the prophet" fell onto Young's shoulders during a
public meeting held in Nauvoo less than three months after the
martyrdom. These divisions were revealed in the struggle over
who the new LDS leader ought to be, but they went far deeper,
reflecting confusion and disagreement about various doctrinal
matters—plural marriage, baptism for the dead, the gathering, the
necessity of temple ordinances—plus practical concerns about
non-Mormon responses to concentrated Mormon settlement and
worry about the propriety of organizing a political Kingdom of
God.

When Brigham Young led the main body of restored Israel westward in 1847, intent on establishing an independent LDS kingdom, large numbers of Saints stayed behind, many of them joining
small isolated Mormon congregations established throughout the
Midwest. In 1860, many but by no means all of these separate congregations united to "reorganize" the Church of Jesus Christ of
Latter Day Saints, which is today centered in Independence, Missouri. Because the members of the "Reorganization" were led by
Joseph Smith III, who refused to acknowledge that his father had
introduced plural marriage into Mormonism, and because these
Saints adopted a succession doctrine requiring the president of
the RLDS Church to be a direct descendant of the first Mormon
prophet, the fundamental differences between the two leading
forms of Mormonism were misunderstood for many years. This
was particularly true within the RLDS fold. Honoring Emma

Smith, the prophet's first wife, who was unwilling—or unable—
to talk about her husband's involvement in plural marriage, and
looking to her descendants for leadership, many of the Saints who
did not go west failed to appreciate the theological differences that
set them apart from their cousins in the Great Basin. They believed that polygamy was the main sticking point, and they said
this with so much vehemence for so long that full comprehension
of the differences between Latter Day Saints and Latter-day Saints
has eluded most of the members of both churches, as well as
people who are members of neither.

Eyes and ears alert to the tensions in Mormon restorationism
can, however, see and hear in RLDS conferences a restored Church
of Jesus Christ that has a figurative connection with Israel, rather
than—as is the case when observing a televised general conference from the LDS tabernacle on Temple Square in Salt Lake
City—seeing and hearing of a restoration of Israel that has a direct
connection with the Church of Jesus Christ.

It does not matter, however, whether the conferences are gathered bodies of Saints from the church centered in Independence
or the one centered in Salt Lake City. The people of the Mormon
restoration remain peculiar people. Unlike those, for example,
who followed Alexander Campbell into the Disciples of Christ
"Campbellite" restoration and, shortly thereafter, found themselves to be the members of just one more Protestant denomination (now subdivided into two), Latter-day Saints of every stripe
are heirs of a radical restoration. Their forebears entered into a
new age in much the same way that the Saints of early Christianity entered into a new age. In so doing the Latter-day Saints started
over, not to reform the institutions of Christendom but to participate in a transformation which in its totality has now made Mormonism into a distinct, discrete, internally consistent religious
tradition. And for those who identify with, participate in, belong
to, accept, convert to, believe, or are in any way a part of that religious tradition, the Mormon restoration truly has to have been
"the greatest news event since the resurrection of Jesus Christ."

so wet with the rain [...] the water might have
been wrung from them — she was speechless and
almost stiffened with the cold and effects of her ex
posure. We laid her on a bed and [...] my [...] and
Husband and my son administered to her by the lay
ing on of hands. We then changed her clothing gave
her some nourishment and put her into a bed covered
with warm blankets and after pouring a little rice
water into her mouth she was administered to again
this time she raised her eyes and seemed to revive
a little. I continued to employ every means for
her benefit and that of my other sick children
in this I was much assisted by Emma and my daughters who
which lay in my power and we soon they reaped
the reward of our labor for in a short time they
began to mend and I now congratulated
myself on the pleasure I should feel in seeing my
children all well and enjoying each others society agai
n after William began to set up a little he related the
following vision

Refer to Wm Smith

I felt concerned about this for I feared that some evil
was hanging over us but knew nothing of the oper
ations of the mob party until one day Joseph ca
rose up and called told me that he wanted me to
not be at all frightened that the mob were com
ing but we must all keep perfectly quiet and
he wished the sisters to stay within doors and not
suffer themselves to be seen at all in the streets
that he could not stay with us but for he
wanted to see the brethren and have them keep their
families quiet and at home he rode off but I soon
[...] that who the mob were this was the

Holograph page from the preliminary manuscript
of Mother Smith's *History*

Chapter Five

Getting the Story Straight

Working within an analytical framework that allows comparison between the beginnings of Christianity and the beginnings of Mormonism has proved useful in this study because it reveals the radical character of the Mormon restoration. But if comparison of this sort lays bare the remarkable similarity in the *process* by which these two religious traditions were established, significant differences between the two need to be constantly kept in mind. One of the most significant of these differences is the dissimilarity between the development and the character of the Christian and Mormon scriptural canons.

At the time of the crucifixion of Jesus, no institutional apparatus held his followers together and no official canon of writings about Jesus existed. When, after centuries had passed and the works that would comprise the canon had been selected, institutional Christianity was more or less securely in place. And it stands to reason that the connection between the two can hardly have been accidental, since the works selected for inclusion in the canon lent themselves to the support of the organized church. With the exception of the Septuagint, a Greek translation of the Old Testament carried over into Christianity unchanged, and with the additional exception of Saint John's Apocalypse, the completed canon was made up of works all dealing in one way or another with the life of Jesus and the experiences of his early followers. The import of this is that the Christian canon and the official version of Christian history are one and the same.

The Mormon canon of scripture was established, however, almost in its entirety during the lifetime of Joseph Smith. In addition to the Book of Mormon, the Latter-day Saint canon of scriptures includes transcriptions of revelations given to Joseph Smith between 1828 and 1844; the Book of Moses, which Smith received by revelation in 1830; the Book of Abraham, a translation of a papyrus (likewise "inspired") which, so the prophet said, contained the writings of Abraham while he was in Egypt; and Joseph Smith's "testimony," a brief spiritual autobiography dealing with the story of the prophet's life before 1830. As opposed to the Christian canon, which includes four narrative accounts proclaiming and interpreting the life of Jesus, plus an additional narrative covering the early years of Christianity, the only narrative description of early Latter-day Saint history is a personal account of the prophet's life in the years before the organization of the church. Smith's revelations are, in a manner of speaking, primary source materials for Mormon history, but they do not tell the Mormon story in chronological or any other systematic fashion.

The absence of narrative accounts of Mormonism's early years from the official canon of LDS scriptures does not mean, however, that LDS history has not been canonized through an identifiable canonization process in which—as in all canonization processes —theological and political considerations were extremely important. An official record was kept from 1839 forward. Said to be Joseph Smith's own history but actually the work of divers hands, this record was carried to the Great Basin when the Latter-day Saints went west, and selections from it were arranged chronologically to become the authorized documentary *History of the Church*.[1] Other works dealing with the history of the Saints after the murder of Joseph Smith were likewise given official approval, and were published by the church in the *Deseret News* and the *Millennial Star* during the second half of the nineteenth century. The multivolume *Comprehensive History of the Church of Jesus Christ of Latter-day Saints: Century I*, written by B. H. Roberts, and *Essentials in Church History*, written by Church Historian Joseph Fielding Smith, have likewise received the church's imprimatur. Moreover, the late nineteenth and early twentieth centuries saw the development of an entire genre of quasi-official LDS history that received tacit, if not direct, ecclesiastical sanction if it had been written by one of the LDS General Authorities (members of the First Presidency, apostles sitting in the Council of the Twelve, or high priests sitting in the First Council of Seventy), or was published by a church press, or was selected for use in some division of the church's educational program.

Throughout the nineteenth and early part of the twentieth centuries, the mechanism by which ecclesiastical judgment was passed on historical, as well as theological and doctrinal, works was consideration of the works during deliberations of the highest conciliar body of the church, the Quorum of the Twelve. In recent decades, however, this function has been assumed by an ecclesiastical administrative committee charged with the task of examining the content of official church publications "for doctrinal soundness and correctness of doctrinal interpretation." Aptly designated the church Correlation Committee, this body measures historical material submitted to it against existing authorized interpretations of Mormon history. For the most part, this body works so quietly and efficiently that the effectiveness with which the LDS Church continues to control its own history is truly surprising, given the size and energy of the scholarly body, whose members pursue the study of LDS history outside of and independent from connections with either the LDS or RLDS churches.[2]

Certain incidents in the record of Mormon history reveal very clearly, moreover, that the historiography of a religious tradition is a fruitful avenue to follow if the goal is an understanding of the process by which that religious tradition came into being and by which it maintains itself across time. One such incident is an unusual historiographical situation that arose in connection with the publication in 1975 of *The Story of the Latter-day Saints*. This survey of Mormon history, which was published by the church-connected Deseret Press, was written as an "in-house" history by James B. Allen and Glen M. Leonard. At that time Allen was Assistant Church Historian and Leonard was a Historical Associate working for the church in its official Historical Department. Although the work was not submitted to the Correlation Committee before its publication, an initial press run of 35,000 copies indicated that the authors, the Historical Depart-

ment staff, and the editors at the press all anticipated that this
work would attain quasi-official status as informally sanctioned
history that could serve as a text in classes on Mormon history
taught in the church Seminaries and Institutes System, at the
various LDS church colleges, and at Brigham Young University.

Perhaps because the work was written by professional historians whose Mormon orthodoxy did not prevent their interpretation from assigning more weight to the impact on Mormonism of
the social, economic, political, and cultural context in which it
developed than the currently canonized story admits, or perhaps
for less easily identifiable theological and/or political considerations, the work was not approved for use in LDS seminary and institute classes or in religion classes taught at church colleges and
at Brigham Young University. Although instructors in such classes
could not assign *The Story of the Latter-day Saints* as a text, the
35,000 copies of the Allen and Leonard work were not left to
gather dust on storage shelves at Deseret Press. The quality of the
work and extraordinary interest in its subject matter combined so
that within five years the first printing was sold out. But despite
abundant evidence that a substantial market continues to exist
for this book, it has not been reprinted. A decision was made, re-
portedly at the highest level, that the work should not be reprinted without extensive revision. Since the book's authors are
no longer at work in the Church Historical Department, and since
the History Division as such no longer exists, extensive revision
probably will not be undertaken.

This is not the first incident, nor is it likely to be the last one, in
which an ecclesiastical decision has been made regarding the un-
acceptability of a narrative account of Mormon history that could
reasonably have been expected to attain at least quasi-official status. In 1865 another episode of this nature occurred. In that instance, however, official reaction was not limited to disapproval
of the reprinting of the work. A much earlier story of the Latter-
day Saints, one written by the mother of the Mormon prophet and
published by Apostle Orson Pratt, a member of the Council of the
Twelve, was suppressed by Church President Brigham Young.

The prevailing—and authorized—interpretation of the decision
made by Church President Brigham Young to suppress "Mother

Smith's History" is one that treats Young's decision in this case as one in a series of incidents in a long-standing and bitter disagreement between Young and Pratt.[3] And no doubt the difficult relationship between these two early Mormon leaders figured in. But to see the story only in this light is to miss the opportunity to observe a new religious tradition as it adds to the order it imposes on the present by imposing order on the chaotic generative years out of which it emerged, and from which it draws its inspiration and its strength.

Responding to a 1968 query from Edwin S. Gaustad about out-of-print works in the field of Mormon history that might be suitable for inclusion in the Arno Press *Religion in America* facsimile reprint series, Leonard J. Arrington suggested Orson Pratt's 1853 Liverpool edition of Lucy Mack Smith's *Biographical Sketches of Joseph Smith, the Prophet, and His Progenitors for Many Generations.* A reprint of this work by the prophet's mother was needed, said Arrington, because Brigham Young ordered its suppression soon after it was published. Concurring with Judge Elias Smith's opinion that the work was "a tissue of lies from beginning to end," Young had decided that the original edition ought to be destroyed and a correct edition prepared to take its place. Since his counsel was followed in this matter, copies from the first edition were very rare.

Arrington disagreed with Young's negative assessments of Mother Smith's history. He described it instead as "informative, basically accurate, and extremely revealing of Joseph Smith's early life and his family background," and explained that "it now seems clear" that the work was condemned "primarily because of the favorable references and space devoted to William Smith" therein. In reality, he said, this work "perhaps tells more about Mormon origins than any other single source."[4]

Gaustad, the advisory editor of the reprint series, was pleased with Arrington's suggestion and recommended the reprinting of the book.[5] Acting on this recommendation, the Arno Press shortly thereafter issued its edition of Lucy Smith's work from the press. Purchased for library collections all across the country, this facsimile of the first edition of the 282-page book said to have been composed by the Mormon prophet's mother quickly became the premier printed resource for information about young Joseph Smith and the beginnings of Mormonism.

Except for the slender store of scattered autobiographical statements left by the prophet, his mother's history is practically the only direct source of information about Joseph's early life. Moreover, although it is obviously retrospective, Lucy Smith's narrative is a rare and valuable firsthand account provided by an observer closely connected to the primary participants in the early development of the Mormon movement.[6] Her work occupies, therefore, a place of central importance in the Mormon historical corpus. Yet while its significance has often been pointed up, scholars have sometimes overlooked Mother Smith's history, or, more likely, dismissed it because it was available to them only in one of the several more or less official versions published by the Reorganized Church of Jesus Christ of Latter Day Saints in 1880, 1908, and 1912, or under the sponsorship of the Church of Jesus Christ of Latter-day Saints in 1902 or 1958.[7] The appearance of a facsimile reprint of the first edition—which was not only not published by but was once suppressed by the LDS Church—reemphasized the importance of the work. At the same time, however, republication has stimulated renewed questions about the book's literary pedigree.

Even though many historians explain that the condemnation of the 1853 edition of Lucy Smith's work came about because Brigham Young was upset with the book's publisher, Orson Pratt, or because he was dismayed by the activities of the prophet's youngest brother, William Smith, it is impossible to ignore entirely Young's allegation that the history was written at a time when Mother Smith could "scarcely recollect anything correctly that had transpired."[8] In addition, since the book was finished and copyrighted in 1845 but not printed until 1853, finding out what happened to the history in the interim between its completion and publication is necessary.[9] Moreover, in view of the fact that examination of the manuscript versions of the work located in the LDS Church Archives reveals that the manuscripts are not Lucy Mack Smith holographs but compilations by Martha Jane and Howard Coray, determining the extent to which the history truly reflects Mother Smith's narrations is also mandatory.[10]

Arranged in different order and placed in general rather than particular categories, these become the standard authenticity, reliability, and provenance queries that historians must put to any primary source before it can be used with confidence. Historiographical in nature, questions of this type are usually answered best by reviewing the history of a document and analyzing its content. Yet because Lucy Smith's history is not a document dealing exclusively, or even primarily, with secular matters, but one that recounts a sacred story (albeit one with profane, i.e. secular, dimensions), it does not fully lend itself to historiographical analysis that fails to take its religious character into account. In much the same way that early accounts of the life of Jesus are religious documents, Lucy Smith's *Biographical Sketches* is religious to the core. The history written by the prophet's mother must be recounted and the contents of the work must be examined in a fashion which will allow full recognition of that fact. When this is done, it becomes very clear that Mother Smith's history not only provides invaluable information about the Mormon prophet and early Mormonism, but information about the process by which Mormonism survived the death of the prophet as well.

Martha Jane Knowlton Coray, a Nauvoo schoolteacher, claimed that after Joseph Smith's death she had approached Mother Smith about writing her memoirs because she wanted to secure as much information as possible for herself and her children. As a schoolteacher, Mrs. Coray also saw the value of having "simple stories" told by the mother of the slain prophet "compiled in a small book for the reading of the young."[11] But Mrs. Coray's husband, Howard, one of Joseph Smith's clerks whose assignment had included the compiling of the official historical record of the church, remembered things the other way around; he said that the initiative came from Mother Smith, who came to see his wife sometime in the winter following the martyrdom "about getting her to write the history of Joseph, to act in the matter only as her, Mother Smith's, amanuensis."[12] Lucy Mack Smith, on the other hand, indicated that her history of the family was undertaken at the direction of the Council of the Twelve, the governing body led by Brigham Young that had assumed the leadership of the church in Nauvoo following the murders of Joseph and Hyrum Smith.[13]

In light of this contradictory evidence recorded by the prin-

cipals in the story, determining just whose idea the work originally was is out of the question. It is now possible to reconstruct
with considerable precision the history's evolution, however, and
there can be no doubt whatsoever that the work came into being
with the assistance of both Martha Jane Coray and her husband
Howard.[14] Exactly how much assistance was tendered is another
matter. That has never been made clear, which means that Mother
Smith's history has likewise been something of a mystery for
most of its literary life.

Brigham Young believed that the work was composed by Mrs.
Coray, who wanted to be a writer, "especially a novel writer."[15]
Ettie B. Smith, Howard Coray's sister, is said to have been sure
that her brother was the author.[16] Others saw it as the combined
work of Lucy Smith and the Corays. Yet the *History* in so many
ways reflected the known personality and attitudes of Mother
Smith that many historians assumed that any early draft of the
work that surfaced would be written in her own hand.

But when an early draft came to light in the Latter-day Saint
Church Archives in the late 1960s, it proved not to be a Lucy
Mack Smith holograph. Instead, this document, which has been
properly designated as the preliminary manuscript of the *History*,
was principally penned by Martha Jane Coray.[17] Rather than confirming President Young's suspicions, however, the preliminary
manuscript reveals a composition process involving Mother Smith
at practically every turn.

From clues provided in the preliminary manuscript it is clear
that "The History of Mother Smith by Herself," the title used in
the manuscripts and on a supplementary title page of the first edition, is a sort of combined oral history and "as told to" autobiography.[18] Lucy Smith's recollections seem to have been recorded into
a series of notebooks during the winter of 1844–45, and her accounts were probably written down as nearly verbatim as possible.[19] Along with auxiliary information (much of it chronological
and genealogical) gathered from various sources, these notebooks
were subsequently used to develop the sustained narrative found
in the preliminary manuscript. This preliminary narrative was
then substantially revised to become, eight years afterward, the
manuscript version of the work from which type was set at the
Millennial Star office for the 1853 edition. Finally, Howard Coray,

whose duties also included compiling the official history of the church, copied the complete history into a securely bound ledger book and deposited it with the Church Historian.[20]

From this reconstruction it is possible to theorize that while Mother Smith was obviously consulted again and again throughout the entire composition procedure, and while she clearly gave her approval to the final version, her most direct and sustained involvement with the history came in the earliest stages, when her narratives were being taken down by Martha Jane Coray. It therefore stands to reason that the preliminary manuscript, its somewhat confused chronology and incomplete information to the contrary notwithstanding, comes closer than the finished *History* to capturing the perceptions and emotions, ideas and feelings, attitudes and beliefs of the mother of the Mormon prophet. Although changes in the final text may appear to be little more than ordinary revision and polished restatement, it nevertheless can be said that every alteration, substitution, addition, and deletion exaggerates the distance between Mother Smith and the readers of her history.

Thus, in this instance, the answer to the question of authenticity—the matter of whether the history is, as it purports to be, a work composed by Lucy Mack Smith—can best be stated as a proposition: the measure of documentary authenticity of the 1853 edition of Mother Smith's *History* is in direct proportion to the amount of material carried over from earlier versions of the work without change. Although it is not easy to arrive at an exact measure without a parallel-column edition, it is estimated that "about one-fourth of the revised manuscript is not in the preliminary draft while approximately ten percent of the earlier manuscript is omitted from the revised manuscript."[21] This suggests that if a strict definition of documentary authenticity is applied, the 1853 edition of Mother Smith's *History* will have to be adjudged, at best, as marginally authentic. But this does not mean that the work is without value and ought to be disregarded. Quite the contrary. It must be recognized for what it is, a "History of Mother Smith by Herself" upon which order and, at the very least, occasional orthodoxy were imposed when the work was cast in final form.

That this imposition of order and orthodoxy was in all likelihood approved by Lucy Smith does not materially alter the historiographical situation, a situation which can be summarized in the following way. Two separate and distinct versions of the *History* exist; one is clearly preliminary to the other; the first reveals more than the second about Lucy Mack Smith (her personality, her perceptions of the emotional ambience with the Smith family, her religious life, her relationship with and understanding of her son Joseph's prophetic career and its central place in the Smith family experience, and her conception of Mormonism); the second might be described as redaction, because it reveals more than the first about the prevailing understanding inside the inner circle at Nauvoo in 1845 about the life, prophetic career, and church founded by Joseph Smith. Examples provided below show the difference in these two versions of Mormon history.

But before providing examples to place these two understandings of the prophet, Mormonism, and the Mormon past in relief, it is important to establish the accuracy of the information in both the preliminary manuscript and the 1853 edition of the book. The matter of whether one is more reliable than the other must be clarified. Certainly accuracy was considered a serious problem at the time of the recall of the book's first edition. An official committee of revision was appointed to prepare a corrected version of the work, and the flyleaf of George A. Smith's working copy of the *History* says that "this work was written in Nauvoo in 1845 by Mrs. Howard Coray, from narrations of Lucy Smith, Mother of the Prophet, after his death. Her memory having been very much impaired, and somewhat shattered by the successive losses of a husband and four sons as well as by care and old age, the work contains many things which are incorrect."

In questioning the accuracy of Mother Smith's memory, Brigham Young was anticipating the task of establishing reliability faced by all historians working with early Mormon history. On this count, Professor Richard Anderson's work has made the task of establishing reliability relatively simple. He has posed a series of questions to verify the accuracy of Lucy Smith's memory and has found an astonishing number of reassuring answers. Beginning in an ingenious way, he examined the work of the official committee of revision that prepared the authorized version of the work published in 1902. Comparing the 1853 and 1902 editions and looking at working copies of the book used by George A. Smith and Samuel W. Richards in the preparation of the latter, Anderson discovered that less than 2 percent of the text was altered in any way. In many of the twenty to thirty instances where changes were made, the changes were minor ones.[22]

As he described his work in an address to the Andrew Jenson Club in Salt Lake City, 7 May 1976, Anderson then proceeded to search out corroborating evidence for the names, dates, and episodes found in the two earlier versions of the history. Corroboration was found either in the public record or in contemporary documents for about 96 percent of all the checkable items in the two versions of the *History*, and this very high percentage led Anderson to conclude that "in Lucy [Mack Smith] we have a person with a very precise memory and an eye for detail who described the events of her own life in a *History* on which we can rely with confidence."[23]

While Professor Anderson failed to make a comparison between the two versions of the *History*, preferring instead to treat them as a synthetic whole in reconstructing early Mormonism, as far as chronology is concerned, the 1853 edition is far more reliable than the preliminary manuscript. The situation is not so dramatic as in the case of authenticity, but in comparing one with the other, the later version, which was revised by Howard Coray, is a more dependable guide to what happened when and where.

Before turning to examples illustrating the difference between the preliminary manuscript and the 1853 edition, it is also important to determine provenance—to see whether anyone tampered with either version. As there are two manuscript versions of the history, the provenance question is two-pronged. The answer to what happened to the preliminary manuscript is fairly simple: it stayed in the possession of Howard Coray for many years until it was finally turned over to the Church Historian, for which consideration, oral tradition tells us, he received an overcoat.[24] But what happened to the revised manuscript from which the text of the 1853 edition of the *History* was set is complicated indeed.

Provenance is usually important because historians need to set up chains of custody to establish the integrity of the documents on which their reconstructions of the past are based. In this instance, however, the question of provenance is integrally related to the much larger issue of succession in the church presidency and its correlative: who, at this crucial time, would have control of the Mormon past? The year was 1845, not 1984, but Brigham Young seems to have anticipated Orwell, understanding quite clearly that "he who controls the past controls the future and he who controls the present controls the past."

As it had been with Joseph Smith, the history of the church was a matter of special concern to Young. Whether he initiated or simply encouraged the Smith-Coray historical enterprise, he was obviously interested in its outcome. But after he read Coray's final draft, he decided that the work still needed revision. He was concerned about the copyright, nevertheless, and on an afternoon when he, along with others, was occupied in revising the church history, he consulted with several of the Twelve about purchasing the copyright from Lucy Smith.[25] Apparently deciding that owning the copyright was unnecessary, this group seems to have concluded that settling with Coray for his work on the project would be sufficient indication of church proprietorship.[26] Young asked that a copy of the manuscript be made for the church before the original was returned to Mother Smith, but thorough revision was planned before publication. As indicated, the so-called church copy was made and Mother Smith's recollections were returned to her.

The two ensuing years, 1846 and 1847, were turbulent years for the Latter-day Saints, and the planned revision of Lucy Smith's manuscript seems to have been a matter of minor concern to Brigham Young and the Twelve. Certainly, as far as can be determined, no attention was given to it, and the church copy was carried to Salt Lake exactly as it had been "copied off, every word" by Howard Coray.

While fully acknowledging the confusion of the situation insofar as it was a struggle between Mormons on the one hand and non-Mormons on the other, histories of the period written by Utah Mormon churchmen—with the conspicuous exception of D. Michael Quinn's article on the succession crisis published in *BYU Studies*—often fail to reflect fully the intra-church contention for leadership that existed during the first few years after the prophet's death.[27] Even such a one-sided dissertation as Douglas Larche's rhetorical history of the struggle for succession reveals, however, that concern about legitimate leadership and, just as important, correct church organization and doctrine were manifest through the final years at Nauvoo.[28] Because present tumult and anxiety almost mandated the examination of the past as guide, the memories of Mother Smith took on an importance they would have surely lacked had her son Joseph lived out his years in peace.

Mother Smith's only surviving son, William, knew this. The prophet's youngest brother, whose claims to church leadership on the basis of lineage were undercut by his unstable personality and unsavory behavior, recognized his mother's unique position in Mormonism. He was aware that her physical presence among the western Saints could help to strengthen and legitimize the church leadership of Brigham Young and the Twelve.[29] And he also knew that so many of the Saints had been anxious to hear from his mother "the particulars of Joseph's getting the plates, seeing the angels at first, and many other things that Joseph never wrote or published that," as she said, she had "almost destroyed her lungs giving recitals about these things."[30] Therefore, assuming that President Young and the Twelve would regard his mother and her firsthand knowledge of the early Mormon past as desirable commodities, he intimated that he could arrange to bring his mother west with him when he wrote—after being dismissed from the Council, cut off from the church, and failing to find a satisfactory place among the Strangites—offering to come out and help lead the church.[31]

Possibly because they knew that the church already had in its possession the written memoirs of his mother, that letter was never answered. More probably it was not answered because Brigham Young and the Twelve, despite the power and appeal of the presence of the immediate family of the prophet, were simply not willing to put up with William Smith. And Mother Smith lived out her life in the Midwest, in steadily failing health and penury, being passed from one member of the family to another, until she went to live with the prophet's widow, Emma, in the Mansion House in Nauvoo, where she died in 1855.[32]

At some point during those final years, the manuscript of the *History* apparently became the possession of Mother Smith's son-in-law, Arthur Milliken, who sold it to Almon W. Babbitt. Babbitt, in turn, is supposed to have allowed it to get into the hands of a sometime church member from Wisconsin, Isaac Sheen, from whom it was obtained by Orson Pratt for the reported sum of $1,000.[33] Pratt wrote a letter to Lucy Smith asking for permission to publish her manuscript, and she answered, saying, "I have studied over the matter and have finally concluded that you may make use of [the manuscript] in any way you see proper."[34] Carried to Liverpool, the manuscript, essentially unchanged, as a comparison with the church copy reveals, became the text of *Joseph Smith, the Prophet: Biographical Sketches of Joseph Smith, the Prophet, and His Progenitors for Many Generations, by Lucy Smith, Mother of the Prophet.*

Because it was printed at the office of the *Millennial Star*, the work seemed to carry the imprimatur of the church, but as the official Journal History makes clear, the work was considered to be both inaccurate and unauthorized and for those reasons was condemned and recalled.[35] Brigham Young undoubtedly had the crucial voice in the council's decision to suppress the book. For that reason it is tempting to regard the book's suppression—as do Richard Anderson and Howard Searle—as just another episode in a complex, wide-ranging, long-term doctrinal and personal conflict between President Young and Orson Pratt that began in 1836 and only ended with Young's death forty-one years later.[36] That temptation is especially great since it is obvious that inaccuracy, the ostensible reason for the suppression, really has very little foundation. Yet to regard the recall decision simply as an *ad hominem* action is not only to ignore Orson Pratt's genuine, almost naive surprise at Young's displeasure about his bringing out the book,[37] but also to disregard the timing of the suppression and an extremely complicated set of circumstances which, for all his perceptiveness, may have been only intuitively understood by Brigham Young himself.

Young's many statements about the book indicate that he was truly convinced that it was absolutely filled with inaccuracies that had occurred through Mother Smith's impaired memory. In spite of all Howard Coray's revisions, President Young and many of the members of the Quorum of the Twelve found the book unacceptable. They had personally witnessed many of the events described by Mother Smith and seemed quite certain, although they cited very few specific examples, that the prophet's mother's accounts were somehow all wrong. Certainly a part of the negative reaction was rooted in the rosy picture of William Smith that

Mother Smith had painted. Yet in reality, inordinate attention is not devoted to William in the *History*, and the revised edition continued to include most of Lucy Smith's accounts mentioning her youngest son. No doubt William Smith was still a thorn in Young's side in 1853 when the book was published. But when it is noted that the work was not recalled until a dozen years later, opposition to William Smith was likely more pretext than the underlying cause for Young's violent and continuing reaction against the work.

Perhaps animosity to Orson Pratt and William Smith is sufficient explanation for the recall of the book. But if not, and if the charges of inaccuracy cannot be substantiated, then why, in the face of the Saints' obvious thirst for knowledge about the prophet and early Mormonism, was Mother Smith's *History* condemned, recalled, and kept from them? Clearly the 1865 date of the suppression is significant. While it is true that the work's recall was justified in an editorial published in the *Deseret News* and *Millennial Star* that included an attack on Orson Pratt, the recall coincided with the presence among the Saints of sons of the prophet who were advancing the succession claims of the Reorganized Church of Jesus Christ of Latter Day Saints.[38] Since those claims held that legitimate leadership for the church had to come from within the prophet's immediate family, emphasis on his family's role in Mormon beginnings could have been anathema in the Great Basin at that time. Thus an argument can be made that the explanation for the suppression of Lucy Mack Smith's *History* lies in the fact that, Coray's revisions notwithstanding, the work sets forth an understanding of the prophet and his church that prevailed within the "Reorganization" rather than the one that prevailed in the valleys of the Utah mountains.

As stated above, when dealing with documents heavily weighted with religious significance, the provenance question resolves itself into a query about whether anyone has tampered with the documents in an effort to support doctrinal or theological positions. One interpretation of the decision to suppress the work, then, is to regard it as the final chapter in the nineteenth-century history of Lucy Mack Smith's *History*, and to recognize it as a somewhat heavy-handed effort at tampering with a document that Saints might read, so Brigham Young repeatedly warned them, at the risk of their own spiritual salvation.

Unlike the difficult situation historians of early Christianity must face in reconstructing the story of the early church with Irenaeus' attack *Against Heresy* as their main guide, historians of Mormonism have available not only Brigham Young's attack on Mother Smith's book, but the book itself in both the published version and preliminary manuscript. Mother Smith can hardly be transformed into Mormonism's Marcion, yet the circumstances are not entirely dissimilar. In making an examination of what it was that Brigham Young and the Quorum of the Twelve were re-acting against, it will become clear that the *process* of institu-tionalizing orthodoxy transcends both time and place.

The first of its two title pages might call Mother Smith's work *The History of the Prophet Joseph*, but the protagonist of her work was not Joseph so much as it was the Smith family from which he sprang. That the prophet was Joseph was almost coinci-dental; it might have been Alvin or Hyrum just as well, for the book is concerned with presenting the credentials, both religious and secular, of the *family*. Almost a third of the work (and an even higher proportion of the preliminary manuscript) is devoted to an account of the families Mack and Smith, with special atten-tion paid to their religious histories. Detailed narratives of Lucy Smith's own spiritual searching and religious encounters are pro-vided at intervals throughout the entire work, including an ex-traordinary spiritual autobiography that Howard Coray merely summarized in the *History*'s final version. And the religious biog-raphy of Joseph Smith, Sr., is likewise detailed, though it is very interesting to note that the father's religious visions are not inte-grated in any way into the preliminary manuscript, but are found on loose sheets included among the miscellany. Yet at no point can there be found evidence of any type of *premonition*, religious or otherwise, that Joseph would be the member of the family whose prophetic career would propel the Smiths into religious prominence. When Joseph reported his visions, his father and mother apparently accepted his reports implicitly and without hesitation, but his birth is described in a matter-of-fact manner: "In the meantime we had a son whom we called Joseph after the name of his Father; he was born on December 23, 1805." Included is no soliloquy describing a period of special spirituality while the future prophet reposed in Mother Smith's womb. Placed in close juxtaposition in the published work is the senior Joseph Smith's vision of the box, the contents of which would make him wise and give him understanding, but that placement may have been made by Howard Coray. And in any event it is placed closer to the birth of William than of Joseph, so that altogether there is presented the picture of a family emotionally and spiritually prepared to support a son's prophetic career. But the son was not necessarily Joseph.

The extent to which that support was forthcoming is not fully revealed in the printed *History*. Howard Coray, fully aware that Mother Smith's narrative differed in significant ways from the early history of Mormonism that had been given official sanction and published in the *Times and Seasons*, generally followed the prophet's account of the discovery of the plates and the bringing forth of the Book of Mormon. For that reason, Lucy Smith's perception of the crucial role of the family is only suggested. In the preliminary manuscript, for example, constant reference is made to the plates having been in the possession of the Smiths, rather than to Joseph's having had them. In discussing the perfidy of Martin Harris, there are constant references in both the preliminary manuscript and the printed version to what Harris had done not to Joseph but to "us." Yet it is in the earlier version of the history that the corporate pronouns predominate, as is indicated by the following reference to arrangements for the printing of the Book of Mormon: "We were again compelled to send for Joseph before we could proceed any farther these trips back and forth from New York to Penn cost everything we could raise."

The altered perspective is subtle, but the shifting emphasis from the family to Joseph in Coray's revision can be demonstrated by comparing the descriptions of the efforts made to protect the Book of Mormon manuscript from malicious persons. A revelation directed that a second copy of the manuscript should be made, only one copy should be taken to the press at a time, guard should be kept, and so on. The 1853 edition concludes the story with the statement that "all these things were strictly attended to, as the Lord commanded Joseph." But in the preliminary manuscript, Mother Smith relates that the danger "astonished us very much but we did gainsay the council of the most high—wherefore we did all things according to the pattern that was given—and accordingly they guarded Oliver to his work in the morning and went after him at night and kept a guard over the house all night long. Although we saw no enemy and knew not that there was one that designed evil against us." When it is noted that this passage refers to a time when Joseph was away in Pennsylvania, the family's participation in the founding of the faith is pointed up in clear and unmistakable ways.

In revising the preliminary manuscript, Howard Coray faced what proved to be insurmountable difficulties. He knew that the revision ought to be cast in the path marked out by the official history that the prophet had been so concerned to see compiled, so when obvious discrepancies appeared he simply substituted a part of that official history, at times placing in Mother Smith's mouth a remark such as "Here I extract from my son's history." He recognized that there was too much emphasis on the Smith family and not enough on the priesthood and the church organiza-tion in the preliminary manuscript, and as a consequence, he de-leted from the revised account long emotional passages that dem-onstrated the closeness of the relationship between Joseph and his immediate family. But all was, finally, to no avail, for when he was done the *History* was, as the copyright said, "The History of Lucy Smith wife of Joseph Smith, the first Patriarch of Jesus Christ of Latter Day Saints, who was the father of Joseph Smith, Prophet, Seer, & Revelator;—containing an account of the many perse-cutions, trials, and afflictions which I and my family have en-dured in bringing forth the Book of Mormon, and establishing the church of Jesus Christ of Latter Day Saints. . . ."[39]

In the final analysis, the 1853 edition of the work really is "The History of Mother Smith by Herself." The preliminary manu-script may provide a more complete and probably more accurate picture of her personality and her relationship with her family in its domestic and everyday forms. But in the book, her vision of Mormonism shines through. It is a Mormonism based on the Book of Mormon and absolute confidence in Joseph Smith's pro-phetic role, but a Mormonism that is familial, even tribal, rather than organizational and institutional. It is the Mormonism of the early 1830s, not that of Kirtland in the mid-1830s, Missouri, or Nauvoo. This is not to say that the work describes a purer or more legitimate Mormonism; it is to say that the Mormonism described by Joseph's mother tells of the church the prophet founded in the beginning, not the one he led at the end of his life. A religious

form almost alien to the Mormonism of the Saints in the intermountain West, the Mormonism described in Mother Smith's
History explains both William Smith's 1845 claim that the Saints
"were all dependent upon his family for the priesthood"[40] and
Paul Edwards's 1977 interpretation of the prophet as a religious
leader who really had no intention of establishing a long-lasting
church organization.[41]

Many, many issues are raised by the study of the preparation,
revision, and suppression of Mother Smith's *History*, but one of
the most important of these is the recognition that here is one of
the major episodes in the struggle for legitimate succession which
occurred in Mormonism after the death of Joseph Smith. The parallels between the struggle for church leadership among the Mormons in the middle of the nineteenth century and the struggle for
leadership in the early Christian church cry out for recognition.
In both cases the struggle was not a struggle between legitimacy
and illegitimacy, but a struggle between forms of legitimacy—almost in classic Weberian terms. Among the early Mormons the
chief charismatic claimant, Strang, proved to be unimportant.
Here *lineage*, i.e. the Smith family, was brought into competition
with *office*, i.e. Brigham Young and the Quorum of the Twelve.
That the suppression of Mother Smith's *History* can be seen as a
part of this struggle is indicated by the fact that Brigham Young
knew that William Smith was no longer a power among the Saints
in 1865. The problem then was that the formation and organization of the RLDS Church had been accomplished and the appeal
of Joseph Smith III was regarded as dangerous. Worried, as he said
in a conference address the following year, about the Saints who
were "apostatizing from the work which the Lord had commanded
[Joseph Smith] to found to run [to] Young Joseph Smith," Brother
Brigham rejected the Mormonism described by Lucy Smith with
its unstated yet perfectly obvious claim that the Smith family was
the royal family in this the last dispensation.[42]

There is no doubt that Leonard Arrington was correct in saying
that Mother Smith's *History* "perhaps tells us more about Joseph
Smith's childhood than any other single source." Or that Richard
Anderson is correct in designating the work as one of "the essential sources for Mormon origins."[43] But for all that, the good
Brother Brigham, head over heels at work in building up a kingdom beleaguered on all sides by non-Mormon forces, was also

probably right in deciding—at a time when all efforts were being devoted to developing and consolidating an extraordinary eccle- siastical organization—that for the protection of the Great Basin kingdom, Mother Smith's *History of the Prophet Joseph* had to be condemned and recalled. For buried in its pages could be found an implicit challenge to Brigham Young's legitimate right to lead the Mormon Church.

The succession crisis had been over so long in 1902 that a con- nection between the contents of Mother Smith's *History* and questions of legitimate church leadership were never raised. Recent developments indicate, however, that control of the Mor- mon past is still a matter of great concern to the LDS Church hier- archy. Yet, as it was in the case of the suppression of Mother Smith's *History*, that concern is often misunderstood.

In a move that departed from an unbroken pattern of calling General Authorities to the post of Church Historian, the church called Leonard J. Arrington, author of the greatly respected his- tory *Great Basin Kingdom*, to this post in 1972. In all likelihood this action was a part of the strenuous efforts then under way throughout the LDS Church to professionalize its bureaucracy, for no evidence points to a conscious desire on the part of church leaders to shift away from a policy of having officially sanctioned accounts of the Mormon past written in what may be called a salvation-history mode. But as a result of calling Arrington as Church Historian, supporting him in the organization of a His- tory Division within the LDS Church Historical Department filled with professional historians, and establishing this enter- prise in handsome quarters adjacent to the Church Archives in the central Church Office Building, a perception spread that the church had changed its policy and its attitude about how its his- tory ought to be written. This perception was supported by Arrington's announcement that a grand programme of historical work was being undertaken under the auspices of the LDS Church Historical Department. Two one-volume histories of Mormonism were already in progress, he said, and a new sixteen-volume his- tory of the church from its beginnings to the present was being inaugurated. Scholarly editions of all Joseph Smith holographs, the letters of Joseph and Emma Smith to each other, Brigham Young's letters to his sons, and the preliminary manuscript of

Mother Smith's *History* were contemplated, as was much other historical work.

While a great deal of this programme of work was completed, it soon became obvious that a new age had not been ushered in. When *The Story of the Latter-day Saints* appeared with the phrase "published in collaboration with the Historical Department of the Church of Jesus Christ of Latter-day Saints" on its title page, some of the LDS General Authorities started to realize that the church itself appeared to be responsible for what was rapidly becoming known as the "new Mormon history." Although this was a turn of events that apparently had not been anticipated, the church hierarchy found this to be an intolerable situation, and it therefore started to pull back. While rumor says that the suppression of the work of historians employed by the church was discussed, Brigham Young's tack was not taken. Apostles Ezra Taft Benson and Boyd K. Packer made well-publicized, widely circulated addresses warning the Saints against accounts of the Mormon past that were so secular—*read* professional—that God's hand in history was obscured, and access to materials in the Church Archives was made less open than formerly, but many professional historians remained (and still remain) on the church payroll.

The situation is much changed, even so. Financial support for the History Division was diminished, for example, while support for oral history, historic preservation, and museum programs was continued and even expanded. Arrington's assignment was more or less silently changed from Church Historian to Director of the History Division, and the History Division was renamed the Joseph Fielding Institute for Church History and physically as well as administratively transferred to Brigham Young University. Official sponsorship of the sixteen-volume history of the church was withdrawn, leaving the authors of the individual volumes to make alternate arrangements for publication. And so on. By these actions, as well as by changes in the way history is being treated in all its *official* publications, the church has moved, not necessarily to disapprove of Mormon history written in the "coolness" of the modern professional mode, but to distance itself from history which fails openly and deliberately to place God at the center of the action.

24 July holiday parade, 1880

Chapter Six

In and Out of Time

I F A GROUP of modern Saints—say a dozen or so drawn from the 170,547 members of the church who were added to the rolls in the church's sesquicentennial year—should be transported by means of a magical time machine back to 1880, they would find the world of Mormondom a century ago very unfamiliar territory. In addition to a landscape from which a multiplicity of ward chapels all built according to standardized architectural plans is absent, and besides all the obvious differences between a Mormonism that had its being in a more technologically primitive world than this one, such a hypothetical Latter-day Saint group would suddenly come face to face with the reality of plural marriage. Rather than knowing about the nineteenth-century form of the patriarchal order of marriage only in abstract terms, they would meet polygamy head on. But these things that are so clearly a part of a different age might not make the Mormonism of 1880 seem as unfamiliar to modern Mormons as would a host of other, far more subtle, differences.

If these Saints, by chance, should step from their time machine out into the land of Zion on the morning of the first Sunday of the month, they would find families unabashedly eating hearty breakfasts. Disoriented as much by the discovery that the day was not being treated as a day of fasting as by time-machine lag, the latter-day visitors would, most probably, seek out a ward meeting place, believing that they could get their bearings by attending Sunday School. Instead of finding what would seem normal to them, a neatly departmentalized session organized by age groups, they would find a somewhat motley general assembly of children of mixed ages. Staying to observe what was happening, they would be reassured by the familiar faith-promoting gist of the words. Yet, more used to the interesting approach and varied activities of twentieth-century Sunday School situations, they would be surprised and perhaps impatient with what would appear to them as interminable "reading around" from the pages of the *Juvenile Instructor*.

Expecting to be able to attend sacrament meeting in the same local ward later in the day, the visitors would learn that sacrament meeting was held only in the tabernacle located in the center of town. This would cause them to expect to join in with all the Saints in the area in a large-scale worship service, but that would likewise lead to disappointment, since at the appointed hour the tabernacle would still seem virtually empty. In time disorientation would give way to dismay: a brother with a tobacco habit could well be seated on the stand; another brother's shirt might be so marked with coffee stains that the visitors would certainly know that he indulged in that forbidden beverage; still another, conceivably a bishop's counselor, might from the stand be sending the telltale aroma of a recently consumed toddy wafting across the front rows in the building. Yet despite their shock at such open breaches of the Word of Wisdom, the members of this latter-day group would almost certainly be equally astonished to see that the meeting proceeded onward toward its conclusion without anyone obviously or unobtrusively collecting quantifiable data that would allow the brethren in Salt Lake City to measure the Saints' level of active commitment to Mormonism.

Moreover, modern Mormons are accustomed to participating in flawlessly orchestrated conference sessions via television. If these interlopers from the future had dropped in at conference time instead of visiting on an ordinary Sunday, their disorientation level would surely have reached the crisis stage. It is very possible that—upon hearing one of the many variations on John Henry Smith's opening statement in his 1885 annual conference address, "What the Lord may have for me to say to you I cannot imagine"—the visitors would simply have left, fleeing forward to their familiar twentieth-century Mormon world as fast as their time machine could carry them.

Wondering about the discrepancy between what they had seen, on the one hand, and their lovingly nurtured faith-promoting pictures of Mormonism's pioneer past, on the other, these hypothetical Saints would no doubt worry about how they ought to describe what they had seen in forthcoming talks at Sacrament Meeting. Prone to put the best face on a disturbing experience, some of the members of the group would probably decide to talk about the inspiring beauty of the Great Salt Lake Valley. Others would perhaps emphasize the timelessness of the *Juvenile Instructor* story that the Sunday School youngsters had been stumbling through. But quite possibly one among the dozen would find an occasion to present a really honest, straightforward report of the trip. And if that should happen, in all likelihood the result would be an inadvertent but nonetheless serious misrepresentation of the nineteenth-century Mormon past.

This perplexing riddle of determining how it is that a truly and totally honest report of the nineteenth-century LDS experience could convey a false impression of the Mormon pioneer past is baffling and worrisome. But it is also a riddle that can have heuristic value: a consideration of this enigma, this perplexing situation, lays bare an enormous problem that historians who deal with religious movements have had to face ever since the Rankean notion that the goal of history is reporting things "as they actually were" was married to "scientific" history with its appetite for cold, hard, unassailable fact.

When religion is the subject matter, the sacred is as important as the not-sacred. But since the sacred and the not-sacred are simply "different modes of being in the world," empirical evidence does not always discriminate between them.[1] Therefore, historians who have attempted to abide by the canons of historical scholarship while at the same time attempting to reconstruct the past history of religious movements have developed a two-step procedure that makes getting around this difficulty possible. Belief statements, descriptions of worship activity such as participation in public and semi-public rituals, documented and thus demonstrable compliance with cultic demands, and acceptance of clearly articulated ethical systems are used to demonstrate that the reality of the sacred was accepted by the participants in the historical drama. With that established, historians move on to explicate the historical situation, treating the sacred and profane, as Mircea Eliade denotes the not-sacred, with essentially the same set of narrative and analytic tools.

As long as a religious movement is institutionalized or developed so fully that a more or less direct relationship exists between manifestations of the sacred and certain empirically identifiable religious statements and activities, this approach works very well. Indeed, it works so well that it may be described as the orthodox scholarly approach to religious history. But this approach is less useful when religious movements are either (a) coming into existence or (b) undergoing radical change. At such crucial times in the history of religious movements, the sacred and the not-sacred cannot always be clearly delineated and separated out. Belief statements are often ambiguous and more than ordinarily subject to multiple interpretation; worship activity cannot always be identified as worship activity; rituals are poorly developed or nonexistent, and so on.

As the foregoing suggestion that the really honest hypothetical Saint's straightforward account of his nineteenth-century visit to Zion would misrepresent the reality of the LDS pioneer experience was designed to point up, *in illo tempore,* in those times, things are not always what they seem. For this reason, if the orthodox scholarly approach is used in writing the history of such periods, the result sometimes poses such a myth-versus-reality problem that an alternative approach is required. That this is the case is not a new observation. The recognition of the need for an alternative approach to the history of religions that are coming into being or undergoing radical change stands at the base not only of the important "Social World of Early Christianity" movement in New Testament studies, but of a comparable "Social World of Ancient Israel" movement in Old Testament studies.[2] These movements are, in turn, based on anthropological literature, which is filled with an ever-increasing number of studies of religions either coming into being or undergoing radical change, studies whose authors map out alternative approaches to the study of the phenomenon of religion in the way their theoretical frameworks are made explicit and precise.

The specific problem being confronted here is continuity and change in twentieth-century Mormonism, but as do all studies of continuity and change, this calls for some treatment of the *before* as well as the *after*. Since Mormonism was still coming into being during the last half of the nineteenth century, however, the use of an alternative approach to this earlier time period is called for. Rather than drawing directly on the anthropological literature to clarify what was happening during the pioneer period, as Lawrence Foster has done with such great success in his study of plural marriage, or making use of the same set of categories which anthropologist Mark P. Leone uses in comparing the pioneer and modern periods in *The Roots of Modern Mormonism*, the alternative to the standard orthodox approach to the history of nineteenth-century Utah Mormonism to be employed here is an approach drawn from the discipline titled somewhat misleadingly History of Religions.[3] Because it is concerned as much with functional and structural questions as with historical ones, this approach lends itself to the explication of situations when things are not always what they appear to be on the surface, which in turn makes possible the identification of the major points of difference between the Mormonism of the pioneer era and that of the modern age.

A catalog of items—some of enormous significance and others only trivial but interesting—could be developed to detail the difference between nineteenth- and twentieth-century Mormonism. Yet as fascinating as such a mere listing could be, it is not a necessary prologue to this consideration of continuity and change, for there is general agreement that at least superficially the difference between the two is very great indeed. More particularly, scholarly consensus extends to the notion that not only is pioneer Mormonism different from modern Mormonism, but that external pressure (particularly political pressure from the government) played such an enormous role in forcing the Mormons to change that it is simply impossible to make sense out of LDS pioneer history without taking that pressure into account.[4] This outside pressure took many forms, but it became concentrated in an anti-polygamy campaign of intense virulence in the 1880s; virtually universal agreement exists, too, that buried within that anti-polygamy campaign were issues as much economic and political as social and moral. Scholars are pretty well agreed, also, that although it could have been initiated as *assimilative* reform (that is, reform activity through which culturally dominant reformers offer their less fortunate neighbors the possibility of achieving middle-class respectability), the anti-polygamy campaign came to be almost exclusively coercive reform as time went on. Just as prohibition would become coercive when temperance leaders started to see persons who drank as "intractable defenders of another culture"—persons who rejected the reformers' values and did not want to change—so anti-polygamy became a coercive movement when it became obvious (remember the abortive effort made to establish a refuge for polygamous wives, for example) that the practice of plural marriage was not forced on the community by its religious leaders.[5] Finally, scholarly consensus likewise points to LDS Church President Wilford Woodruff's 1890 announcement that the Mormon Church had stopped performing plural marriages as the effective point of division between the past and the present. Consensus disintegrates beyond that, however.

There is no question that, from a doctrinal standpoint, President Woodruff's Manifesto now has comparable status with the revelations found in the Doctrine and Covenants. The evidence for the Manifesto's revelatory source is ambiguous, however, depending on an interpretation of a diary entry in which Woodruff noted that he had concluded, after an intense period of prayer and contemplation, that he must act for the "temporal salvation" of the church. For that reason, scholarly opinion—and popular opinion too—divides on the matter of motivation, on what it was that led President Woodruff to reverse his position on the patriarchal order of marriage.[6] Disagreement also exists about the real intent of Woodruff's announcement, since evidence about that is even more ambiguous. Because the historical record includes a good deal of evidence suggesting that the Manifesto was actually a temporary expedient—a political maneuver designed to relieve external pressure long enough for Utah to gain entrance to the Union, after which the practice would be gradually reinstituted — it is not at all certain that the Manifesto was an announcement that the practice of plural marriage would not be a part of Mormonism from the point of its issue forward.[7] But there is no way to know for sure whether the Mormon president-prophet's announcement was an indication that the Saints meant to eschew polygamy permanently, since the elections of Brigham H. Roberts to the U.S. House of Representatives and Reed Smoot to the U.S. Senate came so closely on the heels of Utah's acquisition of statehood that the hands of the anti-polygamists were forced. They had no choice: they had to see that Woodruff's announcement was treated as a substantive pledge to bring the practice of plural marriage to an end. Since we can never know whether, as in the case of prohibition, a "gesture" indicating symbolic capitulation to the ascendancy of the evangelical Protestant culture would have sufficed, it is only possible to speculate about whether the gradual reinstitution of plural marriage could have been effected in much the same manner as the gradual reintroduction of the consumption of alcoholic beverages was effected in the United States and eventually gained widespread acceptance.[8] And though speculation about this matter is interesting, it opens more windows onto American social change and the political processes which develop in pluralistic cultures than onto Mormonism.

Whatever President Woodruff's motivation or intent in issuing the Manifesto, plural marriage has, except for splinter group activity, not been reintroduced into Mormonism. The Manifesto signaled the beginning of the end of a Mormon world in which the practice of plural marriage was not only tolerated but celebrated. More than that: it was a part of an unstated bargain which, on one side, involved a fundamental alteration in the manner of exercising Mormon political and economic power, as well as the discontinuation of plural marriage, and, on the other, made possible the institutional survival of the Church of Jesus Christ of Latter-day Saints, as well as the entrance of a Mormon state into the federal union. Thus, whatever else it did, the Manifesto announced that the old order would have to pass away. As important as are all the practical questions—such as the extent to which external pressure caused this to happen when and as it did, and the manner in which a new *modus vivendi* was fashioned that made possible the secure establishment of the new Mormon order within the context of American society and culture—the question of concern here is what happened to Mormonism when the old order passed away.[9]

Having removed themselves to the Great Basin, the nineteenth-century Saints tried to stay unspotted from the world by as far as possible separating themselves politically, economically, socially, and psychically from the rest of humanity. When the Manifesto symbolically set aside the boundaries that had been so painfully constructed and maintained, a period of extreme danger commenced. At stake was the sheer survival not of the LDS Church, but of a Mormonism that continued to preserve its exclusive claim as the sole corporate body in possession of the holy priesthood and invested with the status of being God's only chosen people. Without boundaries to set them apart, without Gentiles to stand over and against, a chosen people cannot exist; their very identity depends on their perception of their specialness, and that specialness, in turn, depends on their being separated in some way from that part of the population which is not special. The government had made it clear that institutionally established and maintained boundaries could not be tolerated in this nation, and this meant that the Latter-day Saints were faced with a serious internal problem. Somehow the responsibility for boundary maintenance had to be shifted from the corporate body to the individuals within that body, and that shift had to be legitimated in such a way that it would gain general acceptance.

This was no small task, nor one that could be accomplished quickly or easily, especially as it had to be carried out under the watchful eye of the *Salt Lake Tribune* (a hostile Gentile newspaper), the Utah Republican party, the government, and the nation's evangelical Christian community. The Saints had to have time to learn that, instead of leaving the separation of Mormons and Gentiles primarily up to the church leadership, they had to develop patterns of behavior with which they, as individuals, could keep themselves unspotted from the world. A period of transition was inevitable, and this period lasted a very long time, possibly all the way through the ecclesiastical administrations of both Presidents Joseph F. Smith (1901–18) and Heber J. Grant (1918–45).

Notwithstanding the time it took, the heretofore corporate responsibility for maintaining LDS identity that had been assumed by the central church leadership was transferred successfully to the general membership. This transfer of responsibility to the individual was so successful that in fact it brought about a profound alteration in Mormonism. The change proved, in time, to be so basic that some interpreters have suggested that in its new emphasis on individual behavior, Mormonism had turned into a proto-Protestant movement. This interpretation is sometimes set out with great sophistication, as it is in Klaus Hansen's controversial 1973 essay that develops "Some Tentative Hypotheses" about "Mormonism and American Culture."[10] When this happens, the interpretation has a good deal of explanatory power, but when such an interpretation is superficially stated and then used—by suggesting that Mormonism is an idiosyncratic Protestant denomination, charging the Latter-day Saints with wholesale acceptance of the Protestant Ethic, and treating these allegations as proved—to explain the fabled wealth of the Saints and their church, it confuses rather than clarifies the picture.[11]

Still another interpretation drawing on the shifting of responsibility to individual Saints is the one around which Mark Leone builds the basic argument of his *Roots of Modern Mormonism*. Commenting on what happened following the issuing of the Manifesto, he describes the disappearance of political and economic centralization, but differing from Hansen, who suggests in his Epilogue to *Quest for Empire* that the political kingdom gave way to a powerful, centralized Mormon church, Leone sees a switch being made away from theocracy to the individual, not simply a switch from Mormon state to Mormon church. The switch he sees, however, is not a transfer of responsibility for boundary maintenance, but a delegation to individual Saints of the task of constructing their own personal versions of the way in which Mormons ought to view the world—that is, of developing their own individual understandings of the Mormon world view.[12]

Many additional "suggestions" about what happened to Mormonism during the transition period following the Manifesto are to be found in the literature. In *The Story of the Latter-day Saints*, James B. Allen and Glen M. Leonard picture the two or three decades following 1890 as a time of "inspired accommodation," for instance, while in *The Mormon Experience*, Leonard J. Arrington and Davis Bitton describe the "creative adjustment" that took place within Mormonism during those years.[13] In addition to the explanations found in the substantive and important surveys which more or less treat the whole of the Mormon past, there are oversimplified explanations ranging all the way from "The Manifesto Was a Victory!," Gordon Thomasson's rosy characterization wherein the Latter-day Saints (he makes no distinctions between the church and its members) hold on to everything that really mattered, to Samuel W. Taylor's entertaining yet rueful account of a post-Manifesto period when everything of real value in Mormonism is tragically and irretrievably lost.[14] The fundamental way, then, in which the various historical accounts differ provides a dramatic illustration of how very difficult it is to find out from the secondary literature what really happened during these critical years of transition.

Although working directly with the sources can clarify things to some extent, the very fact that the transition period lends itself to such a multiplicity of treatments is an important indication that the period was marked by so much ambiguity and confusion that the documents themselves provide no clear picture of just exactly what happened. Since the passage of time rather than contemporary opinions of even the most sensitively placed individuals determined the way in which Mormonism would develop, the historical record reveals less about the way in which Mormonism did and did not change during the transition period than about the context in which change or lack of change occurred. A better picture of what happened during the transition period can be delineated if a comparison is made between pioneer Mormonism and the Mormonism of the modern age.

The Mormon waters of baptism transformed ordinary American farmers and craftsmen into God's elect, His chosen people. Moreover, the Latter-day Saints had an *exclusive* claim based on the position that when God had executed a new and perpetual covenant with them in 1830, all existing covenants were null and void. The Saints were not the only Americans who believed themselves to be the chosen people, however. Among others, there were Presbyterians, Baptists, Quakers, Methodists, and a host of others who regarded themselves as legitimate heirs to God's promises and thus as His chosen as well. But the difference between what that claim meant, particularly to the great body of evangelical Protestants who dominated the American religious scene in the first half of the nineteenth century, and what it meant to the Latter-day Saints is extremely instructive. The evangelical conception of being chosen differed from the conception of being chosen that underlay and supported the Latter-day Saints. For the evangelical Protestant the claim was a scripturally based doctrinal assumption that had to be brought to life through an experiential assurance of salvation given to individuals by Jesus Christ. The initiative according chosen status came from outside man; a conscious desire to be a part of the elect, demonstrated by repentance and a request for baptism into the church that was the corporate body of God's people, was not enough. Perhaps for that reason the experience of salvation—of being saved—became, in time, more important to evangelicals than the doctrine of election. For Latter-day Saints, on the other hand, the claim to chosenness was not a contingent claim. The power of the LDS message preached to the "field white to the harvest" rested to a great degree on that fact; through repentance and baptism into the church that became the Church of Jesus Christ of Latter-day Saints, individuals gained entrance into the chosen community; they became citizens of God's elect nation, newly restored to the earth. For nineteenth-century evangelical Protestants, then, being a part of the chosen people was a theological construct with less immediacy than the salvation experience, while for the Latter-day Saints, after a revelation called for the gathering of the Saints and after the building of the Kirtland temple, the claim to chosenness became the principle around which they ordered their existence.[15]

Although this elevation to primacy of the notion that their identification as God's chosen people has been more fundamental to the Latter-day Saint experience than anything else might seem to challenge the work of the many scholars who have pointed to the Kingdom of God as the controlling metaphor of early Mormonism, it is not so meant. Rather, it is intended to underscore the importance of the Kingdom of God from another quarter. As discussed earlier, the differences between the LDS version and other Christian primitivist versions of the gospel can easily be seen when the crucial difference in their restoration claims is noted. While others preached that the New Testament apostolic church was restored and ready to accept new communicants, the

Latter-day Saints spread the "good news" of the beginning of the literal gathering of Israel and the restoration of the Ten Tribes, as well as the organization of a church led by a prophet and God's holy priesthood, also restored to the earth in these latter days. Organized with apostles, prophets, pastors, teachers, evangelists, and so on, this (LDS) Church of Jesus Christ claimed to have in its sole possession the gospel ordinances by which individuals willing to repent and be baptized could be *adopted into Israel* in the Old Testament meaning of the term.[16] As converts responded to this powerful message, the body of God's people grew, and since the Kingdom of God is the abode of God's people, its reestablishment on the earth followed, as the night the day, the gathering, the promise of restoration of the Ten Tribes of Israel, and the restoration of the priesthoods of Aaron and Melchizedek. Notwithstanding the imprecision found in LDS literature about whether the literal Kingdom of God was already or was just about to be rebuilt—an imprecision, intrestingly enough, that is paralleled in the Pauline letters in the New Testament—the LDS missionary message carries within it an implicit promise of a life lived out in God's Kingdom.[17] As John Henry Smith (in the address with that "What the Lord may have for me to say to you I cannot imagine" opening) reported to General Conference about the missionary effort in England: "We have done the best we could in our ministrations among the people, and have striven with the power that the Lord has given us to warn our fellowmen of the re-establishment of the Kingdom of God," so thousands of LDS missionaries before and since have carried the message of the reestablishment of the Kingdom of God, not in the future but in the present.[18]

While it may be that the realization that they were citizens of an elect nation came to the Saints only with the beginning of the gathering of Israel and the construction of the Kirtland temple, the important thing to come to grips with here is that, in the context of History of Religions theory, the designation of the Latter-day Saints as the chosen people in the United States in the early 1830s had the same ontological significance as God's designating as chosen the descendants of Abraham. In each situation the appropriate response to powerfully perceived manifestations of the sacred was the building up of a separated community, one clearly set apart so that distinctions were easy to make between the chosen people and the not-chosen Gentiles. Moreover, in that act of building up such a community, the Saints were, from a phenomenological standpoint, participating in a paradigmatic act of creation. The millennial fervor that pervaded early LDS thought was a natural expression, then, of the desire a creative act awakens in man "to live," as Mircea Eliade puts it, "in a pure and holy cosmos as it was in the beginning, when it came fresh from the Creator's hands."[19] Looking for inspiration to the New Testament Book of Revelation and backward to what one Old Testament scholar describes as the *Dawn of Apocalyptic*, the Old Testament prophets and, most especially, the Book of Daniel, the Latter-day Saints set about building a counterpart of the Hebraic kingdom with Solomon's temple at its center.[20] At the same time, they developed a literal latter-day counterpart of their conception of the Old Testament Hebraic culture.[21]

Accounts of the consequences of this effort—internal strife and external pressure eventuating in the murder of the Mormon prophet and destruction of the LDS kingdom on the Mississippi—are so familiar that summary is not a necessary prologue to a consideration of the importance of the concepts of the Kingdom, being chosen as the elect, the Promised Land, and Zion in the Mormon pioneer experience. The fact that Mormonism was rent at least in twain before the Saints crossed the Mississippi is so significant, however, that the implications of that break need to be reviewed.

From the beginning the Mormon movement had held in suspension conceptions of the LDS gospel that were fundamentally contradictory. On the one hand there were Saints who understood the Mormon message and accepted its substance metaphorically, and on the other there were Saints who accepted the gospel quite literally. Although apostasy was a common phenomenon in the early years, the discrepancy between these two understandings did not make itself fully known until Joseph Smith's death removed from the Mormon community the intellect (and the spiritual nature) that was the medium within which the two elements had been suspended. After 1844 the two elements started to separate out, and by 1847, when the Saints started west under the leadership of Brigham Young, those whose understanding of the Mormon message was mainly metaphysical generally stayed behind.[22]

The parallel between the Mormon trek and the biblical Exodus needs to be remembered here, for it is the key to the pioneer experience. Just as the original designation of the Saints as chosen was a repetition of God's paradigmatic act in choosing Abraham's seed, so the Mormon trek renewed the force of God's election of the Mormons in precisely the same way that the miraculous departure from Egypt and the journey through the wilderness and into the Promised Land renewed the identity of the Hebraic tribes as the citizens of His elect nation. As was discussed at length in Chapter Three, when Brigham Young led the Saints across the plains, he led them not only out of the hands of their midwestern persecutors but backward into a primordial sacred time. As the original Israelites had been, so these new Israelites were "once again at the beginning," *in illo tempore*. Repeating the passage from chaos to cosmos, the Latter-day Saints, by that very passage out of a place confused by a concatenation of religious claims into one where their calling and election was unquestionably sure, were formed not into a culture whose perpetuation depended on the preservation of a particular *polis*, but into an ethnic body, a chosen race.[23] Once they had been no people; now, in truth, they were God's People, but not so much because, "like living stones," they had built themselves "into a spiritual house to be a holy priesthood." Like the children of Israel, the Saints made their way through the wilderness to claim their "inheritances," and in so doing conjoined experience and scripture to take possession of that special relationship to God which once had been the sole property of the Jews.[24]

In explicating the dichotomy between mythic (sacred) time and linear, historical (not-sacred, profane) time, Guilford Dudley III, in a very useful study, *Religion on Trial*, states that "the mythic time of beginnings is sacred by definition."[25] The task the Mormons confronted in the Great Basin was nothing less than starting at the beginning to people a holy land and build God's Kingdom. If Dudley is right, the entry of Brigham Young and his followers into the Great Salt Lake Valley was not only entry into sacred space— that is, into the Promised Land—but a move that carried them even more deeply into sacred time. But is there any indication that he is right? After all, nineteenth-century Latter-day Saints were practical people, equally able to benefit from trade with the

Gentiles who crossed their territory on the way to the California gold fields as to build tabernacles and temples in which to glorify God. Did the Saints know that they were living outside time? Since the surviving documents can hardly be expected to yield a *direct* answer to this question, is there any way to find out?

Perhaps an analogue drawn from the experience of a different chosen people will be useful. Richard Reubenstein, a rabbi turned scholar, essayist, and college professor, visited Israel soon after the United Nations certified its existence as a sovereign state. *Power Struggle*, Reubenstein's autobiography, includes an account of that visit and his reaction to it.[26] Then, among the essays collected in *After Auschwitz: Radical Theology and Contemporary Judaism* is one which deals with "The Rebirth of Israel in Contemporary Jewish Theology." This essay is a more impersonal and intellectual consideration of the situation, but it clearly reflects the fact that Reubenstein was in Israel in those heady days when Israel, the political state, and Zion, the symbolic Hebraic kingdom, were fused in Israeli minds. Such great expectations of an impending entrance into the millennium prevailed that it produced an attitude whose "most characteristic feature [was] its fervid desire to bring time and history to an ending."[27] The tenuous and dangerous position of the new Jewish homeland in the volatile Middle Eastern political cauldron appeared to matter less to the Zionists than their need to make history come full circle, allowing them to be again in the original Israel. While news of the events of the world was freely available, people paid attention to their own concerns, taking little thought for the morrow or for what was going on outside Zion.[28] Whether the analogy is appropriate is, perhaps, less important than the fact that it directs attention to the way in which messianic and millennial movements lift otherwise everyday practical people out of time by making long-range plans untenable in view of the nearness of the *eschaton*. Since ample evidence indicates that the Mormon pioneers were prepared for the "winding-up scene" to commence at an early date, and since expectations of the end divert attention away from the calendar and the clock, history and theory here converge.

Although the nineteenth-century Latter-day Saints may have stood outside time as a consequence of their expectations of the advent of the millennium, this does not mean that what they built was insubstantial and other-worldly. On the contrary, they built what was, in effect, a nation-state that was internally power-ful and externally respected as strong enough to be dangerous, even dangerous to the government itself. Gentile politicians main-tained tenuous control over its territorial government, but if any-one's word was law in Utah, née Deseret, it was the president of the LDS Church. Surely Mark Leone overstates the extent of the independence of the Mormon state during the pioneer era, but he is nevertheless correct when he says that in many ways this was Mormonism's golden age.[29] Before the Saints were placed under siege in the 1880s, their nation-state was reasonably independent economically and socially.[30] It had its own diplomatic depart-ment; and although its political strength has probably been con-siderably exaggerated, at least it had its own independent political organization in the shadow government of the State of Deseret.[31]

But if outstanding individual effort and extraordinary com-munity accomplishment together built cities and towns and tab-ernacles and temples, railroads, factories, stores, industries, and all the paraphernalia of a surprisingly strong and independent lit-eral kingdom, what of the Mormon religious experience therein? While there is always danger in analogy and the development of generalization therefrom, Rabbi Reubenstein's observations about the initial Israeli Zionic experience can be helpful at this point. As an American rabbi, he was concerned and disappointed at seeing an almost total absence of ritualized worship in Israel until it occurred to him that persons actually living in the kingdom need not observe rituals that are reminders of what it once was *like* to live in the kingdom. Realizing that more than anything else, a good part of Jewish ritual seemed designed as a reminder of what "next year in Jerusalem" would be like, he looked about not for ordinary worship forms but for expressive ways of celebrating being, as it were, in Jerusalem, and found that most intensively expressed in Israeli folk music.[32]

Much ink in Mormon historiography has been spread across many history pages to develop the importance of the millennial idea. But when the excellent *Building the City of God* study or almost any volume of the *Journal of Discourses* is read with a sen-sitive ear for the language, it is plain to see and hear that John

Henry Smith's placing of the reestablishment of the Kingdom of God in the present tense was not a slip of the tongue.[33] While Christ had not come to earth to reign, nineteenth-century Saints nevertheless lived so clearly in the kingdom, *in illo tempore*, that the sacred and the not-sacred simply cannot be considered separately. This is not to say that music and dancing rather than formal worship was the order of the period, for in addition to singing and dancing there were places of worship in every town and worship services were held in them. Still, as it was for the Jews who emigrated to Israel soon after World War II, the essential worship in the LDS pioneer world was building up the kingdom and inhabiting it.[34] The hypothetical Saints returning from the twentieth century in a time machine would have been astonished to find so few Saints at Sacrament Meeting, because the twentieth-century Sacrament Meeting is a visible worship sign, whereas in the pioneer era more expressive worship signs were irrigation canals, or neatly built and nicely decorated houses, or good crops of sugar beets.[35] More significantly, living in the kingdom in the nineteenth century was the sign of citizenship in God's elect nation. Gentiles there were, but the community was a separated one, made special through the institution of the patriarchal order of marriage. While the Word of Wisdom was usually observed in the Mormon community, the Latter-day Saint perception of being special, of being a part of the chosen people, did not depend on abstaining from tobacco and coffee and on universally negative decisions about whether or not to drink the Valley Tan or the wine the Saints manufactured in Dixie.[36] Identity was maintained corporately, not individually, which explains why all the citizens of the kingdom—those who were involved in plural marriage and those who were not—were willing to defend to the last possible moment the practice of polygamy that kept them set apart.[37]

No single explanation ever suffices to explain complex historical events, and the Manifesto is no exception. Many factors entered into the development of the overall context within which President Woodruff had to take to the Lord the problem of what to do in that intense session of prayer he described in his diary entry for 25 September 1890.[38] It is possible, however, to observe that when the Manifesto signaled the end of plural marriage, it also signaled the beginning of the end of the extraordinary situation wherein Latter-day Saints had lived their lives in sacred space and sacred time.

Evidence of many different kinds may be used to demonstrate that the 1890 Manifesto was a disconfirming event that profoundly altered the character of Mormonism. The development of a fundamentalist movement having as its implicit purpose the re-creation of the nineteenth-century Mormon experience is, *ipso facto*, an indication that Mormonism has been radically changed, for example.[39] Another somewhat paradoxical indication of the impact on the Mormon community and changes the Manifesto implied is a subsequent growth spurt in the turn-of-the-century decades.

In a conceptually useful study of a modern prophetic movement, Leon Festinger and others hypothesize that disconfirmation leads to increased rather than decreased missionary activity as a group that has experienced a disconfirming event seeks to bolster its beliefs through convincing others of their truth.[40] Unless an abnormal birthrate accounts for a temporary rise in natural membership increase in the LDS Church, the fact that the steady growth rate of around 2.6 percent, which obtained with surprising consistency in the 1880s, 1890s, 1920s, 1930s, and 1940s, increased in the turn-of-the-century decade to 3.9 percent and stayed above 3 percent in the following ten-year period is statistically significant and at least superficially confirms the Festinger hypothesis.[41]

But such indirect evidence is not needed to substantiate the notion that in the years following the Manifesto, the Saints had a disconfirmation situation to deal with. Even though, as indicated earlier, the transition years have been much written about without any consensus emerging as to what was really going on, the historical literature reveals that the cessation of plural marriage was such a disconfirming event that it thrust the Saints into the modern age. Interpreted in a phenomenological context, the very ambiguity of the historical accounts reflects an ambiguity that infects society as the natural and inevitable consequence of passage out of sacred into profane, linear, historical time.

The study of early Christianity provides a useful parallel to this aspect of the Mormon past. At this point in their history the Saints had to face a situation somewhat similar to the one which the early Christians faced in the late first century when the synoptic gospels were being written; even though no scriptural "render unto Caesar" admonition was added to the Mormon canon, the United States had made Caesar's claims so insistent that they could no longer be ignored. The millennium's beginning had been delayed, and from thenceforth Latter-day Saints would, as they awaited that happy occurrence, have to make some accommodation to the world. In the absence of the apocalypse (which might be defined as the inauguration of permanent sacred time), the Saints would have to learn to live apocalyptically.[42]

The work of Wayne Meeks, John Gager, and others makes it clear that the Christian community's negotiation of the passage out of sacred time that came at the end of the apostolic era could well have been the point at which Christianity as a religious tradition was most vulnerable.[43] Certainly it is possible to use this parallel to suggest that in Mormonism the passage from the pioneer era to the modern age was likewise a time of enormous vulnerability: some of the Saints wanted to turn backward, seeking to recapture the exhilarating experience of living *in illo tempore* by trying to continue to use the patriarchal order of marriage as a boundary separating the Saints from the world, while others, already impatient to get on with the business of living in the world, were ready to accommodate to the larger American pattern in religion at the expense of fundamental elements in Mormonism.

The generality of Latter-day Saints today would give God the credit for seeing the church through this time of crisis. Two specific instances of continuing revelation can be cited to support this interpretation: the suspension of the adoption ordinance, and President Joseph F. Smith's vision of the redemption of the dead. Instead of establishing a line backward in time, the business of the trek and the pioneer period was the forging of an ethnic identity as a literal New Israel; in addition to designations of lineage in patriarchal blessings, the development of close intra-Mormon kinship ties was facilitated during that time both by plural marriage and by the ordinance of adoption.[44] But with those ties formed, the restoration of the tribes called for the performance of the symbolic ordinances for the dead that would tie modern families to their Hebraic ancestors. The ordinance of baptism for the dead was introduced into Mormonism in the Nauvoo period, but during the trek and the pioneer period—as the Saints

waited for the advent of the millennium in which God would take
the world forward (or backward) to its paradisical state—even the
possibility of carrying the ordinances of the gospel to the dead in
wholesale fashion would have, to say the least, seemed remote.
Moreover, until President Smith described the process he had
seen in a vision by which the dead are redeemed, the compelling
necessity for so doing had not been made absolutely clear to the
Saints. (This realization can be connected to the expansion of the
genealogy program that has taken place since the turn of the century.) The revelations suspending the adoption ordinances and
providing a vision of the redemption of the dead turned the attention of the Saints to responsibilities which, carried out in profane time, became occasions of returning periodically to sacred
time though the medium of the ritual performance of sacred
ordinances.[45]

The preservation of a Mormonism that is changed but continuous with the LDS past is, however, most importantly made possible through means less esoteric. The transfer of boundary maintenance responsibility to individuals, especially through close
adherence to the Word of Wisdom, tithing in a manner that makes
it seem a bit like paying taxes, and careful compliance with a
clearly articulated behavioral code, has long been effected so that
Latter-day Saints are constantly reminded of their chosen status
by what they eat and do not eat (as Arrington and Bitton point
out, the parallel with the Jewish dietary laws is instructive) and
by the ways in which they behave. Moreover, since the Saints are
expected to clothe themselves with special undergarments that
symbolize their covenants made during the celebration of the ordinances of the endowment in the temple, they are kept ever
mindful that they are God's people by what they wear as well.

Worship activity, which at times in the twentieth-century Mormon world seems almost mandatory, supplements the LDS dietary, behavior, and dress codes. Just as important, and quite possibly more important, the structured maintenance of community
—through priesthood, auxiliary, and youth activities, an elaborate
educational program, and an extraordinary visiting-teacher program—makes Saints perpetually aware that they are members of
a chosen band.

Although their everyday lives are ordinarily lived out in a profane and, in very many instances, Gentile world, twentieth-century Latter-day Saints still possess the means of reentering sacred time and space. By their very nature temples are sacred space, and time spent therein has a ritual sacredness attached to it. And tabernacles and ward chapels, their multiform uses to the contrary notwithstanding, are sometimes also transformed so that entering them carries Saints away from the profane world of every day. Sundays, particularly Fast Sundays, also permit the regular recovery of a certain kind of sacred time.

Beyond that, there is another extraordinarily important way in which today's Latter-day Saints reenter sacred space and time. Certain places and events in the everyday world trigger that reentry when the spirit is truly sensitive. The reading of the history of the pioneer period, standing in Temple Square, looking up at Eagle Gate, sitting in conference when the whole community is symbolically gathered back to the center place, participating in or even simply watching the pioneer parade on 24 July each year—these are examples of customary situations that can take modern Saints back to the mythic time when the Mormon world was fresh and new. This does not happen all the time, nor does it happen to all the Saints. But the return to the uniquely sacred time in the Utah Mormon experience happens often enough to a large enough number of Latter-day Saints to guarantee that today's Saints live out their lives in a corporate community that still stands squarely and securely in the presence of the past.

Funeral service for President Wilford Woodruff in the LDS tabernacle;
inset: President Joseph F. Smith

Chapter Seven

The Millennial Vision
Transformed

Continuing a pattern established in 1830, the year the church was organized, members of the Church of Jesus Christ of Latter-day Saints meet in General Conference twice each year. They travel to Salt Lake City for weekends early in October and April, arriving in such numbers that they strain the capacity of airport facilities, commercial hostelries, and guest rooms in many local Mormon homes. Coming from every place on the earth where LDS geographical subdivisions—stakes, wards, missions, and branches—exist, they throng Temple Square, making the meticulously groomed grounds of that historic stucco-walled enclosure in the heart of the city appear to be a landscaped garden surrounding some mythical United Nations meeting place. When the doors of the tabernacle are opened for the two-hour morning and afternoon conference sessions, many thousands of Saints fill the great, plain, turtle-backed building that sits opposite the elaborate, almost Gothic, temple in the middle of the square. There LDS church members learn firsthand about the state of their church. With the routine dispatch born of frequent practice, they handle matters of ecclesiastical business, voting at every General Conference, usually unanimously, to sustain the general officers of the church and, when necessary, forming themselves into constituent assemblies to accept new revelation as "the will of the

Lord." At conference they are also informed about new church policies and reminded of standing ones, and they receive instruction and admonition from their leaders. But these semi-annual and annual conferences, as the fall and spring church-wide assemblies are called, are not convened for the sole purpose of conducting the business of the church. The Latter-day Saints who go to conference expect to leave there enlightened and inspired.

When the group was small and the world less complicated, LDS conferences were occasions which brought all the church together in one place. While the growth of the church and the dispersion of its members throughout the world now make such a physical ingathering of the whole body of Saints impractical, the use of the electronic media carries the conference proceedings to the Saints wherever they are. In order to make the proceedings effective when they are broadcast on radio and television and recorded for distribution throughout the church, however, the traditional conference pattern had to be considerably altered. Cameras, microphones, and tape recorders impose such strict time and content constraints that, instead of continuing the long-standing practice of extempore speaking, Mormon leaders now deliver conference addresses from prepared texts. As a result, even as they recognize the enormous value of electronic conference coverage to the cause of Mormonism, some of the Saints look back with nostalgia to the time when "the brethren" could respond more freely to "the dictates of the spirit," when conference speakers rarely confined their addresses to a single subject, when the length of the conference prayers was not determined by the flashing of a little red light on the podium, and when the sessions could last as long as the LDS leaders had counsel to impart and testimony to bear. But changes in the nature of the sessions notwithstanding, Latter-day Saints continue to regard General Conference as an important and significant part of their lives.

Many factors combine to invest it with such meaning. The immense difference between conference sessions and ordinary everyday Mormon meetings is one of these, for the contrast between the two is very great indeed. The magnitude of the one as opposed to the other has increased across the years because the church—in order to keep everyone involved and to diminish the perception of anonymity which participation in a large congregation sometimes engenders—has instituted a policy of limiting the size of its local wards (geographical units roughly comparable to Roman Catholic parishes). Somewhat in the manner of cell division, one of these wards is turned into two if its membership gets very far above 600 or 700. For this reason, even though the percentage of members present at LDS Sunday School and Sacrament Meeting tends to be greater than the percentage of members attending weekly worship services in Protestant churches, the limited size of Mormon wards means that weekly meetings are only attended by an average number, estimated to be somewhere between 100 and 200 people. Fairly modest affairs as far as numbers are concerned, local meetings are often fairly informal as well. Without a professional clergy to plan and carry out Sunday services, Mormon wards have programs planned and carried out by the Saints themselves, a practice that leads to considerable variation from meeting to meeting and week to week. Ritualized in that the sacrament is always served and hymns are always directed by a choral leader from the stand, and in that on Fast Sundays, the first Sunday of every month, testimonies are always borne and babies are sometimes blessed, these local Latter-day Saint Sunday programs are distinguished from conventional worship patterns by an absence of liturgy and classic sermonizing. In many local Mormon meetings, moreover, movement in the chapel provides a contrapuntal accompaniment to the proceedings on the stand. As teenaged Aaronic priesthood holders pass the sacramental bread and water to all who are in the congregation including babes-in-arms, as latecomers arrive and early departers leave, and as Saints too young to have developed meeting-length attention spans move constantly to and fro, these local gatherings sometimes seem alive with sound. Suggesting that such meetings have little or no meaning for Latter-day Saints would be absurd. Yet it is plain to see that their place in the religious lives of the Saints is not the same as the place of conference sessions in which 6,000 or 7,000 Saints are packed into the tabernacle, where silent stillness reigns as the precisely planned program is executed with painstaking care.[1]

The rank of their presiding officers also differentiates General Conference sessions from other Mormon meetings, including conferences held in large LDS geographical units designated as stakes, regions, and areas. (Roughly equivalent to Roman Catholic dioceses in size, stakes are so named because together all the Mormon stakes support the tent of Zion.) In view of Mormonism's development in the United States during the Jacksonian era, the democratic age of the common man, it may appear almost ironic that rank, ecclesiastical calling, and the precedence of position should assume inordinate importance to Latter-day Saints. Actually, however, the Mormon reverence for rank is not an irony. In the case of the President of the church, reverence is not only based on ecclesiastical position but also on the Saints' recognition of him as "prophet, seer, and revelator" to the church. As it applies to all the other officeholders in the church, the regard in which they are held has its roots in the fact that the Latter-day Saints have come very close to translating into reality the concept of the priesthood of all believers.

Despite its exclusion of women, even Martin Luther might have admired the virtually universal LDS system that has come to make every worthy male above the age of twelve a member of one of the quorums of either the Aaronic or the Melchizedek priesthood. These quorums are ranked from lowest to highest, making upward progress possible as males proceed from service in a deacons' quorum to service in quorums of teachers, priests, elders, seventies, and, finally, high priests.[2] Thus rank is tied to quorum service. Higher rank is attached to service in a bishopric (a bishop and two counselors), which the church has called to preside over a ward, and a presidency (a president and two counselors), which is called to preside over a stake.

The great majority of Latter-day Saint priesthood quorums exercise only local or regional jurisdiction, or jurisdiction over some limited auxiliary or church activity. But some quorums have greater authority, exercising jurisdiction over all the church. Naturally, higher rank is connected to membership in these general quorums, which include the First Quorum of the Seventy (the name is taken from the New Testament, which explains that in addition to apostles, the Lord appointed seventy others and sent them out to proclaim the nearness of the Kingdom of God), the Presidency of the First Quorum of the Seventy (a presidency which, in this case, has seven members), the Council of the Twelve (whose members must have been ordained as apostles), and the First Presidency of the church.

Although quorum assignments throughout Mormondom are made by higher authorities who, by virtue of their rank, are believed to have access to divine counsel in the matter, at every level quorums that exercise jurisdiction over the Saints and all presiding officers must be sustained in their positions by the vote of the people over whom they preside. Since the members of the general quorums preside over the entire church, they must be sustained in their positions by the vote of the people who are present in General Conference. Along with the Presiding Bishopric (a three-man body directed by the First Presidency to assume responsibility for the temporal affairs of the church), the members of these quorums make up the group known collectively as the General Authorities, or, more familiarly, "the brethren."

Rank is recognized in General Conference in Salt Lake City by seating arrangement as well as by the selection of persons assigned to give the invocations, closing prayers, and important conference talks. Seated in the central portion of the tabernacle, directly facing the multitiered stand located in front of the Tabernacle Choir in the western curve of the unusual oval building, are men from ward bishoprics and stake presidencies, men who sit on church-wide boards of auxiliary organizations, and members of the priesthood who fill important church assignments. This great mass of priesthood leaders is surrounded on three sides on the main floor and in the freestanding gallery by a Mormon host that represents the general membership of the church. In among this aggregation of Latter-day Saints are always seated wives of ranking priesthood leaders, women who, according to Mormon doctrine, will share in the perquisites of their husbands' priesthood in the next life, but who are not permitted to share his status recognition in General Conference in this one.

The General Authorities are arrayed on the stand in order of precedence, with the members of the Presiding Bishopric and auxiliary presidencies seated on the lower tiers, while the members of the First Quorum of the Seventy and the seven presidents of the First Quorum of the Seventy are seated above them. Members of the Council of the Twelve sit on the highest tier, with the mem-

bers of the First Presidency in the center. The seat of honor is re-
served for the President of the church, whose rank, the highest of
all in Mormondom, is likewise indicated by the rising to their feet
of the multitudes attending conference as they show respect and
love for their "prophet, seer, and revelator," when he makes his
entry into their midst.

Tour guides are given to extolling the unique design and acous-
tical singularity of the tabernacle, while they reserve their discussion of the religious significance of Temple Square for that point
in the tour when the beauty of the temple is pointed out. For this
reason visitors often come away equating engineering ingenuity
with the tabernacle and spiritual experience with the temple.
This is a misconception, but it is a curious and interesting one
since the engineering ingenuity that went into the building of the
tabernacle is in some measure responsible for the fact that, for
many Latter-day Saints, attending General Conference is often
the occasion of spiritual experience as meaningful as that encoun-
tered in the temple.

Although seating arrangement and protocol turn the tabernacle
into "a house of order" at conference time, the architecture of the
strange structure, the absence of angles and sharp corners, and
the plain naturalness of the walls seem to soften doctrinal distinctions between leaders and led, Melchizedek and Aaronic
priesthood place, men and women, old and young, converts and
birthright Mormons, and so on. The Saints sit encircled by those
unadorned walls, "squeezed up tight" to make room for more
Mormon brothers and sisters than seems humanly possible on the
long oak benches that fill the mammoth auditorium; they are en-
veloped by the natural polyphonic sound produced when cher-
ished Mormon hymns are brought to life beneath the vast and ex-
pansive concave ceiling; and they are surrounded by an uncanny
quiet, broken only by the voice of revered leaders when the music
dies away. The effect is extraordinary. Gathered there quite literally in the center of the Mormon world, Latter-day Saints participate in a direct and primary experience of community which,
while corporate, is in its way often as powerful, meaningful, and
profound as the spiritual experiences sometimes accompanying
the performance of the secret sacred temple rites, which center on
individuals in the context of family and not on the congregation.

Besides the intangible spiritual treasures connected with the General Conference ambience, conference yields up more tangible, though to the Saints no less exalted, treasures in the form of conference sermons and talks. Transcribed and printed in official *Conference Reports* as well as in magazines published by the church and, in recent years, recorded and issued as cassette tapes, these addresses are more didactic than dogmatic in their comfortable blend of the sacred and not-sacred, the prosaic and the holy. When statements of church policy need to be made, the conference stand is the platform from which they are formally announced. But policy statements are clearly identified and set apart from conference addresses, which, almost without exception, link instruction inextricably with testimony and sometimes mix theological speculation with everyday commonsense observation. Yet conference sermons and talks, particularly those given by the General Authorities, take on a special character that separates them from sermons and talks delivered in other places and under different circumstances.[3]

According to Mormon belief, all Latter-day Saints are entitled to personal revelations as they apply to matters of individual concern. Mormon men who are married and are a part of the LDS priesthood are, as "heads or presidents or spokesmen for their families," entitled to revelation that affects their families too.[4] Latter-day Saints who serve as presiding officers over regular or special priesthood quorums, or over any one of the seemingly infinite administrative subdivisions of the church or its auxiliaries, are also entitled to divine inspiration in matters concerning those over whom they preside. While conference addresses are not put forth as revelation, an informal *ex cathedra* infallibility inheres in them, almost as if by being delivered in the presence of the church in conference assembled, these addresses are somehow distillations of the concentrated power of revelation and inspiration present at that time and in that place. Without being accorded status as Mormon doctrine, the words said in conference carry more weight and impact than words said elsewhere. When such words are uttered by the church president—who as presiding officer over the church has a right to divine inspiration in matters concerning its members, and who as its "prophet, seer, and revelator" may receive revelation for the whole of the church

—Latter-day Saints regard those words, quite simply and without question, as true.

Because General Conferences are so multifaceted—practical and inspirational, tangible and symbolic—they serve as useful indexes to what is happening in Mormonism. In order to suggest the nature of the complex process by which the millennial vision of early Mormonism was transformed into a vision in which it could maintain itself in the world as long as need be, inside rather than outside history, the 1916 Annual Conference will be examined in some detail. This particular conference is selected primarily because of the major conference address delivered by Church President Joseph F. Smith. But it is also important to remember that it occurred at a point when the demise of the Mormon political kingdom was marked by a demonstrable shift in the nature of LDS politics that made possible the election in 1916 of Utah's first non-Mormon governor, while the death of plural marriage in any way sanctioned by the LDS Church was everywhere apparent.

Conferences now begin on Saturday morning and end on Sunday afternoon. Earlier in the century the schedule was more flexible. This made it possible for conference to convene on Thursday, 6 April 1916, the eighty-sixth anniversary of the formal organization of the church. Presiding was President Joseph F. Smith, the sixth president of the LDS Church. He was a son of Hyrum Smith and he had still been a child, aged six, when his uncle, Joseph Smith, Jr., was martyred in Illinois. His memories of the church were not memories of the early days when the Saints had been driven from Ohio to Missouri and from Missouri back to Illinois. Although he surely remembered the trek, his memories of "drivings" were drivings of a different kind, for in the fifteen years since he had been made church president, Joseph F. Smith had been forced to preside over the church as it had been driven by both external and internal forces out of the Old World and into the New. His years of leadership had been difficult, filled not so much with mobbings as misunderstandings, not so much with persecution as pretense, not so much with tragedy as with tension.

President Smith knew that the fifteen years of his presidency had been hard years for the Latter-day Saints too. He knew that they were worried about what had happened in the church as well as to the church and that they were concerned about the changes that were rushing in upon the Mormon world. Therefore, instead of delivering a sentimental homily about the founders of the church and the trials they had endured, he delivered "a remarkable sermon" that had continuity as one of its main themes.[5] This was a sermon that the Saints very much needed to hear, since the behavioral boundary that had once separated the Mormons from the outside world was being seriously eroded. The special features that had served the LDS community as distinguishing marks were either being stripped away entirely or so transformed that they no longer functioned to keep the cultural context in which the Saints lived set clearly apart from the rest of the nation. The disappearance of plural marriage and the political kingdom was accompanied, moreover, by the normalizing of the LDS community's political and economic structures, with the formation in Utah of regular federal, state, and local governmental units, and with the development of close financial ties and ordinary business intercourse with the nation's larger business and financial community.

Recognition of the reality of the fundamental alteration in Mormonism issuing from these changes came only gradually to the Mormon world. As the Saints had moved into the new century, however, it had become increasingly obvious to them that they might henceforth be required to live as a peculiar people in an open rather than closed society. Moreover, it was likewise ever more obvious that, instead of being designed to reverse the direction, the activities and policy decisions of the First Presidency and the Council of the Twelve were turning Mormonism away from the course on which it had been placed by its first prophet and his nineteenth-century successors.

Because they believed that their leaders were themselves divinely led since they had access to continuing revelation, many of the Mormons followed along without complaint. They made adjustments—often without realizing that adjustments were being made—by following their "file leaders" and staying "in harmony" within the priesthood quorums and local units of the church's auxiliary organizations in their own stakes and wards. But by 1916 there were many Saints who, quite satisfied to be free of the constraints that had gone along with living in a community gathered out of and separated from the world, were welcoming the new situation by questioning the authority of their LDS leaders in all areas except the strictly ecclesiastical. Other Saints were terribly concerned about the absence rather than the presence of traditional constraints; they were having difficulty accepting, or even tolerating, change; and while they did not all express their reservations about what was happening by attempting in one way or another to pattern their lives on the lives of Mormons in the days of Brigham Young and John Taylor, they listened carefully whenever people wondered publicly whether the source of inspiration for Mormonism's change in direction was human or divine. As conference opened that spring, then, things were not exactly tranquil in Zion. The sermon delivered by Joseph F. Smith at the opening session appeared, on the surface, not to take much cognizance of that fact, however. When it was subsequently published in the *Improvement Era*, the official organ at that time for all LDS priesthood quorums, it was headed "In the Presence of the Divine." This title suggests that the president's focus was more spiritual than temporal, and on first reading the sermon does seem to have differed from many other conference sermons of the time in that it dealt with timeless theological and doctrinal matters rather than contemporary concerns. But just as careful reading of the New Testament reveals the enormous extent to which the framing of the several accounts of the life of Jesus was affected by the conditions facing the early Christian community at the time of the composition of the gospels, so careful reading reveals the enormous extent to which Smith's sermon spoke directly to the needs of the Mormon community gathered that day in the tabernacle in Temple Square.

Nowhere in the sermon did Smith mention the demise of plural marriage. He made no reference to the disappearance of unity in economic affairs or to the dissolution of the Mormon political party organization, though he specifically rejected the notion that any human person would ever reign as king of the Kingdom of God. He did not discuss the recent excommunication of stalwart Saints whose only observable offense was refusal to stop marrying into plurality. Nor did he make allusion to the church's refusal to provide institutional support for a popular prohibition measure that would have made the sale and consumption of alcoholic beverages illegal in Utah. Yet by indirection the president's message touched on all of these and practically every other matter that threatened the harmony and tranquility of early twentieth-century Mormonism.

Couched in a manner that makes it applicable in all times and in divers places, Joseph F. Smith's sermon called up the sacred past and brought it forward to vindicate the present. Just as surely as the early Christian canon, in order to establish a correspondence between two apparently different eras, brought the Hebraic past into the Christian present by providing a genealogical bridge and pointing up analogues between the personal history of Jesus and the corporate history of the Jews, so the prophet-president's sermon established a basis for a metaphysical bonding between the nineteenth-century Mormon experience and its distinctly dissimilar twentieth-century counterpart. No evidence has been found to suggest that in preaching this sermon Smith consciously set out to legitimize the much-changed Mormon situation and defend his years of leadership. Yet that nonetheless is precisely what he did. He cut away the ground on which criticism and incipient dissent had been based, and at the same time he provided reassurance to the Saints, who were fearful that the 1890 Manifesto announcing the discontinuation of the practice of polygamy had been a signal that the new dispensation of the fulness of times was about to come to a premature and inglorious end.

At one point in the sermon, President Smith spoke bluntly to his hearers in the tabernacle, saying that "the people who are associated in this organization must hearken to the voice of him who has divine authority to guide and direct and counsel in the midst of Israel." As a whole, however, the sermon was not a Jeremiad crying woe to those who failed to remember that the gospel of Jesus Christ was "obedience to the truth [and] submission to the order that God has established in his house." Neither was it a disquisition employing rhetoric in support of an argument. President Smith simply stated his belief that in standing there before the church assembled in conference, he also stood "in the presence not only of the Father and of the Son, but in the presence of those who God commissioned, raised up, and inspired to lay the foundations of the work." Without ever stating it as

premise, Smith placed before the church the principle that, however much they might differ one from the other, the past and the
present are inexorably joined. Only a very thin veil separated
the Saints on earth, he said, from those who have moved on into
"that other sphere," a veil so thin that in fact the Saints on earth
were actually living in the presence of their ancestors and their
"friends, associates, and co-laborers" who had preceded them
"into the spirit world." Calling the roll of names of his predecessors in office—Joseph Smith, Brigham Young, John Taylor,
Wilford Woodruff, and Lorenzo Snow—President Smith assured
his hearers that the church's former leaders continued to watch
over the Saints, and that the present welfare of the church was as
much their concern as had been the welfare of the Saints over
whom they had once presided.

Moving in the course of the sermon from the use of the condi-
tional clause "if they are permitted to look" to the assured "they
see us," the president told his listeners that Mormonism's former
leaders continued to care deeply about the activities of the Saints
still on this side of the veil. "They love us now more than ever,"
he said, because "they can comprehend, better than before, the
weaknesses that are liable to mislead us into dark and forbidden
paths." Then, without acknowledging that among the dark and
forbidden paths of modern Mormonism there were certain ones—
highways leading to plural marriage and a political Kingdom of
God established on the earth—that had once been open and well
traveled by the Saints, Smith made it obvious that he was con-
fident that the changed situation did not really matter. He was, in
fact, so positive that all of those who, "under the guidance and
inspiration of the Almighty, and by his power, began this latter-
day work," were rejoicing with him as they looked down on the
scene in the tabernacle in 1916 that he could dramatize the unity
between the old and the new by picturing himself as the bridge
between the past and the present. He said that when he went to
join "Joseph and Hyrum [brother of the first Mormon prophet and,
as every hearer knew, the father of President Smith], and Brigham
and John, and Wilford and Lorenzo," he wanted to meet them as
he had met them here, "in love, in harmony, in unison, and in per-
fect confidence that I had done my duty as they have done theirs."

Aware that he stood in the presence of those departed leaders, President Smith was "impressed with the thought that I would not this moment say or do one thing that would be taken as unwise or imprudent, or that would give offense to any of my former associates and co-laborers in the work of the Lord." He ardently desired to meet them with the knowledge that he had "carried out the mission in which they were engaged as they would have it carried out," sure that he had "been as faithful in the discharge of duty committed to me and required at my hand as they were faithful in their time."

As he pictured that future scene, President Smith was almost overcome with emotion. He asked forbearance; struggled to regain control; and continued by reminding the Saints, as he had often done before, that he had felt it his duty to proclaim the gospel from the days of his childhood and throughout his life. Then, almost as if to demonstrate continuity with Mormon beginnings and the pioneer past, he rehearsed the basic beliefs that, taken together, are the LDS gospel.[6] He said:

> that God is not a spirit, but a material being of the male gender who, while he does not himself extend through all the immensity of space, has knowledge and power that do extend through all space, which he governs in its entirety;

> that Jesus Christ, the Son of God, grew from birth to manhood in the flesh, "developing into the very image and likeness of his Father" (which is indication that he is likewise a material being, one separate from his Father);

> that the gospel of Jesus Christ, "which is the power of God unto salvation" and "gift of eternal life," consists of *knowing* "the only true and living God" and also "his Son whom he sent into the world";

> that this indispensable *knowledge* cannot be gained outside or in any way separate from the only true and legitimate church of Jesus Christ, that is, the Church of Jesus Christ of Latter-day Saints, which (after having been removed from the earth at the time of the "great apostasy" during the apostolic period) was restored to the earth through the divine mission of the prophet Joseph Smith to "revive and renew in the hearts of the children of men" the doctrines of Christ, the ordinances of his gospel, and the fulness of that gospel of salvation to the world;

that *knowing* God and Jesus Christ *begins* with faith, repentance of sin, and entry into the house of God, which means adoption into the body of Israel, that is, the Church of Jesus Christ of Latter-day Saints;

that entrance into the household of faith comes through baptism by immersion for remission of sin and the laying-on of hands for the gift of the Holy Ghost, ordinances acceptable to God only if they are administered by His divine authority, an authority exclusively exercised by the LDS priesthood, which was restored to the earth in 1829;

that the *knowledge* necessary to salvation and eternal life *increases* as Latter-day Saints come to know God and Jesus Christ more fully and intimately in the church through *obedience* to gospel truths as revealed or mediated by the voices of those who have "divine authority to guide and direct and counsel in the midst of Israel," through *submission* to priesthood leadership, the order that God has instituted in his house, and through *participation* in the ordinances, including "the ordinances of the house of God [temple ordinances] revealed in greater plainness in this dispensation than perhaps in any former dispensation since the world was formed."

For the most part, President Smith simply stated these elements of the LDS gospel with little elaboration. As he talked of the role of the priesthood in the church and in the world, however, he extended his treatment of the principle of "submission to the order that God has established in his house." Those who hold the priesthood are divinely appointed to administer in God's name, he said. With respect to the church and its members, the priesthood has both responsibilities and the authority necessary to fulfill those responsibilities; God, in calling, ordaining, and appointing men to priesthood offices, "cannot fail [to] sanction" the decisions they make, the actions they take, or the ordinances they perform in his name. But priesthood bearers have other responsibilities besides a responsibility to the church and its members. They are charged also with preaching the gospel to the world, with the task of declaring "the truth that Jesus is the Christ and that [note the significant use of the present tense] Joseph is a prophet of God," and that he was "authorized and qualified to lay the foundation of the Kingdom of God," of which Christ, not man, is king.

Since—if words and actions are to be understood literally rather than figuratively—the prophet Joseph Smith was crowned king of the Kingdom of God in 1844, President Smith differed with his predecessors about this important matter.[7] But with the exception of his assertion that "no man is king of the Kingdom of God," a point not truly central to his statement of the essentials of the LDS gospel, Smith included nothing in his sermon that is inconsistent with descriptions of the Mormon gospel found scattered through the sermons of every church president from 1830 onward. Discussion of principles, beliefs, and notions that were incompatible with pioneer Mormonism was missing. But their absence does not signify that such elements did not then exist so much as it emphasizes the extent to which it was the character of this sermon to span the chasm between the present and the past. By concentrating on what the Mormons regard as the essential principles of the gospel—the nature of God, Christ's role as Savior, the restoration of the church and its place, and the place of the priesthood, in humanity's quest for salvation and eternal life—Joseph F. Smith conveyed to the Saints his confidence that the changes which had occurred during his tenure were not changes which had in any way diminished the strength of the relationship between God and His chosen people. Notwithstanding shifting times and seasons, Mormonism remained the same. Hallowed by his initial evocation of the approving gaze of the former leaders of the church, Smith's 1916 conference sermon said to the Saints that, in spite of the altered context in which it had its being, the Mormonism of which they were a part was inherently the same Mormonism as the Mormonism he had known throughout the seventy-eight years of his life.

President Smith knew, of course, that on the surface the Mormonism of 1916 was by no means the Mormonism of his youth, or even his middle years. Of his six wives, four were still alive. But the patriarchal order of marriage, for example, was rapidly disappearing from the scene. Likewise, direct LDS control of politics was no more. Whereas the political kingdom had once been enough of a reality for Brigham Young simply to pause in the

midst of a sermon to conduct the (unanimous) election of Almon
W. Babbitt to the U.S. Congress, Smith's support of the incumbent
senatorial candidate caused such an uproar in 1912 that he subsequently had to deny intending to influence a single Saint to go
thou and vote likewise.[8] Along with all the Saints who had lived
substantial proportions of their adult lives within the Mormon
pioneer community, Smith knew that things were different, very
different. And yet, looking "beyond the veil," he was able to say in
effect that although things change, they also stay the same.

While this message included no "thus saith the Lord" signal to
indicate that it was being revealed directly from on high, thousands of Latter-day Saints are reported to have "felt the Divine inspiration that accompanied the delivery of this remarkable sermon."[9] As a result, even though his visionary 1916 conference
address was not formally recognized as revelation and added to
the LDS canon (as were two other visions he reported about the
life beyond), presented as it was in General Conference, the powerful weight of continuing revelation was implicitly attached to the
substance of the message.

This was no small thing. According to Mormon doctrine, the
"Lord's true Church is established and founded upon revelation;
its identity as the true Church continues as long as revelation is
received to direct its affairs." Moreover, as opposed to personal
revelation, revelation given to the whole church is never manifested indiscriminately, but is given through its properly authorized officers.[10] Therefore, the very fact that among the listeners
in the tabernacle that day there were thousands who felt the presence of divine inspiration as their president spoke was, itself, con-
firmation that the LDS Church was still being led by revelation
despite the demise of the pioneer kingdom in which the Saints
openly practiced plural marriage and their leaders openly directed
their social, political, and economic destinies. As President Smith
was reassured, so confidence was renewed within the community
that the Church of Jesus Christ of Latter-day Saints was still
Christ's church; its members were still God's people; and Joseph
F. Smith was still their "prophet, seer, and revelator," as well as
the president, the chief administrative officer, of their church.

Certainly, however, making too much of this 1916 conference

sermon would be a mistake. As powerful as it was, it was only one of many sermons presented on the theme of continuity in the midst of change during Joseph F. Smith's presidency.[11] Its importance to this study lies in the manner in which close reading set in the context of General Conference opens up the *process of transition* that allowed Mormonism, even as it relinquished its millenarian/millennial character, to retain its perception of itself as the body of God's chosen people who continued to live at the edge of history. In the sermon's effective bonding of past and present within the ecclesiastical framework of institutional Mormonism, the whole of the complex transformation of the millennial vision that energized early Mormonism is suggested.

Because the 1890s opened with the promulgation of the Manifesto and because Utah's quest for statehood was concluded in 1896, when the LDS state was allowed to join the Union, histories that attempt to survey the Mormon past have a tendency to picture the final decade of the nineteenth century as a sort of transitional maelstrom in which Mormonism was fundamentally altered. If careful attention is paid not only to the substance but the structure of what President Smith said, it is possible to get an idea about the *process* by which the Mormonism that had its being in a world that was set apart—one in which literal inheritances in Zion were taken up and actual cities of God were constructed in Ohio, Illinois, and the intermountain West—gave way to a Mormonism that exists within the larger American culture and, increasingly, in the cultures of many other parts of the globe. Moreover, by focusing on process rather than comparing before and after forms of Mormonism, the pattern of transformation is sufficiently clarified to make it obvious that accommodation to the world and spiritualization of the message explanations are not powerful enough to account for what happened.

The focus on process reveals, in addition, that the transformation of Mormonism's original millennial vision cannot be adequately described simply by examining what went on during the 1890s. Instead, the transformation process extends back across the nineteenth century as well as forward at least through Joseph F. Smith's presidency, which did not come to an end until 1918. As the Saints overcame their disappointment when the 1890s

turned out to be a prologue to modern Mormonism rather than
the celebrated "winding-up scene" that would usher in the *eschaton*, so earlier Saints had sustained a series of devastating dis-
appointments occasioned by the frustration of their intense expectations. As was the case in the 1890s and thereafter, so in the
1830s when Zion (in Missouri) went unredeemed, in the 1840s
when Joseph Smith was murdered, and in the late 1850s and early
1860s when Deseret became Utah in fact as well as in name, disappointment was overcome as revelation operated to strengthen
the ritual and institutional dimensions of this developing religious tradition.

A major question that would issue from Mormonism's transformation was the now oft-asked question of whether Mormonism
is or is not Christian. When the obvious LDS behavioral pecu-
liarity disappeared, the members of the Church of Jesus Christ of
Latter-day Saints were seen to resemble so closely their evangelical Protestant neighbors that the idea that Mormonism is
merely one more slightly idiosyncratic form of Christianity entered popular perceptions of the Saints.[12] All the foregoing, from
the story of the discovery of the gold plates and the reopening
of the canon through the nineteenth-century experience of the
Saints and beyond, suggests that, at least in the case of the members of the Church of Jesus Christ of Latter-day Saints centered in
Salt Lake City, those perceptions are wrong.[13] And yet the Saints
think of themselves as Christians and think of their church as the
only legitimate Church of Jesus Christ.

As does the delineation of how the Mormon experience gave
the Latter-day Saints an understanding of Judeo-Christian history
and theology peculiar to themselves, so President Joseph F. Smith's
conference address helps to resolve this dilemma of definition. If
the key concepts of saving knowledge of Jesus Christ and the importance of temple ordinances are kept in mind as the address is
considered, it becomes very clear that Mormonism is a form of
corporate Christianity. While it perceives of itself as Christian,
Mormonism differs from traditional Christianity in much the
same fashion that traditional Christianity, in its ultimate emphasis on the individual, came to differ from Judaism.

Although the "unit of salvation" in Mormonism remains the

individual, salvation itself depends on knowing Christ, knowledge that can only be gained with the legitimation of the LDS
priesthood and within the corporate structure of the LDS Church.
In addition, although the gospel is available to all, the "unit of ex-
altation" is the family rather than the individual. Consequently,
the ultimate goal of the Latter-day Saints is not eternity somehow
spent in the presence of the Lord Jesus Christ in heaven. Mormonism holds up a different goal: "eternal progression" toward
godhood. When this theological conception is added to the peculiar understanding that Saints have of themselves and their
Hebraic-Christianness, which grew out of their past as peculiar
people, it becomes as clear as can be that, nomenclature notwithstanding, Mormonism is a new religious tradition.

PIC-NIC PARTY

AT THE

HEAD WATERS

OF

BIG COTTONWOOD.

PRES. BRIGHAM YOUNG *respectfully invites* Geo. A. Smith *and family to attend a Pic-Nic Party at the Lake in Big Cottonwood Kanyon on*

Friday, 24th of July,

REGULATIONS.

You will be required to start so as to pass the first mill, about four miles up the Kanyon, before 12 o'clock, on Thursday, the 23rd, as no person will be allowed to pass that point after 2 o'clock, p.m. of that day.

All persons are forbidden to smoke cigars or pipes, or kindle fires, at any place in the Kanyon, except on the camp ground.

The Bishops are requested to accompany those invited from their respective Wards, and see that each person is well fitted for the trip, with good, substantial, steady teams, wagons, harness, hold-backs and locks, capable of completing the journey without repair, and a good driver, so as not to endanger the life of any individual.

Bishops will, before passing the first mill, furnish a full and complete

Invitation to the 24 July celebration in Cottonwood Canyon, 1857

Appendix

A Chronology
of Nineteenth-Century Mormonism

1805	December 23	Joseph Smith, Jr., was born in Sharon, Vt., to Joseph and Lucy Mack Smith.
1816		The Smith Family left New England and settled in western New York.
1820	Spring	That existing churches were "all wrong" was revealed in a vision to Joseph Smith by two personages whom he identified as the Father and the Son.
1822		A seerstone, a magical device used to locate lost objects, was found by Joseph Smith while he was helping to dig a well for Willard Chase.
1823	September 21/22	Revealed to Joseph Smith in a vision was the existence of golden plates on which was engraved in "Reformed Egyptian" an ancient record and a set of

"ancient seers" called the Urim and Thummim, which could be used to translate the record into English. The messenger in the vision told Smith that the plates and the seers were buried in the Hill Cumorah, near Manchester, N.Y.

1823	September 22	Joseph Smith visited the Hill Cumorah but said he was not allowed to take possession of the plates.
1824–27		In addition to working on their farm, Joseph Smith, his father, and possibly one or another of his brothers engaged from time to time in treasure-hunting. Smith's seerstone was the means used to determine the approximate location of the treasure.
1824	September 22	Smith said that he again visited the Hill Cumorah but was not allowed to take possession of the plates and the Urim and Thummim.
1825	September 22	Smith said that he again visited the Hill Cumorah but was not allowed to take possession of the plates and the Urim and Thummim.
1825	October	Smith was hired by Josiah Stowell to go to the Susquehanna Valley in Pennsylvania to locate a lost silver mine.

1826	March 20	Smith was charged with being an imposter and brought to trial before a justice of the peace in Bainbridge, N.Y.
1826	September 22	Smith said that he again visited the Hill Cumorah but was not allowed to take possession of the plates and the Urim and Thummim.
1827	January 18	Smith was married to Emma Hale of Harmony, Pa.
1827	September 22	Joseph and Emma Smith visited the Hill Cumorah and Joseph reported that he had been allowed to take possession of the plates.
1828	Spring	A document containing characters Smith said he copied from the plates was carried by Martin Harris to the East, where it was shown to scholars at Rutgers and Columbia. The scholars were unable to read the document.
1828	June	Martin Harris took the first 116 pages of the manuscript of the Book of Mormon home to show them to his wife and family. These pages disappeared and were never found.
1828	July	Smith said the plates and the Urim and Thummim were taken from him because he had allowed Harris to show the 116 pages of manuscript to his family.

1828	September 22	Smith said the plates and the Urim and Thummim were returned to him.
1829	Winter, Spring	Smith began to have revelations calling persons to join in the work that was being inaugurated with the coming into being of the Book of Mormon.
1829	April 6	Oliver Cowdery decided to become Smith's scribe, and intense work on the Book of Mormon commenced.
1829	May 15	The Aaronic priesthood was restored.
1829	Summer	The manuscript of the Book of Mormon was ready for the press.
1830	March 26	The Book of Mormon was first advertised for sale.
1830	April 6	The Church of Jesus Christ was organized in Fayette, N.Y.
1830	April 11	Oliver Cowdery preached the first LDS public discourse at a meeting in the Whitmer home in Fayette, N.Y.
1830	June	The "Visions of Moses," now included in the Pearl of Great Price, were revealed to Joseph Smith.
1830	June 9	At the first conference of the church a total of twenty-seven members was reported.

1830	October	Missionaries to Indians in Ohio and Missouri stopped in Kirtland, Ohio, where they converted a Campbellite minister, Sidney Rigdon, and his entire congregation to Mormonism.
1830–31		The concept of the "gathering" was introduced and put into practice when Joseph Smith and his New York followers settled together in and around Kirtland, Ohio.
1830–33		Joseph Smith worked on his inspired translation of the Bible.
1831	June 3	At a conference in Kirtland, high priests and elders were called to lead a body of Mormons to Jackson County, Mo.
1831	August 2–3	Sidney Rigdon identified and dedicated a portion of Jackson County, Mo., as the "Land of Zion." Joseph Smith identified and dedicated a temple site therein.
1832	Winter, Spring	The organization of a First Presidency was effected and afterward confirmed by revelation.
1832	March 24	A mob in Hiram, Ohio, tarred and feathered Joseph Smith and beat Sidney Rigdon severely.
1832	June 1	*The Evening and Morning Star*, edited by William Wine Phelps, was issued at Independence, Mo. This was the first LDS periodical and it welcomed free blacks into Mormonism.

1833   February 27   The Word of Wisdom was is-
                            sued as a word of counsel and
                            advice to Latter-day Saints. In
                            the early twentieth century the
                            Word of Wisdom was accorded
                            the status of revelation.

1833   Summer   The publication of a collection
                            of Joseph Smith's revelations
                            was undertaken. The title of
                            the collection was *A Book of
                            Commandments*.

1833   July 20   Strife between Mormons and
                            non-Mormons escalated in
                            Missouri when the office of the
                            Evening and Morning Star in
                            Independence was destroyed by
                            a mob of Missourians. Many of
                            the copies of the *Book of Com-
                            mandments* were destroyed.

1833   November   The Latter-day Saints fled from
                            Jackson County in response to
                            threats and attacks by mobs of
                            Missourians.

1833   December 18   Joseph Smith, Sr., was ordained
                            as the first Patriarch to the
                            Church.

1834   February, July   Stake organizations with high
                            councils and stake presidencies
                            were established in Kirtland
                            and in Missouri, where most of
                            the Saints had settled in Clay
                            County.

1834   May 6-June 20   Joseph Smith led a small force
                            of Latter-day Saints from Ohio
                            westward in an effort to assist
                            the beleaguered Missouri Saints.

		Called Zion's Camp, this force failed to accomplish its objective and dispersed. Most members returned to Kirtland.
1835	February 14	At a meeting of Zion's Camp after its members returned to Kirtland, the Quorum of the Twelve was first organized.
1835	July 3	Egyptian mummies and papyrus scrolls were exhibited in Kirtland. From these papyri, Joseph Smith said he translated the Book of Abraham.
1836	March 27-April 3	The Kirtland temple was dedicated.
1836	April 3	Behind the veil in the Kirtland temple, Joseph Smith and Oliver Cowdery beheld Jesus, Moses, Elias, and Elijah.
1836	Summer	Saints living in Clay County, Mo., were asked to leave. Most moved to the northwestern part of the state, settling chiefly in Caldwell County, making the town of Far West the center of Mormon settlement.
1837	January	The Kirtland Safety Society Bank was organized but failed to receive a state charter.
1837	Summer	Missionary work outside North America commenced with the departure of Heber C. Kimball, Orson Hyde, Joseph Fielding, and Willard Richards for the British Isles.

1837	Summer-Fall	Economic confusion and apostasy generated great stress among the Saints in Kirtland.
1838	January 12	From Kirtland Joseph Smith and Sidney Rigdon fled west to Missouri.
1838		Throughout the year Saints from Kirtland left to join the Missouri Saints, swelling the Mormon ranks in and around Far West.
1838	July 4	A cornerstone was laid for a temple in Far West. This plus Sidney Rigdon's inflammatory Independence Day address raised the already elevated level of tension between Mormons and non-Mormons to dangerous heights.
1838	August 6	Mormons were not allowed to vote at Gallatin, Mo., and a violent exchange occurred between some of the Saints and some Missouri citizens.
1838	Autumn	The Missouri-Mormon war started in earnest with guerrilla-like activities occurring from both camps. The most violent Saints called themselves the Danite Band.
1838	October 24	A pitched battle took place at Crooked River.
1838	October 26	Missouri Governor Lilburn Boggs issued an order stating

that the Saints must be "exter-
minated" or expelled from the
state.

1838	October 30	In a massacre at Haun's Mill, seventeen Latter-day Saints were killed.
1838	November	Joseph Smith and other LDS leaders were arrested. The Missouri militia plundered Far West.
1838–39	Winter-Spring	Under extreme duress, the Saints departed from Missouri leaving most of their possessions behind.
1839	April 16	Joseph Smith and other imprisoned LDS leaders were allowed to escape.
1839	May 10	Joseph Smith and his family moved to Commerce, Ill., a town site that had been purchased by the Saints and renamed Nauvoo.
1840	April 16	The mission in England became successful enough to establish the *Latter-day Saints Millennial Star*.
1840	April 14	Brigham Young was sustained as President of the Quorum of the Twelve Apostles.
1840	December 16	The city of Nauvoo received a charter from the state of Illinois which gave it a large measure of autonomy.

1840	December 31	Total LDS Church membership was reported at 30,000.
1841–44		Nauvoo experienced a period of astonishing growth, becoming the largest city in Illinois.
1841	January 19	A revelation called for the construction of a temple in Nauvoo and introduced baptism of the dead as a temple ordinance.
1842		The inauguration of the practice of plural marriage caused internal dissension in the Mormon community, while rumors of the practice caused outrage among non-Mormons.
1842	March 17	The Female Relief Society was organized with Emma Smith as its president.
1842	May 4	New temple "endowments" were introduced into Mormonism.
1842	July 20	Joseph Smith was arrested for complicity in an attack on the life of Governor Boggs of Missouri. Smith was released on a habeas corpus writ.
1843	July 12	The revelation on the "Eternity of the Marriage Covenant and Plural Marriage" was written into the record.
1844	January 29	Joseph Smith announced his candidacy for President of the United States.

1844	March 11	The Council of Fifty was organized.
1844	June 7	A paper opposing the leadership of Joseph Smith, the *Nauvoo Expositor*, published its one and only issue.
1844	June 11	Joseph Smith and the Nauvoo city council authorized destruction of the *Nauvoo Expositor*'s press.
1844	June 27	The murder of Joseph Smith and his brother Hyrum took place in Carthage, Ill., where they were being held in jail in connection with the suppression of the *Expositor*.
1844–45		An internal struggle took place but no new prophet/president emerged immediately to take Smith's place.
1845		Efforts to finish the Nauvoo temple accelerated, even as Illinois citizens made it clear that the Saints were no longer welcome in the state.
1845	January	The protection that the Nauvoo charter had afforded the Mormons was withdrawn, opening the way for renewed persecution of the Saints.
1845	September 22	The Council of the Twelve announced publicly that the Saints intended to leave Illinois.

1845	December 10	After completion and dedication of the top floor of the Nauvoo temple, the Saints began to receive endowments in the temple.
1846	February 4	The first major group of Latter-day Saints left Nauvoo, crossing the Mississippi River into Iowa.
1846	April 30	The completed Nauvoo temple was dedicated.
1846	Summer	Temporary LDS settlements were established in Iowa at Garden Grove, Mount Pisgah, Council Bluffs, and Winter Quarters.
1847	April 7	The "Pioneer Company" left Winter Quarters to search for a permanent settlement site.
1847	July 22–24	The "Pioneer Company" reached the valley of the Great Salt Lake.
1847	July 28	A site was selected for an LDS temple in Salt Lake City.
1847	December 27	Brigham Young was sustained as President of the Church of Jesus Christ of Latter-day Saints.
1849	March 5	A provisional State of Deseret was established in the Salt Lake Valley.

1849	October	A Perpetual Emigrating Fund was established to assist with the "gathering" to Utah.
1850	September	As a part of the Compromise of 1850 the State of Deseret was made Utah Territory and Brigham Young was appointed governor.
1850	December 31	Total LDS Church membership was reported at 60,000.
1851	September	Three federal judges, the first of a long series of federal officials, arrived to preside over the Latter-day Saints.
1852	August 28	The doctrine of plural marriage was announced publicly.
1853	April 6	At Zarahemla, Wis., the founding conference of the Reorganization was held, bringing together many Saints who rejected the leadership of Brigham Young and the Twelve.
1856	June 9	The first handcart company left Iowa City. Saints traveling with such companies walked across the mountains to Utah.
1857		In an altercation known as the Utah War the federal government established its formal hegemony over Utah Territory.
1857	September 7	The Mountain Meadows Massacre took place in southern

		Utah. An Arkansas immigrant company was massacred by Mormons and Indians.
1860	April 6	Joseph Smith III accepted the position of President and Prophet to the Reorganized Church of Jesus Christ of Latter Day Saints.
1860	December 31	Total LDS Church membership was reported at 80,000.
1862	July 8	A federal law designed to make plural marriage illegal was passed by the U.S. Congress.
1867	October 6	The recently completed taber-nacle in Temple Square in Salt Lake City was the site of a semi-annual conference of the LDS Church.
1867	December 8	Bishops were instructed to organize Relief Societies in the various wards of the church.
1869	May 10	The transcontinental railroad was completed, tying Utah Ter-ritory closer to the rest of the nation.
1869	November 28	The forerunner of the LDS Young Women's Mutual Im-provement Association was organized.
1869	December	A dissident LDS "Godbeite" movement developed among some Mormon intellectuals and business people.

1870		The Mormons and non-Mormons in Utah Territory divided formally into opposing political parties.
1870	December 31	Total LDS Church membership was reported at 110,000.
1871	November 9	Ground was broken for an LDS temple in St. George, Utah.
1872	October 2	Brigham Young was arrested on an unlawful cohabitation charge. This was the first major arrest in a campaign to bring plural marriage to an end by arresting Mormon leaders. The case against President Young was subsequently dropped.
1874	June 23	A more stringent bill against the practice of plural marriage, the Poland bill, became federal law.
1875	June 10	The first Young Men's Mutual Improvement Association was organized.
1877	April 6	The St. George temple was dedicated.
1877	April 25	Ground was broken for an LDS temple in Manti, Utah.
1877	May 18	Ground was broken for an LDS temple in Logan, Utah.
1877	August 29	Brigham Young died in Salt Lake City at the age of seventy-six.

1877   October 6   John Taylor was sustained as
                         President of the Quorum of the
                         Twelve Apostles.

1878   August 25   The first Primary Association
                         was established.

1880   April 6   The LDS Church's first jubilee
                         was celebrated.

1880   October 10   John Taylor was sustained as
                         President of the Church.

1880   December 31   Total LDS Church membership
                         was reported at 160,000.

1882   March 14   A much more stringent anti-
                         polygamy measure, the
                         Edmunds bill, was passed by
                         Congress, paving the way for
                         the "Raid," in which scores of
                         federal marshals were sent to
                         Utah Territory to arrest men
                         who were practicing plural
                         marriage.

1884–90   Intense efforts made by the fed-
                         eral government to arrest po-
                         lygamists led to the creation of
                         the "Underground," a network
                         designed to protect from pros-
                         ecution the Saints who were
                         practicing plural marriage.

1884   May 17–19   The Logan temple was
                         dedicated.

1886–90   Mormons fled to Mexico and
                         Canada in order to escape pros-
                         ecution while living within the
                         plural marriage system.

1887	February 17–18	The Edmunds-Tucker Act passed Congress. This was an even more stringent effort made by the federal government to bring the practice of plural marriage to an end.
1887	July 25	John Taylor died at Kaysville, Utah, at the age of seventy-eight.
1888	May 21	The Manti temple was dedicated.
1889	April 7	Wilford Woodruff was sustained as President of the Church.
1890	September 24	President Woodruff issued the "Manifesto," a document announcing that the LDS Church was no longer sanctioning plural marriage.
1890	October 6	In General Conference, the Latter-day Saints voted unanimously to accept the Manifesto.
1890	December 31	Total LDS Church membership was reported at 205,000.
1891		The People's party, the Mormon political party, was disbanded. Saints were directed to join the Republican and Democratic parties.
1893	January 4	The President of the United States issued a proclamation of amnesty for all polygamists who had entered plural marriage before 1 Nov. 1890.

1893	April	The Salt Lake temple was dedicated.
1894	July 14	An enabling act was signed paving the way for statehood for Utah Territory.
1894	November 13	The Genealogical Society of Utah was organized.
1895	March 4	The Utah constitutional convention met in Salt Lake City.
1896	January 4	Utah was admitted to the Union as a state.
1898	September 2	Wilford Woodruff died in California at the age of ninety-one.
1898	September 13	Lorenzo Snow was sustained as President of the Church.
1899	May 8	President Snow called for the payment of full tithes by all Latter-day Saints.
1900	December 31	Total LDS Church membership was reported at 268,331.

Notes

Preface

1. Here as elsewhere in this work, the term "traditional Christianity" encompasses both Roman Catholicism and what might be called mainstream Protestantism. Also here as elsewhere in this work, LDS use of theological concepts such as "fulness of times" will be used without the standard editorial *sic* to indicate that LDS usage differs from traditional usage.

2. While my sustained argument does not follow the lines of Fawn M. Brodie's work, it should be pointed out at the outset that Brodie described Mormonism in the Preface to her biography of the Mormon prophet as follows: "It was a real religious creation, one intended to be to Christianity as Christianity was to Judaism: that is, a reform and a consummation." *No Man Knows My History: The Life of Joseph Smith, the Mormon Prophet* (1945; 2nd ed. rev., New York: Alfred A. Knopf, 1971), p. viii.

3. Allen and Leonard, *The Story of the Latter-day Saints* (Salt Lake City: Deseret Book, 1976); Arrington and Bitton, *The Mormon Experience: A History of the Latter-day Saints* (New York: Alfred A. Knopf, 1979). Other older but still standard works are: Joseph Fielding Smith, *Essentials in Church History*, Classics in Mormon Literature ed. (Salt Lake City: Deseret Book, 1979); Joseph Smith, Jr., *History of the Church of Jesus Christ of Latter-day Saints: Period I, History of Joseph Smith, the Prophet*, ed. B. H. Roberts, 6 vols., 2nd ed. rev. (Salt Lake City: Deseret Book, 1955), cited hereafter as *DHC* (*Documentary History of the*

Church); B. H. Roberts, ed., *History of the Church of Jesus Christ of Latter-day Saints: Period II, from the Manuscript History of Brigham Young and Other Original Documents* (Salt Lake City: Deseret Book, 1932), hereafter cited as *DHC* 7 (*Documentary History of the Church*, vol. VII); and Inez Smith Davis, *The Story of the Church*, 4th ed. rev. (Independence, Mo.: Herald Publishing House, 1948).

4. See especially Thomas S. Kuhn, *The Structure of Scientific Revolutions*, 2nd ed. (Chicago: University of Chicago Press, 1970); Mircea Eliade, *Cosmos and History: The Myth of the Eternal Return*, trans. Willard R. Trask (New York: Harper, 1954), and *The Sacred and the Profane: The Nature of Religion*, trans. Willard R. Trask (New York: Harcourt Brace, 1957); Peter Berger, *The Sacred Canopy: Elements of a Sociological Theory of Religion* (Garden City, N.Y.: Doubleday, 1967); Berger with Thomas Luckmann, *The Social Construction of Reality: A Treatise in the Sociology of Knowledge* (Garden City, N.Y.: Doubleday, 1967); Frank Kermode, *The Sense of an Ending: Studies in the Theory of Fiction* (New York: Oxford University Press, 1967); Northrop Frye, *Fearful Symmetry: A Study of William Blake* (Princeton, N.J.: Princeton University Press, 1947), and *The Great Code: The Bible and Literature* (New York: Harcourt Brace Jovanovich, 1981); John Gager, *Kingdom and Community: The Social World of Early Christianity* (Englewood Cliffs, N.J.: Prentice-Hall, 1975).

5. A series of articles published in 1982 in the *Bulletin of the Council on the Study of Religion* is one recent attempt to describe "religious studies."

6. Shipps, "In the Presence of the Past: Continuity and Change in Twentieth-Century Mormonism," in Thomas G. Alexander and Jessie L. Embry, eds., *After 150 Years: The Latter-day Saints in Sesquicentennial Perspective* (Provo, Utah: Charles Redd Center for Western Studies, 1983), pp. 4–35.

Chapter One

1. The awkward use of quotation marks around the word *translation* has been dispensed with in this work. The term is used here as it is used by Latter-day Saints; it does not signify a direct word-by-word, phrase-by-phrase translation of a text from one language to another.

2. G. J. Adams, *"A Lecture on the Authenticity & Scriptural Character of the Book of Mormon" Delivered at the Town Hall,*

Charlestown, Mass., on Sunday, February 7th (Boston: J. E. Farwell, 1844), p. 24. Copy available in the Yale University Library.

3. The *Documentary History of the Church* that B. H. Roberts edited and *Essentials of Church History* written by Joseph Fielding Smith have both been formally approved (authorized) by the Council of the Twelve Apostles of the Church of Jesus Christ of Latter-day Saints.

4. Nineteenth-century anti-Mormon literature is extensive. While much of it deals with polygamy and the Mormon political kingdom, nearly every volume and journal article included accounts of the beginnings of Mormonism that described it as superstition. The author has examined all the periodical articles on the Mormons and Mormonism indexed in *Poole's Index* and *Readers' Guide* between 1860 and 1960. An analysis of a representative sample stratified chronologically is described in "From Satyr to Saint: American Attitudes toward the Mormons, 1860–1960," a paper presented at the 1973 annual meeting of the organization of American Historians. Copy available in the LDS Church Archives, Salt Lake City.

5. Unless otherwise indicated, the information on which this narrative prologue is based came from the following works: several versions, published and unpublished, of the history of the Smith family, Joseph Smith, and Mormonism written by the prophet's mother, Lucy Mack Smith, in 1845; the 1833 Book of Commandments, the first collection of Joseph Smith's revelations; later editions of the Doctrine and Covenants of the Church of Jesus Christ of Latter-day Saints; Brodie, *No Man Knows My History*; Donna Hill, *Joseph Smith, the First Mormon* (New York: Doubleday, 1979); Richard Lloyd Anderson, *Joseph Smith's New England Heritage* (Salt Lake City: Deseret Book, 1971); Shipps, "The Prophet Puzzle: Suggestions Leading toward a More Comprehensive Interpretation of Joseph Smith," *Journal of Mormon History* 1 (1974): 3–20.

6. Lucy Mack Smith gave birth to a tenth child after the family moved from New England to New York.

7. Jon Butler, "Magic, Astrology, and the Early American Religious Heritage," *American Historical Review* 84 (Apr. 1979): 317–46; Marvin S. Hill, "The Role of Christian Primitivism in the Origin and Development of the Mormon Kingdom, 1830–1844" (Ph.D. dissertation, University of Chicago, 1968), and "Brodie Revisited: A Reappraisal," *Dialogue* 8 (Winter 1972): 72–85. See also Howard Kerr and Charles L. Crow, eds., *The Occult in Amer-*

ica: New Historical Perspectives (Urbana: University of Illinois Press, 1983), especially the essays written by Jon Butler and R. Laurence Moore.

8. See especially the influential work of Whitney R. Cross, *The Burned-over District: The Social and Intellectual History of Enthusiastic Religion in Western New York, 1800–1850* (Ithaca, N.Y.: Cornell University Press, 1950).

9. Precisely how much the family knew at the time is not exactly clear. Although the canonized version of Smith's history emphasizes the vision of 1820, the vision of superlative importance to Joseph's mother, and likewise to his father, was the one that their son had during the third harvest time after the family opened their new farm. That is, in 1823. As his mother described this exciting event, after retiring to bed one evening, following a conversation about the diversity of churches in the world, an angel appeared to her son and said: "I perceive that you are enquiring in your mind which is the true church. There is not a true church on earth. No not one. And has not been since Peter took the keys of Melchisidec priesthood after the order of God into the Kingdom of Heaven. The churches that are now upon the earth are all man-made churches. There is a record for you, Joseph, but you cannot get it until you learn the commandments of God. For it is not to get gain, but it is to bring forth that light and intelligence which has been long lost in the earth . . . you must tell your father of this for he will believe every word you say. . . ." While this remembrance of Joseph's account of the vision—found in the preliminary manuscript of Lucy Mack Smith's history—undoubtedly telescoped at least two of the prophet's visions into one, there can be little question about the significance of this astonishing, yet not unanticipated, event for Smith's parents.

10. "Introduction: A Framework for the Comparative Study of Altered States of Consciousness," in Erika Bourguignon, ed., *Religions, Altered States of Consciousness and Social Change* (Columbus: Ohio State University Press, 1973), pp. 12–15. Bourguignon's framework is used to distinguish different forms of biblical prophecy in Simon B. Parker, "Possession Trance and Prophecy in Pre-exilic Israel," *Vetus Testamentum*, 1978, pp. 271–85.

11. Odgen Kraut, *Seers and Seer Stones* (Salt Lake City: by the Author, n.d.) contains descriptions and some pictures of seerstones that might have belonged to Smith and other early Mormons.

12. *Mormonism Unvailed: or A Faithful Account of That Sin-*

gular Imposition and Delusion . . . published by Eber D. Howe in Painesville, Ohio, in 1834, was the first significant book-length anti-Mormon work. The Chase and Harris affidavits are reprinted in Brodie, *No Man Knows My History*, pp. 435–37. The Stout reference is Juanita Brooks, ed., *On the Mormon Frontier: The Diary of Hosea Stout*, 2 vols. (Salt Lake City: University of Utah Press, 1964), 2: 593.

13. The exact nature of the charge is still unresolved. See Marvin S. Hill, "Joseph Smith and the 1826 Trial: New Evidence and New Difficulties," *Brigham Young University Studies* 12 (Winter 1972): 226.

14. In addition to the accounts written by the Mormon prophet himself and by his mother, various letters and reminiscences describe what happened between September 1827 and April 1830. The most significant are those written by Emma Smith, Oliver Cowdery, and Martin Harris. Donna Hill and Fawn M. Brodie both made use of these materials in composing their biographies of Joseph Smith and both provide complete bibliographical references to them.

15. Doctrine and Covenants 9: 7–9.

16. Robert N. Hullinger devotes a full chapter to this episode in *Mormon Answer to Skepticism: Why Joseph Smith Wrote the Book of Mormon* (St. Louis, Mo.: Clayton Publishing House, 1980). Throughout he intimates that this was all part of a great ruse to make the Book of Mormon effective as an answer to skepticism. Here its significance is pictured as an event which reassured Joseph Smith that the record was of divine origin.

17. Lucy [Mack] Smith, *Biographical Sketches of Joseph Smith, the Prophet, and His Progenitors for Many Generations* (Liverpool: Orson Pratt, 1853), pp. 124–27.

18. Doctrine and Covenants, sec. 4.

19. This suggestion was made to me by Rev. Wesley P. Walters, who knows of the existence of a document on which the names of Oliver Cowdery and Solomon Mack, Joseph's grandfather, are linked. That Cowdery was what, in those days, was called a "rodsman" is suggested by the reference to his use of the rod (Aaron's gift) in a revelation printed in *A Book of Commandments for the Government of the Church of Christ* (Zion [Independence, Mo.]: W. W. Phelps, 1833; reprint, Independence: Herald Publishing House, 1971), VII: 2.

20. Doctrine and Covenants 10: 46.

Chapter Two

1. The loss of the first 116 pages of text was a matter of such great concern to Joseph Smith that he included a Preface in the first Book of Mormon edition explaining that the lost material had not been retranslated from the Book of Lehi, but that, being commanded of the Lord, Smith had translated accounts of the same situations and events from the plates of Nephi. This Preface, signed by "the author," was not included in subsequent editions. The testimonies about having seen the plates signed by the three witnesses and the eight witnesses are now bound in the front of the Book of Mormon. In the 1830 edition they were bound in after the text.

2. An early example of the charge that the Book of Mormon was heresy is found in the writing of the Rev. Diedrich Willers. See D. Michael Quinn, trans. and ed., "The First Months of Mormonism: A Contemporary [1830] View by Rev. Diedrich Willers," *New York History* 54 (July 1973): 331.

3. The fact that the book itself convinced readers of its authenticity is suggested by an early proselyting technique that might be called the "loan strategy." When persons could not—or would not—buy copies of the Book of Mormon, missionaries would place a volume on loan in a household. Returning to retrieve the book several days or weeks later, they would sometimes find that, through reading the book, persons had more or less inadvertently become converts to Mormonism.

4. This is a part of the well-known Moroni 10:4 passage that is often made the heart of LDS missionary lessons.

5. A positive statement of these claims is set in small type on the title page of the Book of Mormon.

6. The description of this continuum is provided by Parley P. Pratt in *A Voice of Warning and Instruction to All People*, perhaps the greatest of all nineteenth-century LDS proselyting tracts. In the 1893 edition, the quotation appears on p. 133.

7. This discussion of the Book of Mormon as hierophany is based on the theoretical work of Mircea Eliade, most especially the introductory section of *The Sacred and the Profane*.

8. Most important in asserting the presence of things ancient in the Book of Mormon is the work of Hugh Nibley, particularly two books, *Lehi in the Desert and the World of the Jaredites* (Salt Lake City: Deseret Book, 1952) and *Since Cumorah: The Book of Mormon in the Modern World* (Salt Lake City: Deseret Book,

1967), plus a large number of articles conveniently listed in Louis Midgley, "Hugh Nibley: A Short Bibliographical Note," *Dialogue* 2 (Spring 1967): 119–21; for the absence from the Book of Mormon of the rhetoric of nineteenth-century American politics, see Richard L. Bushman, "The Book of Mormon and the American Revolution," *BYU Studies* 17 (Fall 1976): 3–20; a widely circulated unpublished manuscript, over 400 pages in length, entitled *An Ancient Setting for the Book of Mormon*, written by anthropologist John L. Sorenson, makes the argument that the Book of Mormon story can be fitted in with what we know about Central America between 600 B.C.E. and 400 C.E.; the matter of literary style is dealt with in Wayne A. Larsen, Alvin C. Rencher, and Tim Layton, "Who Wrote the Book of Mormon? An Analysis of Wordprints," *BYU Studies* 20 (Spring 1980): 225–51.

9. The quotations from early LDS leaders are taken from the entries in Andrew Jenson, *Latter-day Saint Biographical Encyclopedia* (Salt Lake City: A. Jenson History Co., 1901). As for accounts of continuing experiences of this sort, it is not at all unusual for the testimonies given in Fast Sunday sacrament meetings to include accounts of recent conversions. References to Moroni 10:4 are often included in such testimonies.

10. Eliade, *The Sacred and the Profane*, Introduction and chap. 1.

11. Pratt, *A Voice of Warning*, chaps. 1 and 2.

12. James B. Allen, "Emergence of a Fundamental: The Expanding Role of Joseph Smith's First Vision in Mormon Religious Thought," *Journal of Mormon History* 7 (1980): 43–61.

13. The sectarian strife in nineteenth-century America is accorded great emphasis in most historical as well as theological discussions of Mormonism. This emphasis in turn appears to undergird the actuality of the vision.

14. Allen, "Emergence of a Fundamental," p. 61.

15. An outstanding exception is Arrington and Bitton, *The Mormon Experience*, especially chap. 2.

16. Bruce R. McConkie, *Mormon Doctrine* (Salt Lake City: Bookcraft, 1958), pp. 264–66.

17. Timothy L. Smith, "The Book of Mormon in a Biblical Culture," *Journal of Mormon History* 7 (1980): 3–21.

18. Writers who wish to cast doubt on Mormonism generally, and on the Book of Mormon specifically, have recognized this and have made more or less constant references to the fact that an account of the First Vision was not written down until twelve years

after it was said to have happened. In the *Salt Lake City Messenger*, published by Jerald and Sarah Tanner, and *The Utah Evangel*, published by the Rev. John Smith, contradictions in various accounts of the vision are also regularly pointed out. The most substantial efforts to question Smith's veracity in regard to the date given for the vision are Jerald and Sandra Tanner, *Joseph Smith's Strange Account of the First Vision* (Salt Lake City: Modern Microfilm, n.d.); and Rev. Wesley P. Walters, "New Light on Mormon Origins from the Palmyra Revival," which was first published as an Evangelical Theological Society tract and afterward reprinted in *Dialogue* 4 (Spring 1969): 60–81.

19. Marvin S. Hill, "The Rise of Mormonism in the Burned-over District: Another View," *New York History* 61 (Oct. 1980): 411–30, is a revisionist study that summarizes and questions scholarship about the Burned-over District from the work of Whitney R. Cross forward.

20. A recent and very useful study of the state of confusion in early nineteenth-century America is Gordon Wood, "Evangelical America and Early Mormonism," *New York History* 61 (Oct. 1980): 359–86.

21. Martin Marty, *Righteous Empire: The Protestant Experience in America* (New York: Dial Press, 1970), chap. 7.

22. This statement is not put forward as a challenge to William G. McLoughlin's interpretation of revivalism in *Revivals, Awakenings, and Reform: An Essay on Religion and Social Change in America, 1607–1977* (Chicago: University of Chicago Press, 1978) so much as to point out that revitalization took several forms.

23. Nathan O. Hatch, "Sola Scriptura and Novus Ordo Seclorum," in Nathan O. Hatch and Mark A. Noll, eds., *The Bible in America: Essays in Cultural History* (New York: Oxford University Press, 1982), pp. 59–78; Paul E. Johnson, *A Shopkeeper's Millennium: Society and Revivals in Rochester, New York, 1815–1837* (New York: Hill and Wang, 1978).

24. David A. Hollinger, "T. S. Kuhn's Theory of Science and Its Implications for History," *American Historical Review* 78 (Apr. 1973): 370–93.

25. John S. Dunne, *Time and Myth* (Notre Dame, Ind.: University of Notre Dame Press, 1975), p. 50.

26. Wood, "Evangelical America and Early Mormonism."

27. Hullinger, *Mormon Answer to Skepticism* is, in fact, a book-length argument that the Book of Mormon was a response

to skepticism. His argument is entirely supported by circumstantial evidence, however.

28. In the documentation for his 1980 article on the First Vision, James B. Allen notes, on p. 59, that both George Q. Cannon and Joseph Fielding Smith made use of this "heavens no longer brass" phrase.

29. Doctrine and Covenants 124: 125.

30. Shipps, "The Prophet Puzzle," pp. 19–20.

Chapter Three

1. Ninian Smart, *Worldviews: Crosscultural Explorations of Human Beliefs* (New York: Charles Scribner's Sons, 1983) is a recent volume which devotes separate chapters to these dimensions of religion.

2. Such reviews of a new tradition's past serve, to a great degree, as creedal statements.

3. Mortensen and Mulder, *Among the Mormons* (New York: Alfred A. Knopf, 1958) is a collection of documents about the Saints written by non-Mormons. Its content tells the LDS story from the outside and thus could not have captured the same sense of replication as documents written by the Mormons themselves.

4. The Doctrine and Covenants text indicates that Moses, Elijah, and Elias appeared to Smith and Cowdery. Since *Elias* is simply the Greek form of the name Elijah, it is not clear whether the reference refers to two or to three biblical figures.

5. Lakoff and Johnson, *Metaphors We Live By* (Chicago: University of Chicago Press, 1980).

6. James B. Allen, "One Man's Nauvoo: William Clayton's Experience in Mormon, Illinois," *Journal of Mormon History* 6 (1979): 52.

7. Davis Bitton, "The Ritualization of Mormon History," *Utah Historical Quarterly* 43 (Winter 1975): 67–85.

8. Frye, *Fearful Symmetry*, p. 317.

Chapter Four

1. Bangerter, "The Best of All Good News: The Gospel Is Restored" (edited version of a Brigham Young University devotional address delivered Apr. 1979), *Ensign*, Apr. 1980, pp. 56–59.

2. As Elder Bangerter's entire address is based on the assumption that Mormonism is the only church, he does not deal with other "true church" claims.

3. Howard Clark Kee, *Jesus in History: An Approach to the Study of the Gospels*, 2nd ed. (New York: Harcourt Brace Jovanovich, 1977), pp. 181–84.

4. Gager, *Kingdom and Community*, chap. 2.

5. Shipps, "The Prophet Puzzle." See also the underground edition of Reed Durham, "Is There No Help for the Widow's Son?," presidential address delivered at the annual meeting of the Mormon History Association, Nauvoo, Ill., Apr. 1974.

6. Eliade, *Cosmos and History*, chap. 2.

7. The significance of the conversion of Sidney Rigdon and his congregation is discussed in the context of restoration movements in Richard L. Bushman, *Joseph Smith and the Beginnings of Mormonism* (Urbana: University of Illinois Press, 1984), chap. 6. A good place to begin a study of Mormon apostasy is with a careful reading of the footnotes in the *Documentary History of the Church*.

8. A convenient collection of early Disciples of Christ writings, mainly composed of the writings of Thomas and Alexander Campbell, is *The Millennial Harbinger Abridged*, ed. Benjamin Lyon Smith, 2 vols. (Rosemead, Calif.: Old Paths, 1965).

9. 2 Nephi 27: 12; 29: 1, 14.

10. 1 Nephi 14: 1–2.

11. 1 Nephi 14: 10.

12. 3 Nephi 21: 5.

13. 1 Nephi 14: 14.

14. 2 Nephi 26: 16. The Book of Mormon was understood by Joseph Smith and other Mormons to be the "voice [which] shall come from the ground like the voice of a ghost," fulfilling the prophecy of Isaiah 29. See especially verses 4, 11–12, 18.

15. The restoration of the Aaronic priesthood is described in sec. 13 of the Doctrine and Covenants. As printed in the modern editions, this revelation is composed of two sections, the first given through Joseph Smith at Harmony, Pa., in August 1830, and the remainder probably given 4 September 1830. See heading for sec. 26, Book of the Doctrine and Covenants, Reorganized Church of Jesus Christ of Latter Day Saints (Independence, Mo.: 1978). The revelation announcing that twelve apostles would be called is sec. 18 in the Salt Lake City edition of the D&C and sect. 16 in the Independence edition.

16. The revelation on church organization and government is sec. 20 in the Salt Lake City edition of the D&C and sec. 17 of the Independence edition; the revelation to Joseph Smith given at

the organizational ceremony is printed as sec. 21 of the Salt Lake City edition and sec. 19 of the Independence edition. In the 1833 Book of Commandments, the first published collection of Joseph Smith's revelations, the order of these revelations is reversed and the revelation on church organization and government is dated June 1830.

On the prophet's role as exercised by Joseph Smith, comparison with Old Testament prophetic figures seems especially clear as the Old Testment prophets are described in Walter Bruggerman, *The Prophetic Imagination* (Philadelphia: Fortress Press, 1978).

17. Melodie Moench, "Nineteenth-Century Mormons: The New Israel," *Dialogue* 12 (Spring 1979): 42–45.

18. *The Millennial Harbinger Abridged*, 1: 228.

19. D&C 84: 2 (Salt Lake City ed.) reads: "Yea, the word of the Lord concerning his church, established in the last days for the restoration of his people, as he has spoken by the mouth of his prophets. . . ."

20. This idea is expressed clearly in the Mormon "Articles of Faith" included in the canonized work The Pearl of Great Price, and printed in a good proportion of the proselyting literature now distributed by LDS missionaries.

21. The extent to which modern understanding of the Pauline letters reflects Reformation readings, and most especially those of Martin Luther, is made clear in Krister Stendahl, *Paul among Jews and Gentiles and Other Essays* (Philadelphia: Fortress Press, 1976).

22. *A Book of Commandments*, chaps. III, V, X, XI, XII.

23. Quinn, "The First Months of Mormonism," p. 327.

24. DePillis, "The Development of Mormon Communitarianism, 1826–1846"; Hill, "The Role of Christian Primitivism in the Development of the Mormon Kingdom, 1830–1844"; Gordon Douglas Pollock, "In Search of Security: The Mormons and the Kingdom of God on Earth, 1830–1844," Ph.D. dissertation, Queen's University, Kingston, Ontario, 1977.

25. The quotation comes from Rev. Willer's letter, p. 331.

26. Manuscript letter located in the LDS Church Archives. The letter was printed as "A Gospel Letter" in Benjamin E. Rich, ed., *Scrapbook of Mormon Literature*, 2 vols. (Chicago: by the Editor, n.d.), 1: 543–45.

27. Lucy Mack Smith, *Biographical Sketches of Joseph Smith*, pp. 9, 34–36, 41–42, 46–50. The tendency toward primitive Christianity is even more pronounced in an early manuscript

version of Mother Smith's history located in the LDS Church Archives.

Although Joseph Smith's account of his First Vision has been subjected to a great deal of scholarly scrutiny in recent years, little attention has been paid to the context in which he found the advice, "If any of you lack wisdom, let him ask of God. . . ." Given the subsequent events, it is interesting, at least, to note that the epistle in which this familiar verse appears opens as follows: "James, a servant of God and of the Lord Jesus Christ, *to the twelve tribes which are scattered abroad*, greeting" (italics mine).

The Smith quotation was used in the title of Fawn Brodie's biography of the prophet. An excellent account of the change in direction taken by Mormonism in the first few years after 1830 is Peter Crawley, "Joseph Smith and *A Book of Commandments*," *Princeton University Library Chronicle* 42 (Autumn 1980): 18–32.

28. D&C (Salt Lake City ed.), sec. 38.

29. See n. 4, chap. 3.

30. Compare the account of the "transfiguration" during the dedication of the Kirtland temple with sec. 27 in the LDS Doctrine and Covenants and sec. 26 in the RLDS Doctrine and Covenants.

31. Danel W. Bachman, "New Light on an Old Hypothesis: The Ohio Origins of the Revelation on Eternal Marriage," *Journal of Mormon History* 5 (1978): 19–32.

Chapter Five

1. Editorial work for the volumes in this series was begun around the turn of the century by George Q. Cannon, who was First Counselor to Church President Lorenzo Snow. After Cannon's death, this editorial project was assigned to Brigham H. Roberts, a member of the First Council of Seventy, who was sustained as Assistant Church Historian in 1902. The first volume of the work was published that same year. The seventh and last volume was not published until 1932.

2. The description of the function of the Correlation Committee was provided by Lavina Fielding Anderson, whose assignment as an assistant editor of the *Ensign* included seeing historical articles through the press and into print in this official publication of the LDS Church. Despite the existence and vigorous activity of the Mormon History Association and the John Whitmer Historical Association, and such publications as the journals published by these two organizations, plus the success of *Dialogue, Expo-*

nent II, the *Utah Historical Quarterly*, and *Sunstone* magazine, none of which is connected officially with either the LDS or the RLDS churches, both churches continue to maintain virtual control of Mormon history *for their members* primarily because the general membership of both churches gains most of its knowledge of the LDS past through official church publications.

3. The most recent and most complete statements of this interpretation are Richard L. Anderson, commentary on Shipps, "The Prophet, His Mother, and Early Mormonism," a paper presented at the annual meeting of the Mormon History Association, Logan, Utah, May 1978, and Howard Clair Searle, "The History of Joseph Smith by His Mother," chap. 8, "Early Mormon Historiography: Writing the History of the Mormons, 1830–1858," Ph.D. dissertation, University of Southern California, Los Angeles, 1979.

4. Leonard J. Arrington to Edwin S. Gaustad, 5 Feb. 1969.

5. Edwin S. Gaustad to Leonard J. Arrington, 24 Feb. 1969.

6. The significance of the work is indicated by the fact that every reference in the typescript Introduction to the unpublished Journal History of the LDS Church is taken from Mother Smith's *History*, for example, as are all references to events in 1830 and 1831.

7. *History of the Prophet Joseph by His Mother Lucy Smith*, as revised by George A. Smith and Elias Smith (Salt Lake City: Improvement Era, 1905); *History of Joseph Smith by His Mother, Lucy Mack Smith*, with Notes and Comments by Preston Nibley (Salt Lake City: Bookcraft, 1958). In both the second and third editions of Mother Smith's *History*, changes and deletions are made with no indication given of the manner in which the text has been altered. A careful collation of the three editions has been published by the Modern Microfilm Company of Salt Lake City as the Introduction to *Joseph Smith's History by His Mother: A Photomechanical Reprint of the Original 1853 Edition*.

8. At this time Orson Pratt was located in Washington, D.C., where he was publishing *The Seer*, in whose pages he was disagreeing publicly with President Young over the so-called Adam-God doctrine. The "impaired memory" charge was made many times: see, for example, Journal History, 31 Dec. 1853, and a notation on the flyleaf of George A. Smith's copy of Mother Smith's *History*, LDS Church Archives. For a full account of the postmartyrdom activities of the prophet's youngest brother, William, see B. H. Roberts, *Succession in the Presidency of the Church of Jesus Christ of Latter-day Saints*, 2nd ed. (Salt Lake City: G. Q. Cannon, 1900), chap. 2.

9. An extended account of the history of the manuscript is given in Searle's dissertation, pp. 383–90.

10. See below for a more complete discussion of the arrangements with Howard and Martha Jane Coray for "compiling" Mother Smith's *History*.

11. Statement of 13 June 1865 from Martha Jane Coray, LDS Church Archives.

12. Manuscript, Howard Coray "History," p. 16, LDS Church Archives.

13. Lucy Mack Smith to William Smith, Jan. 1845, LDS Church Archives: "William I have something to communicate with regard to business I have by the Councill of the 12 undertaken a history of the Family. . . ."

14. Typescript, Howard Coray statement, LDS Church Archives.

15. Remarks made by Brigham Young, Wellsville, Cache Valley, Utah, 8 May 1865, transcription in LDS Church Archives.

16. N. W. Green, *Mormonism: Its Rise, Progress, and Present Condition* (Hartford, Conn.: Belknap & Bliss, 1870), p. 21.

17. A determination of the handwriting was made by Dean Jessee, of the Joseph Fielding Smith Institute of Church History, Brigham Young University.

18. Flyleaf, copy of Mother Smith's *History* used as a working copy during service on the committee of revision by George A. Smith. Statement signed by George A. Smith and Robert L. Campbell.

19. Martha Jean Coray's statement of 13 June 1865 describes the process of composition, a description amply borne out by notes denoted "Miscellany" in Dean Jessee's typescript of the preliminary manuscript.

20. This copy remains in the LDS Church Archives.

21. Richard L. Anderson, "The Reliability of the Early History of Lucy and Joseph Smith," *Dialogue* 4 (Summer 1969): 13–28.

22. Richard L. Anderson, presentation concerning his work-in-progress editing Lucy Mack Smith's *History*, Andrew Jenson Club, 7 May 1976. Tape recording in the LDS Church Archives.

23. *Ibid.*

24. Although this is an often-told story, its source could not be verified.

25. *DHC* 7: 519.

26. Whether the church copy is a true copy or a further revision is unclear.

27. Despite the enormous amount of information contained in B. H. Roberts, *Succession of the Presidency of the Church*, the reader is left with the impression that Brigham Young and the Quorum of the Twelve were firmly in control of the situation throughout.

28. Douglas Larche, "A Rhetorical History of the Post-1844 Struggle for Succession in the Mormon Church," Ph.D. dissertation, Indiana University, Bloomington, 1977.

29. Irene Bates, "William Smith, 1811–1893: Problematic Patriarch," a paper presented at the 1981 annual meeting of the Mormon History Association, pointed out that the description of William as unstable has been overemphasized. That Brigham Young also realized the value of Lucy Mack Smith's support is demonstrated not only in the obvious efforts made in Nauvoo to dissuade her from putting her son William forward as church president, but from the many references made to Mother Smith's approval of the course of the church—both public and private references—after the Saints reached Utah.

30. Lucy Mack Smith to William Smith, 23 Jan. 1845, LDS Church Archives.

31. William Smith to Orson Hyde, written from St. Louis, 2 June 1847, LDS Church Archives.

32. Accounts of visits to Lucy Mack Smith made by several people from Utah are included in the Journal History. See especially 10 Sept. 1849 and 25 Nov. 1855. Hannah Topfield King also visited Mother Smith, and a full account of that visit may be found in the King manuscript, p. 99, LDS Church Archives.

33. George A. Smith to Solomon Mack, 23 Feb. 1859, LDS Church Archives.

34. Lucy Mack Smith to Orson Pratt, 4 Feb. 1853, LDS Church Archives.

35. Journal History, Dec. 1853.

36. In addition to the discussion in Searle's dissertation, see Gary James Bergera, "The Orson Pratt–Brigham Young Controversies, Conflict within the Quorums, 1853–1868," *Dialogue* 13 (Summer 1980): 7–49.

37. See Brigham Young's Office Journal, Book D, 31 Jan. 1860, LDS Church Archives.

38. Paul M. Edwards, "Sweet Singer of Israel: David Hyrum Smith," *Courage* 2 (Summer 1972): 483–84.

39. Vol. 18, Copyright Records, Illinois, Aug. 1821–Sept. 1848.

The author acknowledges the assistance of Roger Wright Harris in obtaining the text of the copyright.

40. *DHC* 7: 429.

41. Edwards, "The Secular Smiths," *Journal of Mormon History* 4 (1977): 3–17.

42. The words from the conference address are taken from Brigham Young Papers—Addresses, 1866, speech of 7 Oct. 1866, recorded by George D. Watt, LDS Church Archives. For a useful analysis of the situation in early Christianity that might prove a felicitous model for a study of the succession crisis in Mormonism, see Gager, *Kingdom and Community*, chap. 3, "The Quest for Legitimacy and Consolidation."

43. Anderson, "The Reliability of the Early History of Lucy and Joseph Smith," p. 28.

Chapter Six

1. Eliade, *The Sacred and the Profane*, Introduction.

2. These movements are instituted as subgroups of the American Academy of Religion.

3. Lawrence Foster, *Religion and Sexuality: Three American Communal Experiments of the Nineteenth Century* (New York: Oxford University Press, 1981; Urbana: University of Illinois Press, 1984); Mark P. Leone, *Roots of Modern Mormonism* (Cambridge, Mass.: Harvard University Press, 1979).

4. A useful recent summary of the situation revealing the extent of outside pressure that figured in the decision to stop the practice of plural marriage is E. Leo Lyman, "The Woodruff Manifesto in the Context of Its Times," a paper presented at an adjunct session of the Mormon History Association, San Francisco, Calif., Dec. 1978.

5. Joseph R. Gusfield, *Symbolic Crusade: Status Politics and the American Temperance Movement* (Urbana: University of Illinois Press, 1963), pp. 6–7.

6. Because it was originally issued in the form of a press release declaring that accusations charging the LDS church leaders with continuing to teach, encourage, and urge the practice of polygamy were false, the Manifesto has often been treated as Exhibit A to prove that the decision to end polygamy was simply a matter of accommodating the church to American culture. The orthodox LDS position rejects this notion out of hand, holding instead that Woodruff's action was divinely inspired.

7. A historical interpretation that might be described as the "grand conspiracy" theory holds that a division was made between the *church* and the *priesthood* before the Manifesto was issued. This division, so the interpretation goes, made it possible for the leaders of the church to say in all honesty that the church was no longer teaching the practice of polygamy or solemnizing polygamous marriages, while the practice continued through the agency of the LDS priesthood. The fact that at least two apostles who were members of the Council of the Twelve continued to contract plural marriages is regarded as evidence of conspiracy, as is evidence that George Q. Cannon extended official approval to plural marriages solemnized in Mexico after 1890. The "grand conspiracy" idea is basic to the doctrine to which most modern Mormon polygamists who continue to practice polygamy subscribe. A recent work in which this historical interpretation is worked out is Samuel W. Taylor, *Rocky Mountain Empire: The Latter-day Saints Today* (New York: Macmillan, 1978).

8. Senator Reed Smoot's election to the U.S. Senate brought about a Senate investigation of the Mormon Church which was so intensive and widely publicized that a reintroduction of the practice of plural marriage would have been impossible even if that had been the intent.

9. It is important to keep in mind that the Saints gave up the *practice* of plural marriage, but that the theological superstructure that justified the practice is still very much in place in Mormonism.

10. F. Mark McKiernan, Alma R. Blair, and Paul M. Edwards, eds., *The Restoration Movement: Essays in Mormon History* (Lawrence, Kan.: Coronado Press, 1972), pp. 1-22. Hansen's ideas on the connections between Mormonism and modern American culture are developed and refined in *Mormonism and the American Experience* (Chicago: University of Chicago Press, 1981).

11. Historical treatments emphasizing the wealth of the church unduly are generally superficial and tend toward exposé. Two examples are Wallace Turner, *The Mormon Establishment* (Boston: Houghton Mifflin, 1966), and William J. Whalen, *The Latter-day Saints in the Modern Day World* (New York: John Day, 1964).

12. Klaus J. Hansen, *Quest for Empire: The Political Kingdom of God and the Council of Fifty in Mormon History* (East Lansing: Michigan State University Press, 1967); Leone, *Roots of Modern Mormonism*, especially chap. 7.

13. Allen and Leonard, *The Story of the Latter-day Saints*,

chap. 14; Arrington and Bitton, *The Mormon Experience*, chap. 13.

14. Gordon C. Thommasson, "The Manifesto Was a Victory!," *Dialogue* 6 (Spring 1971): 37–45; Taylor, *Family Kingdom* (New York: Macmillan, 1951) and *Rocky Mountain Empire*.

15. Almost any standard survey of American Protestantism treats the importance of the salvation experience under the rubric of revivalism. Marty's *Righteous Empire* is particularly useful in describing the triumph of evangelical Protestantism. See also Bernard A. Weisberger, *They Gathered at the River: The Story of the Great Revivalists and Their Impact upon Religion in America* (Boston: Little, Brown, 1958).

16. The pattern for adoption into Israel, which is directly related to the LDS usage of the term, is Jacob's adoption of Manesseh and Ephraim described in Genesis 48.

17. Wayne Meeks, "Social Functions of Apocalyptic," address presented in the Religious Studies Departmental Lecture Series, Indiana University, Bloomington, Mar. 1979.

18. *Journal of Discourses of President Brigham Young, His Counselors, and the Other Church Leaders*, 26 vols. (Liverpool, 1854–87), 26: 175.

19. The desire mankind has to live "in the beginning" is fully described, with examples drawn from many different cultures, in *The Sacred and the Profane*, chap. 2, "Sacred Time and Myths."

20. Paul D. Hanson, *The Dawn of Apocalyptic* (Philadelphia: Fortress Press, 1975).

21. Although precise comparison of emphases on Old and New Testament apocalyptic found either in evangelical Protestantism or Mormonism is exceedingly difficult, one indicator which can serve that purpose is a comparison of index references to the Books of Daniel and Revelation in *Quest for Empire*, Klaus J. Hansen's study of millennialism in Mormonism, and Ernest Lee Tuveson, *Redeemer Nation: The Idea of America's Millennial Role* (Chicago: University of Chicago Press, 1968). Hansen's work has a single reference to the Book of Revelation in the index, while the index to Tuveson's work has, in addition to two separate single page references, *passim* references to two sections nine and eighteen pages long. The Hansen index has seven references to the Book of Daniel, while the Tuveson index has only two. Another indicator of the extent to which the Saints turned to the Old Testament apocalyptic rather than the new is the index of the 26-volume *Journal of Discourses*, which contains transcriptions of sermons given during the pioneer period by the principal LDS

leaders. This index contains only one reference to the Book of Revelation but multiple references to the Book of Daniel.

22. Alma R. Blair, "Reorganized Church of Jesus Christ of Latter Day Saints: Moderate Mormonism," in McKiernan *et al.*, eds., *The Restoration Movement*, pp. 207–30.

23. In a highly respected but now somewhat dated sociological study entitled *The Mormons* (Chicago: University of Chicago Press, 1957), Thomas F. O'Dea described the Latter-day Saints as "a peculiarly American *subculture*" (italics mine) as well as "a peculiarly American religion." The interpretation being put forward in the present volume goes beyond O'Dea's conclusion to suggest that the Latter-day Saints, by virtue of a common paradigmatic experience as well as isolation, have acquired an ethnic identity so distinct that it sets the Saints apart in much the same fashion that ethnic identity sets the Jews apart.

24. Exclusive claims were made by many religious groups in nineteenth-century America, but for the most part other claims were grounded in New Testament theology, especially as articulated in the Pauline letters. While there can be no question about whether the Mormons are Christian (the LDS Articles of Faith begin "We believe in God, the Eternal Father, and in His Son, Jesus Christ . . ." and include the statement "We believe that the first principles and ordinances of the Gospel are: first, Faith in the Lord Jesus Christ . . .), their position is more clearly aligned to that held by the Apostle Peter before the Jerusalem Conference.

25. Guilford Dudley III, *Religion on Trial: Mircea Eliade & His Critics* (Philadelphia: Temple University Press, 1977), p. 67.

26. Reubenstein, *Power Struggle* (New York: Scribners, 1974).

27. Reubenstein, *After Auschwitz* (Indianapolis: Bobbs-Merrill, 1966), pp. 131–42. The quotation comes from p. 133.

28. Reubenstein's argument about the impact of the return to Israel on Judaism is much influenced by Freudian psychology. In using his work for the purpose of drawing an analogy to assist in explicating nineteenth-century Mormon experience, I have made no effort to extend the analogy to develop the psychoanalytic dimension of theology of the Latter-day Saints.

29. Leone, *Roots of Modern Mormonism*, p. 25. Leone's summary of the situation in the second half of the nineteenth century reads: "Mormons defined, more or less on their own terms, the relationship that they would have with the rest of the world, principally the United States. These years saw Mormonism become a working society, growing to maturity through its capacity to

handle a harsh environment. With a fully operating government and a dynamic economy centrally managed along socialist lines, Mormonism strove to create internal self-sufficiency, and to a remarkable degree it succeeded. These years were in many ways Mormonism's finest. The church ran itself according to its own lights and, in so doing, became the only American utopia ever to turn itself into a state."

30. In addition to Leone's work, the economic and social independence of nineteenth-century Mormonism is described in both *The Story of the Latter-day Saints* by Allen and Leonard and *The Mormon Experience* by Arrington and Bitton.

31. Dale Morgan, "The State of Deseret," *Utah Historical Quarterly* 8 (1940): 64–239; Hansen, *Quest for Empire*, chap. 7; D. Michael Quinn, "American Religious Diplomacy: Scholarly Neglect and Prominent Example," unpublished ms.

32. Reubenstein, *After Auschwitz*, p. 132.

33. Leonard J. Arrington, Feramorz Y. Fox, and Dean L. May, *Building the City of God: Community & Cooperation among the Mormons* (Salt Lake City: Deseret Book, 1976).

34. This is essentially the thesis of both *Building the City of God* and Leonard J. Arrington, *Great Basin Kingdom: An Economic History of the Latter-day Saints, 1830–1900* (Cambridge, Mass.: Harvard University Press, 1958).

35. As late as 1920, Sacrament Meeting attendance, for example, was still at just above 15 percent. Richard O. Cowan and Wilson K. Anderson, *The Living Church: The Unfolding of the Programs and Organization of the Church of Jesus Christ during the Twentieth Century* (Provo, Utah: Brigham Young University Printing Service, 1974), pp. 185, 190.

36. Leonard J. Arrington, "Have the Saints Always Given as Much Emphasis to the Word of Wisdom as They Do Today?," *Ensign*, Apr. 1977, pp. 32–33.

37. Descriptions of the efforts made by the Mormon community to preserve the practice of polygamy are plentiful. One of the best and most complete is Gustive O. Larson, *The Americanization of Utah for Statehood* (San Marino, Calif.: Huntington Library, 1971).

38. This diary entry has been reprinted many times. See, for instance, Brigham H. Roberts, *A Comprehensive History of the Church of Jesus Christ of Latter-day Saints: Century I*, 6 vols. (Salt Lake City: Deseret News Press, 1930), 6: 220.

39. The change in Mormonism is the basic explanation ad-

vanced by dissident Latter-day Saints to justify their existence. See Lyle O. Wright, "Origin and Development of the Church of the Firstborn of the Fulness of Times" (Master's thesis, Brigham Young University, Provo, Utah, 1963), and Russell R. Rich, *Those Who Would Be Leaders: Offshoots of Mormonism*, 2nd ed. (Provo: Extension Publications, Division of Continuing Education, 1967).

40. Leon Festinger *et al.*, *When Prophecy Fails* (Minneapolis: University of Minnesota Press, 1956), p. 28.

41. Membership statistics are available in the church almanacs published annually by the *Deseret News*. I am grateful to Prof. Ned Hill for assistance in figuring growth rates.

42. That the necessity of adjusting to a world wherein Caesar reigned was a crucial factor in causing the New Testament saints to "reenter time" was first suggested to me by the Rev. George Davis. I have—more or less directly—adopted his words to express the idea that, instead of living in the apocalyptic kingdom, the Saints had to learn to live apocalyptically.

43. Meeks, "Social Functions of Apocalyptic"; Gager, *Kingdom and Community*.

44. One of the most important revelations in D. Michael Quinn's work on the Mormon hierarchy is the extent to which the hierarchy not only functioned but was a royal family. The kinship lines within the Mormon leadership group are an indication of the new Mormon ethnicity. See D. Michael Quinn, "The Mormon Hierarchy, 1832–1932: An American Elite," Ph.D. dissertation, Yale University, New Haven, Conn., 1976.

45. James B. Allen, "Line Upon Line . . . ," *Ensign*, July 1979, pp. 32–39.

Chapter Seven

1. The electronic transmission of conference proceedings to Mormons throughout the nation has somewhat diminished the significance of attending conference in person in the lives of Latter-day Saints.

2. Aaronic priesthood quorum rankings are theologically as well as practically ordered. Ordinarily ordained as deacons at the age of twelve, LDS males generally serve during their teen years first in deacons' quorums, then in teachers' quorums, and after that in priests' quorums. At the age of nineteen or thereabouts they are often called to serve eighteen-month proselyting missions, and at that time are ordained as elders in the Melchizedek

priesthood. While males who are converted to the church as adults are generally ordained to the Aaronic priesthood, their elevation to the Melchizedek priesthood usually comes fairly rapidly, since *in practice* Aaronic priesthood activity has been more or less transformed into a youth program. The three orders in the Melchizedek priesthood are not ranked theologically in the same way that Aaronic priesthood orders are ranked. All members of the Melchizedek priesthood are elders, whether or not they are part of an elders' quorum. But some members of the Melchizedek priesthood are likewise ordained as seventies, which means that they possess the same authority that all elders possess, plus a special call to be traveling ministers. Likewise, some members of the Melchizedek priesthood are ordained as high priests, which means that they have been called to minister over the spiritual, as opposed to the temporal, concerns of the church. High priests stand above the members of all the other priesthood orders in the sense that high priests possess all the authority of the seventies, elders, priests, teachers, and deacons. *In practice*, a high priest is regarded as superior in rank to a seventy or an elder, but that does not mean, as might be expected, that the highest rank is numerically smaller than the lower ranks. At the close of 1978, 68 percent of the members of the Melchizedek priesthood were elders; 26 percent were high priests; and less than 6 percent were seventies. A fairly recent official statement concerning the Melchizedek priesthood is Bruce R. McConkie, "Only an Elder," *Ensign*, June 1975, pp. 66–69.

3. Conference proceedings have been on the record from the very first insofar as their having been recorded for posterity is concerned. Since 1898 *Conference Reports* have been issued. The 26 volumes of the *Journal of Discourses*, published in Liverpool between 1854 and 1887, are not conference reports, but they nevertheless contain many discourses that were delivered in General Conference. The special character separating conference utterances from other LDS sermons and talks has caused a certain amount of confusion, because that special character has often led people to regard the contents of virtually all conference addresses as doctrine. Since contemporary conference sermons and talks are delivered from carefully prepared texts, a practice that facilitates their rapid translation for simulcast as well as manageable broadcasting on commercial radio and television stations, contemporary conference sermons and talks are considered to be doctrinally sound and completely in line with church policy. Throughout

most of the history of the church this was not the case, because discourses delivered extemporaneously were not always as doctrinally sound or as congruent with church policy as is the case today.

4. When there is no father (patriarch) in the home, the mother (matriarch) presides and receives revelation for the entire family. This is consistent with the principle that all Latter-day Saints may receive revelation both for themselves and for all those over whom they preside.

5. James R. Clark, ed., *Messages of the First Presidency of the Church of Jesus Christ of Latter-day Saints*, 5 vols. (Salt Lake City: Bookcraft, 1971), 5: 4-11.

6. Only those who have been called on to summarize the sermons delivered extemporaneously by Latter-day Saints will appreciate the extent to which order has been imposed on President Smith's message. An extraordinary effort has been made, however, to draw this description of LDS belief from this single source to show the extent to which the essentials of the Mormon faith can be set out without recourse to elaborate doctrinal formulation.

7. Although no official source contains a record of the ordination ceremony, rumor (apparently derived from apostates who were in a position to know) holds that the prophet Joseph Smith was made king of the Kingdom of God before his death in 1844. This charge figured in the development of opposition to Smith that led to his death. A report that Brigham Young likewise proclaimed himself to be king was made by Bishop Andrew Cahoon in 1889. See Hansen, *Quest for Empire*, pp. 66, 155—58; Robert Bruce Flanders, *Nauvoo: Kingdom on the Mississippi* (Urbana: University of Illinois Press, 1965), p. 292.

8. Jan Shipps, "Utah Comes of Age Politically: A Study of the State's Politics in the Early Years of the Twentieth Century," *Utah Historical Quarterly* 35 (Spring 1967): 108.

9. *Messages of the First Presidency*, 5: 4, indicates in a footnote the consensus among the Saints that President Smith's sermon was an example of continuing revelation being manifested in the presence of the Saints.

10. Bruce R. McConkie, *Mormon Doctrine*, entry under "Revelation."

11. I am indebted to Scott Kenney, who is engaged in writing a biography of President Smith, for pointing out the importance of this theme in Smith's sermons.

12. This perception is clearly revealed in the periodical literature. See Shipps, "From Satyr to Saint."

13. This conclusion is fully appropriate only for the form of Mormonism that is centered in Salt Lake City. The RLDS Church embraces a theology and practice much closer to traditional Christianity.

Bibliography

BOOKS, DISSERTATIONS, AND THESES

Adams, G. J. *"A Lecture on the Authenticity & Scriptural Character of the Book of Mormon" Delivered at the Town Hall, Charlestown, Mass., on Sunday, February 7th.* Boston: J. E. Farwell, 1844.

Alexander, Thomas G., and Jessie L. Embry, eds. *After 150 Years: The Latter-day Saints in Sesquicentennial Perspective.* Provo, Utah: Charles Redd Center for Western Studies, 1983.

Allen, James B., and Glen M. Leonard. *The Story of the Latter-day Saints.* Salt Lake City: Deseret Book, 1976.

Anderson, Richard Lloyd. *Joseph Smith's New England Heritage.* Salt Lake City: Deseret Book, 1971.

Arrington, Leonard J. *Great Basin Kingdom: An Economic History of the Latter-day Saints, 1830–1900.* Cambridge, Mass: Harvard University Press, 1958.

———, and Davis Bitton. *The Mormon Experience: A History of the Latter-day Saints.* New York: Alfred A. Knopf, 1979.

———, Feramorz Y. Fox, and Dean L. May. *Building the City of God: Community & Cooperation among the Mormons.* Salt Lake City: Deseret Book, 1976.

Berger, Peter. *The Sacred Canopy: Elements of a Sociological Theory of Religion.* Garden City, N.Y.: Doubleday, 1967.

———, and Thomas Luckmann. *The Social Construction of Real-*

ity: A Treatise in the Sociology of Knowledge. Garden City, N.Y.: Doubleday, 1967.

A Book of Commandments for the Government of the Church of Christ. Zion [Independence, Mo.]: W. W. Phelps, 1833; reprint, Independence: Herald Publishing House, 1971.

Bourguignon, Erika, ed. *Religion, Altered States of Consciousness and Social Change.* Columbus: Ohio State University Press, 1973.

Brodie, Fawn M. *No Man Knows My History: The Life of Joseph Smith, the Mormon Prophet.* 2nd ed. rev. New York: Alfred A. Knopf, 1971.

Brooks, Jaunita, ed. *On the Mormon Frontier: The Diary of Hosea Stout.* 2 vols. Salt Lake City: University of Utah Press, 1964.

Bruggerman, Walter. *The Prophetic Imagination.* Philadelphia: Fortress Press, 1978.

Bushman, Richard L. *Joseph Smith and the Beginnings of Mormonism.* Urbana: University of Illinois Press, 1984.

Clark, James R., ed. *Messages of the First Presidency of the Church of Jesus Christ of Latter-day Saints, 1916–1934.* 5 vols. Salt Lake City: Bookcraft, 1971.

Cowan, Richard O., and Wilson K. Anderson. *The Living Church: The Unfolding of the Programs and Organization of the Church of Jesus Christ during the Twentieth Century.* Provo, Utah: Brigham Young University Printing Service, 1974.

Cross, Whitney R. *The Burned-over District: The Social and Intellectual History of Enthusiastic Religion in Western New York, 1800–1850.* Ithaca, N.Y.: Cornell University Press, 1950.

Davis, Inez Smith. *The Story of the Church.* 4th ed. rev. Independence, Mo.: Herald Publishing House, 1948.

DePillis, Mario. "The Development of Mormon Communitarianism, 1826–1846." Ph.D. dissertation, Yale University, 1961.

Doctrine and Covenants. Independence, Mo.: Reorganized Church of Jesus Christ of Latter Day Saints, 1978 ed.

Doctrine and Covenants of the Church of Jesus Christ of Latter-day Saints. Salt Lake City: Published by the Church, 1952.

Dudley, Guilford, III. *Religion on Trial: Mircea Eliade & His Critics.* Philadelphia: Temple University Press, 1977.

Dunne, John S. *Time and Myth.* Notre Dame, Ind.: University of Notre Dame Press, 1975.

Eliade, Mircea. *Cosmos and History: The Myth of the Eternal Return.* Trans. Willard R. Trask. New York: Harper, 1954.

————. *The Sacred and the Profane: The Nature of Religion.* Trans. Willard R. Trask. New York: Harcourt Brace, 1957.

Festinger, Leon, *et al. When Prophecy Fails.* Minneapolis: University of Minnesota Press, 1956.

Flanders, Robert Bruce. *Nauvoo: Kingdom on the Mississippi.* Urbana: University of Illinois Press, 1965.

Foster, Lawrence. *Religion and Sexuality: Three American Communal Experiments of the Nineteenth Century.* New York: Oxford University Press, 1981; Illini Book ed., Urbana: University of Illinois Press, 1984.

Frye, Northrop. *Fearful Symmetry: A Study of William Blake.* Princeton, N.J.: Princeton University Press, 1947.

————. *The Great Code: The Bible and Literature.* New York: Harcourt Brace Jovanovich, 1981.

Gager, John. *Kingdom and Community: The Social World of Early Christianity.* Englewood Cliffs, N.J.: Prentice-Hall, 1975.

Green, N. W. *Mormonism: Its Rise, Progress, and Present Condition.* Hartford, Conn.: Belknap & Bliss, 1870.

Gusfield, Joseph R. *Symbolic Crusade: Status Politics and the American Temperance Movement.* Urbana: University of Illinois Press, 1963.

Hansen, Klaus J. *Quest for Empire: The Political Kingdom of God and the Council of Fifty in Mormon History.* East Lansing: Michigan State University Press, 1967.

————. *Mormonism and the American Experience.* Chicago: University of Chicago Press, 1981.

Hanson, Paul D. *The Dawn of Apocalyptic.* Philadelphia: Fortress Press, 1975.

Hill, Donna. *Joseph Smith, the First Mormon.* New York: Doubleday, 1979.

Hill, Marvin S. "The Role of Christian Primitivism in the Origin and Development of the Mormon Kingdom, 1830–1844." Ph.D. dissertation, University of Chicago, 1968.

History of Joseph Smith by His Mother, Lucy Mack Smith. Notes and comments by Preston Nibley. Salt Lake City: Bookcraft, 1958.

History of the Prophet Joseph by His Mother Lucy Smith. Revised by George A. Smith and Elias Smith. Salt Lake City: Improvement Era, 1905.

Howe, Eber D. *Mormonism Unvailed: or A Faithful Account*

of That Singular Imposition and Delusion. . . . Painesville, Ohio: Printed and Published by the Author, 1834.

Hullinger, Robert N. *Mormon Answer to Skepticism: Why Joseph Smith Wrote the Book of Mormon.* St. Louis, Mo.: Clayton Publishing House, 1980.

Jenson, Andrew. *Latter-day Saints Biographical Encyclopedia.* Salt Lake City: A. Jenson History Co., 1901.

Johnson, Paul E. *A Shopkeeper's Millennium: Society and Revivals in Rochester, New York, 1815–1837.* New York: Hill and Wang, 1978.

Joseph Smith's History by His Mother: A Photomechanical Reprint of the Original 1853 Edition. Salt Lake City: Modern Microfilm, n.d.

Journal of Discourses of President Brigham Young, His Counselors, and Other Church Leaders. 26 vols. Liverpool: Latter-day Saints Book Depot, 1854–86; lithograph ed., Los Angeles, Calif.: Gartner Printing & Litho, 1956.

Kee, Howard Clark. *Jesus in History: An Approach to the Study of the Gospels.* 2nd ed. New York: Harcourt Brace Jovanovich, 1977.

Kermode, Frank. *The Sense of an Ending: Studies in the Theory of Fiction.* New York: Oxford University Press, 1967.

Kerr, Howard, and Charles L. Crow, eds. *The Occult in America: New Historical Perspectives.* Urbana: University of Illinois Press, 1983.

Kraut, Ogden. *Seers and Seer Stones.* Salt Lake City: Published by the Author, n.d.

Kuhn, Thomas S. *The Structure of Scientific Revolutions.* 2nd ed. Chicago: University of Chicago Press, 1970.

Lakoff, George, and Mark Johnson. *Metaphors We Live By.* Chicago: University of Chicago Press, 1980.

Larche, Douglas. "A Rhetorical History of the Post-1844 Struggle for Succession in the Mormon Church." Ph.D. dissertation, Indiana University, Bloomington, 1977.

Larson, Gustive O. *The Americanization of Utah for Statehood.* San Marino, Calif.: Huntington Library, 1971.

Leone, Mark P. *Roots of Modern Mormonism.* Cambridge, Mass.: Harvard University Press, 1979.

Lyman, E. Leo. "The Mormon Quest for Utah Statehood." Ph.D. dissertation, University of California, Riverside, 1981.

McConkie, Bruce R. *Mormon Doctrine.* Salt Lake City: Bookcraft, 1958.

McKiernan, F. Mark, Alma R. Blair, and Paul M. Edwards, eds. *The Restoration Movement: Essays in Mormon History.* Lawrence, Kan.: Coronado Press, 1972.

McLoughlin, William G. *Revivals, Awakenings, and Reform: An Essay on Religion and Social Change in America, 1607–1977.* Chicago: University of Chicago Press, 1978.

Marty, Martin. *Righteous Empire: The Protestant Experience in America.* New York: Dial Press, 1979.

The Millennial Harbinger Abridged. Selections by Benjamin Lyon Smith, with an Introduction by Charles Louis Loos. 2 vols. Rosemead, Calif.: Old Paths, 1965.

Mortensen, Russell, and William Mulder, eds. *Among the Mormons.* New York: Alfred A. Knopf, 1958.

Nibley, Hugh. *Lehi in the Desert and the World of the Jaredites.* Salt Lake City: Deseret Book, 1952.

———. *Since Cumorah: The Book of Mormon in the Modern World.* Salt Lake City: Deseret Book, 1967.

O'Dea, Thomas F. *The Mormons.* Chicago: University of Chicago Press, 1957.

Pollock, Gordon Douglas. "In Search of Security: The Mormons and the Kingdom of God on Earth, 1830–1844." Ph.D. dissertation, Queen's University, Kingston, Ontario, 1977.

Pratt, Parley P. *A Voice of Warning and Instruction to All People.* 13th ed. Salt Lake City: Deseret News, 1893.

Quinn, D. Michael. "The Mormon Hierarchy, 1832–1932: An American Elite." Ph.D. dissertation, Yale University, New Haven, Conn., 1976.

Reubenstein, Richard. *After Auschwitz: Radical Theology and Contemporary Judaism.* Indianapolis: Bobbs-Merrill, 1966.

———. *Power Struggle.* New York: Scribners, 1974.

Rich, Russell R. *Those Who Would Be Leaders: Offshoots of Mormonism.* 2nd ed. Provo, Utah: Extension Publications, Division of Continuing Education, 1967.

Roberts, Brigham H. *A Comprehensive History of the Church of Jesus Christ of Latter-day Saints: Century I.* 6 vols. Salt Lake City: Deseret News, 1930.

———. *Succession in the Presidency of the Church of Jesus Christ of Latter-day Saints.* 2nd ed. Salt Lake City: G. Q. Cannon, 1900.

———, ed. *History of the Church of Jesus Christ of Latter-day Saints: Period II, from the Manuscript History of Brigham Young and Other Original Documents.* Salt Lake City: Deseret Book, 1932. (Usually cited as *Documentary History of the Church VII* or *DHC 7*.)

Searle, Howard Clair. "Early Mormon Historiography: Writing the History of the Mormons, 1830–1858." Ph.D. dissertation, University of Southern California, Los Angeles, 1979.

Smart, Ninian. *Worldviews: Crosscultural Explorations of Human Beliefs*. New York: Charles Scribner's Sons, 1983.

Smith, Joseph, Jr. *History of the Church of Jesus Christ of Latter-day Saints: Period I, History of Joseph Smith, the Prophet*, ed. B. H. Roberts. 6 vols. 2nd ed. rev. Salt Lake City: Deseret Book, 1955. (Usually cited as *Documentary History of the Church* or *DHC*.)

Smith, Joseph Fielding. *Essentials in Church History*. Classics in Mormon Literature ed. Salt Lake City: Deseret Book, 1979.

Smith, Lucy [Mack]. *Biographical Sketches of Joseph Smith, the Prophet, and His Progenitors for Many Generations*. Liverpool: Orson Pratt, 1853; Religion in America ed., New York: Arno Press, 1969.

Stendahl, Krister. *Paul among Jews and Gentiles and Other Essays*. Philadelphia: Fortress Press, 1976.

Tanner, Jerald and Sandra. *Joseph Smith's Strange Account of the First Vision*. Salt Lake City: Modern Microfilm, n.d.

Taylor, Samuel W. *Family Kingdom*. New York: Macmillan, 1951.

———. *Rocky Mountain Empire: The Latter-day Saints Today*. New York: Macmillan, 1978.

Turner, Wallace. *The Mormon Establishment*. Boston: Houghton Mifflin, 1966.

Tuveson, Ernest Lee. *Redeemer Nation: The Idea of America's Millennial Role*. Chicago: University of Chicago Press, 1968.

Weisberger, Bernard A. *They Gathered at the River: The Story of the Great Revivalists and Their Impact upon Religion in America*. Boston: Little, Brown, 1958.

Whalen, William J. *The Latter-day Saints in the Modern World*. New York: John Day, 1964.

Wright, Lyle O. "Origin and Development of the Church of the Firstborn of the Fulness of Times." Master's thesis, Brigham Young University, Provo, Utah, 1963.

ARTICLES AND UNPUBLISHED PAPERS

Allen, James B. "Emergence of a Fundamental: The Expanding Role of Joseph Smith's First Vision in Mormon Religious

Thought." *Journal of Mormon History* 7 (1980): 43–61.

———. "Line Upon Line. . . ." *Ensign*, July 1979, pp. 32–39.

———. "One Man's Nauvoo: William Clayton's Experience in Mormon, Illinois." *Journal of Mormon History* 6 (1979): 37–59.

Anderson, Richard L. "The Reliability of the Early History of Lucy and Joseph Smith." *Dialogue: A Journal of Mormon Thought* 4 (Summer 1969): 13–28.

———. Presentation concerning his work-in-progress editing Lucy Mack Smith's *History*. Andrew Jenson Club, 7 May 1976. Tape recording in the LDS Church Archives.

Arrington, Leonard J. "Have the Saints Always Given as Much Emphasis to the Word of Wisdom as They Do Today?" *Ensign*, Apr. 1977, pp. 32–33.

Bachman, Danel W. "New Light on an Old Hypothesis: The Ohio Origins of the Revelation on Eternal Marriage." *Journal of Mormon History* 5 (1978): 19–32.

Bangerter, W. Grant. "The Best of All Good News: The Gospel Is Restored," an edited version of a Brigham Young University devotional address delivered Apr. 1979. *Ensign*, Apr. 1980, pp. 56–59.

Bates, Irene. "William Smith, 1811–1893: Problematic Patriarch." Paper presented at the annual meeting of the Mormon History Association, Ogden, Utah, May 1981.

Bergera, Gary James. "The Orson Pratt–Brigham Young Controversies: Conflict within the Quorums, 1853–1868." *Dialogue: A Journal of Mormon Thought* 13 (Summer 1980): 7–49.

Bitton, Davis. "The Ritualization of Mormon History." *Utah Historical Quarterly* 43 (Winter 1975): 67–85.

Blair, Alma R. "Reorganized Church of Jesus Christ of Latter Day Saints: Moderate Mormonism." In Mark F. McKiernan, Alma R. Blair, and Paul M. Edwards, eds., *The Restoration Movement: Essays in Mormon History*. Lawrence, Kan.: Coronado Press, 1973, pp. 207–30.

Bushman, Richard L. "The Book of Mormon and the American Revolution." *BYU Studies* 17 (Fall 1976): 3–20.

Butler, Jon. "Magic, Astrology, and the Early American Religious Heritage." *American Historical Review* 84 (Apr. 1979): 317–46.

Crawley, Peter. "Joseph Smith and *A Book of Commandments*."

Princeton University Library Chronicle 42 (Autumn 1980): 18–32.

Durham, Reed. "Is There No Help for the Widow's Son?" Presidential address delivered at the annual meeting of the Mormon History Association, Nauvoo, Ill., Apr. 1974. Underground ed.

Edwards, Paul M. "The Secular Smiths." *Journal of Mormon History* 4 (1977): 3–17.

————. "The Sweet Singer of Israel: David Hyrum Smith." *Courage: A Journal of History, Thought, and Action* 2 (Summer 1982): 484–91.

Hatch, Nathan O. "Sola Scriptura and Novus Ordo Seclorum." In Nathan O. Hatch and Mark A. Noll, eds., *The Bible in America: Essays in Cultural History.* New York: Oxford University Press, 1982, pp. 59–78.

Hill, Marvin S. "Brodie Revisited: A Reappraisal." *Dialogue: A Journal of Mormon Thought* 8 (Winter 1972): 72–85.

————. "Joseph Smith and the 1826 Trial: New Evidence and New Difficulties." *Brigham Young University Studies* 12 (Winter 1972): 223–33.

————. "The Rise of Mormonism in the Burned-over District: Another View." *New York History* 61 (Oct. 1980): 411–30.

Hollinger, David A. "T. S. Kuhn's Theory of Science and Its Implications for History." *American Historical Review* 78 (Apr. 1973): 370–93.

Larsen, Wayne A., Alvin C. Rencher, and Tim Layton. "Who Wrote the Book of Mormon? An Analysis of Wordprints." *Brigham Young University Studies* 20 (Spring 1980): 225–51.

Lyman, E. Leo. "The Woodruff Manifesto in the Context of Its Times." Paper presented at an adjunct session of the Mormon History Association, San Francisco, Calif., Dec. 1978.

McConkie, Bruce R. "Only an Elder." *Ensign*, June 1975, pp. 66–69.

Meeks, Wayne. "Social Functions of Apocalyptic." Addresses presented in the Religious Studies Departmental Lecture Series, Indiana University, Bloomington, Mar. 1979.

Midgley, Louis. "Hugh Nibley: A Short Bibliographical Note." *Dialogue: A Journal of Mormon Thought* 2 (Spring 1967): 119–21.

Moench, Melodie. "Nineteenth-Century Mormons: The New Israel." *Dialogue: A Journal of Mormon Thought* 12 (Spring 1979): 42–45.

Morgan, Dale. "The State of Deseret." *Utah Historical Quarterly* 8 (Apr., July, Oct. 1940): 65–244.

Parker, Simon B. "Possession Trance and Prophecy in Pre-exilic Israel." *Vetus Testamentum*, 1978, pp. 271–85.

Quinn, D. Michael. "American Religious Diplomacy: Scholarly Neglect and Prominent Example." Unpublished ms.

———, trans. and ed. "The First Months of Mormonism: A Contemporary [1830] View by Rev. Diedrich Willers." *New York History* 54 (July 1973): 317–33.

Shipps, Jan. "From Satyr to Saint: American Attitudes toward the Mormons, 1860–1960." Paper presented at the annual meeting of the Organization of American Historians, Chicago, 1973. Copy available in the collection of the LDS Church Archives.

———. "In the Presence of the Past: Continuity and Change in Twentieth-Century Mormonism." In Thomas G. Alexander and Jessie L. Embry, eds., *After 150 Years: The Latter-day Saints in Sesquicentennial Perspective*. Provo, Utah: Charles Redd Center for Western Studies, 1983, pp. 4–35.

———. "The Prophet Puzzle: Suggestions Leading toward a More Comprehensive Interpretation of Joseph Smith." *Journal of Mormon History* 1 (1974): 3–20.

———. "Utah Comes of Age Politically: A Study of the State's Politics in the Early Years of the Twentieth Century." *Utah Historical Quarterly* 35 (Spring 1967): 91–111.

Smith, Lucy Mack. "A Gospel Letter." In Benjamin E. Rich, ed., *Scrapbook of Mormon Literature*. 2 vols. Chicago: Published by the Editor, n.d., 1: 543–45.

Smith, Timothy L. "The Book of Mormon in a Biblical Culture." *Journal of Mormon History* 7 (1980): 3–21.

Sorenson, John L. "An Ancient Setting for the Book of Mormon." Unpublished ms.

Thomasson, Gordon C. "The Manifesto Was a Victory!" *Dialogue: A Journal of Mormon Thought* 6 (Spring 1971): 37–45.

Walters, Rev. Wesley P. "New Light on Mormon Origins from the Palmyra Revival." *Dialogue: A Journal of Mormon Thought* 4 (Spring 1969): 60–81.

Wood, Gordon. "Evangelical America and Early Mormonism." *New York History* 61 (Oct. 1980): 359–86.

Index

Aaronic priesthood, x, 2, 22, 23, 74, 76. *See also* Priesthood
Abraham, 2, 46, 61, 72, 77; Book of, 47
Acts, Book of, 54
Adam, 2
Adoption into Israel, 75, 120; ordinance, 127
After Auschwitz (Reubenstein), 123
Against Heresy (Irenaeus), 102
Age of Reason (Paine), 7
Alexander, Thomas G., 80
Allen, James B., xi, 32, 89, 117
Among the Mormons (Mortensen and Mulder), 56
"Ancient seers," 13. *See also* Urim and Thummim
Anderson, Richard, 96, 97, 100, 105
Andrew Jenson Club, 97
Anthon, Charles, 14
Anthropological studies: of Mormonism, 113; of religion, 112
Anti-Masonry, 7
Anti-Mormons, x
Anti-polygamists, 114; campaign, 115
Apocalypse of St. John, 87. *See also* Revelation

Apostasy: from apostolic Christianity, 2; from Mormonism, 81, 121
Apostles, Christian, ix; twelve to be called, 74
April 6: significance, 21
Archives, LDS Church, 92
Arno Press, 91
Arrington, Leonard J., xi, 91, 105, 107, 117
Authority: in Mormonism, 137, 140; quest for, 78
Auxiliary activities, LDS, 128

Babbitt, Almon W., 99
Bainbridge, N.Y.: trial, 11, 153. *See also* Treasure-hunting
Bangerter, W. Grant, 67
Baptism, LDS, 72, 74, 144; for the dead, 84, 160
Baptist Church, 6
Benson, Ezra Taft, 107
Berger, Peter, xi
Bible: historicity of, 47; Smith's translations of, 47, 155
Bishopric, 134
Bitton, Davis, xi, 64, 117
Boggs, Gov. Lilburn, 158
Book of Commandments, 17, 156
Book of Mormon: analyzed by A. Campbell, 44; coming forth

Gentile(s), 3, 52, 75, 116, 123, 125;
government, 62; politicians,
124; world, 129
God: nature of in LDS belief, 143
Godbeite movement, 169
"Gold bible," 38, 78. See also
Book of Mormon
Gold plates, 11–18 passim, 148
Gospel(s): Abrahamic, xi; New
Testament, 45, 88
Gotama, 42
Grandin, E. B. (printer), 26
Grant, Heber J., 116
Grant, Jedidiah, 60
"Great Apostasy," 51
Great Awakening, Second, 36
Great Basin Kingdom (Arrington),
106
Great Salt Lake Valley, 122
Growth rates, LDS, 126

Hale, Isaac, 12
Handcart Company, 163
Hansen, Klaus J., 117
Harris, Lucy, 11
Harris, Martin, 11–23 passim,
103, 153
Haun's Mill massacre, 159
Hebraic story: redacted in New
Testament, 35–36
Hebrew Bible, 54
Hebrews, ix; Book of, 54
Heilsgeschichte (salvation his-
tory), 53
Heresy, x
Hierarchy, LDS, 4, 107
Hieroglyphics, 13, 14, 15, 153
High priests quorum, 134
Hill, Donna, 79
Hill, Marvin, 6, 78
Hill Cumorah, 11, 152, 153
Hinduism, 42, 43
Historians of Mormonism, 89
Historiography, 89
History: Christian, xii, 46;
Hebraic, vii, 46, 60; linear char-
acter of, 52; Mormon, xii, 1, 2,
44, 57, 58, 106–7; religious,
111; scientific, 111

History of Joseph Smith, the
Prophet. . . . See Smith, Lucy
Mack, History
History of Religions, x, 133
Holy Ghost, 76
"House of order," 136
Howe, Eber D., 44
Hurlbut, Philastus, 10

Identity: Hebrew, 122; Mormon,
122, 125
Improvement Era, 140
In illo tempore, 112, 122, 125, 127
Indians, American, 35
Intuition, 71
Irenaeus, 102
Isaac, 61
Isaiah, 37, 53; Book of, 77; chap.
29, 18
Islam, 42
Israel, 42, 123; ancient, 43, 81;
camp of, 60; history, 60; Mor-
mons re-live story of, 38; resto-
ration of, 37, 85

Jackson County, Mo., 155
Jacksonian democracy, 4
Jacob, 61
Jesus: in LDS theology, 2, 143; life
of, 42, 46, 49, 51, 87, 149; resur-
rection, xiii, 45; theological sig-
nificance, 54, 55
"Jesus Freaks," 50
Jews, ix
John the Baptist, 2
Johnson, Mark, 61
Johnson, Paul, 34
Jordan River, 61
Joseph, 61
Joshua, 37
Journal of Discourses, 124
Journey to Great Salt Lake Valley.
See Trek
Judeo-Christian tradition, 46
July 24: significance, 64, 129

Kermode, Frank, xi
Keys: to gathering of Israel, 82; to
new dispensation, 82

Although members of th
Shipps as the Thomas L
been so. In a rich and v
fourth-grade teacher in
Georgia Academy for th
suburban Chicago bar;
Episcopal residential in
coordinator at the (Kin
sity. None of these pur
to Logan, Utah, in 196
While working for a de
assigned to teach ninet
—and immediately ha
Mormons. Her answer

She received her B.S
to work on an M.A. a
thesis on Mormons ir
versity of Colorado in
university with the lo
at Indianapolis, wher
creased the library ho
have been favorably c

In 1973 she preser
American Historians
the Mormons from 1
1974 she wrote a pa
Prophet Puzzle," wh
Mormon History. In
produced numerous
national journals. Th
from the documents

She has been hear
to honor her as both
Association. For son
moved to Logan, sh

A Note on the Author

Although members of the Mormon History Association may think of Jan Shipps as the Thomas L. Kane of the twentieth century, it has not always been so. In a rich and varied career, Jan has been, among other things, a fourth-grade teacher in an Alabama mill town; a piano teacher at the Georgia Academy for the Blind; a seller of clothing and a piano player at a suburban Chicago bar; a housemother and recreation supervisor at an Episcopal residential institution for troubled teenage girls; *and* a project coordinator at the (Kinsey) Institute for Sex Research at Indiana University. None of these pursuits defined her eventual career. Rather, a move to Logan, Utah, in 1960 initiated her lifelong interest in Mormon studies. While working for a degree in history at Utah State University, she was assigned to teach nineteenth-century Utah history at a local high school —and immediately had to ask herself how much she knew about the Mormons. Her answer? She "desperately needed to know more."

She received her B.S. at Utah State, then moved across the mountains to work on an M.A. at the University of Colorado at Boulder, writing a thesis on Mormons in politics. After receiving her Ph.D. from the University of Colorado in 1965, she went on to teach at what she calls "the university with the long name," Indiana University–Purdue University at Indianapolis, where she is now a full professor. At Indiana, she increased the library holdings on Mormonism to such an extent that they have been favorably compared with Yale's.

In 1973 she presented to the annual meeting of the Organization of American Historians a noteworthy study of American attitudes toward the Mormons from 1860 to 1960 entitled "From Satyr to Saint," and in 1974 she wrote a path-breaking article on Joseph Smith entitled "The Prophet Puzzle," which was subsequently published in the *Journal of Mormon History*. In her twenty-four years with Mormon history, she has produced numerous articles and book reviews appearing in Mormon and national journals. This, her first book, synthesizes what she has learned from the documents and from the Saints themselves.

She has been heartily accepted by scholars of Mormonism, who chose to honor her as both vice-president and president of the Mormon History Association. For someone who had never heard of Joseph Smith when she moved to Logan, she has come a very long way.

DENNIS L. LYTHGOE
Massachusetts State College
at Bridgewater